IN AND OUT OF CHARACTER

Basil Rathbone

IN
AND OUT
OF
CHARACTER

Limelight Editions

An Imprint of Hal Leonard Corporation
New York

Limelight Editions (an imprint of Hal Leonard Corporation)
19 West 21ˢᵗ Street, New York, NY 10010

Published by Limelight Editions in 1989
Fifth printing, 2007

Printed in the United States of America

The Soldier from *The Collected Poems of Rupert Brooke*. Copyright 1915 by Dodd, Mead & Company, Inc. Copyright 1943 by Edward Marsh. Reprinted by permission of Dodd, Mead & Company, Inc., McClelland and Stewart, Limited, and Sidgwick & Jackson, Ltd.

221B by Vincent Starrett. Reprinted by permission of the author.

I Like Them Fluffy from *Plain Jane* by A. P. Herbert. Reprinted by permission of the proprietors of *Punch*, Sir Alan Herbert, Ernest Benn, Let., and Doubleday and Company, Inc.

The short story "Daydream" first appeared in the December 1956 number of *Esquire*.

Library of Congress Cataloging-in-Publication Data

Rathbone, Basil, 1892--1967.
   In and out of character / Basil Rathbone.---1ˢᵗ Limelight ed. p. cm.
   Reprint. Originally published: Garden City, N.Y.: Doubleday, C1962.
   1. Rathbone, Basil, 1892--1967. 2. Actors---Great Britain---Biography. I. Title.
PN2598.R35A3   1989
791.43'028'0924---dc19
[B]

                                        88-21531
                                           CIP

Limelight ISBN-10: 0-87910-119-9
Limelight ISBN-13: 978-0-87910-119-0

www.limelighteditions.com

To my Ouida with love

CONTENTS

Preface

"I have heard it said that if one writes a book in which one's thoughts and experiences play a major role, it is no good doing so unless one can be 'sensational.'" A very well-known newspaperman—a good friend of mine—and I were talking one day, shortly after my return to New York from the West Coast in 1946. I was commenting upon the thousands upon thousands of happy families in the motion picture industry, and especially I mentioned in the "name bracket"—Irene Dunne and her husband—Claudette Colbert and her husband—Jack Benny's marriage—Sir C. Aubrey Smith and his wife—the Nigel Bruces, to name but a few. Why was it, I asked my friend, that, at least so it seemed to me, successful marriages were not news. His answer shocked me, but when I had time to think it through I had to agree with him. He said, "My dear Basil, in my business the only good news is bad news." Cynical? Perhaps, but I am much afraid it is the truth.

My wife and I have been married for thirty-six years. No two strong-minded, healthy, normal individuals live together that long in a romantic paradise! There have been times when clashes of personality and human folly have temporarily disrupted our lives. But because we happen to be in the public eye, does this entitle us—or you—dear reader, to an exposé of our weaknesses and problems? To what end? To destroy your illusions?—to insinuate that my problems are greater than yours and worthy of your consideration?—to feed my ego under the glaring light of publicity?—to expose a friend *or acquaintance in circumstances that I have learned of by chance—or been exposed to in confidence? No! For me indeed no! Where, within the dictates of my conscience, I can speak with you of those I have known, and ofttimes loved, I will do so respecting their confidence in me and my regard for them.*

I launch myself upon this project with a light heart. I am a frustrated writer anyway, and I've nothing to lose; not even my time, for I shall enjoy writing this book. Add to a frustrated writer a frustrated musician, and most surely you will end up a frustrated actor. The author of this book is all three.

A considerable part of the success of Archibald MacLeish's play J.B. grew from a sense of personal identification felt by so many of its audience. I dare to hope that this, even if in lesser degree, may be the fate of the journey I am about to record.

I

War

In June of 1918 a rumor had begun to spread through British forces all along the front that the Germans were pulling out of their positions. At night one heard sounds from behind their lines which strongly indicated that transport and artillery were on the move. As Patrols Officer of the Second Battalion, Liverpool Scottish, I had become increasingly aware of the urgency to obtain more complete information. Conditions were forcing me to look upon my role in the Great War with greater seriousness than I had done in the past.

At that time, reconnaissance patrols operated at night. Once or twice a week, with three other men in diamond shape, I crawled about no-man's-land in the dark, hoping to bring back useful information about enemy dispositions and possible intentions. Our best bet, of course, was to meet up with a German patrol and take a prisoner. But this was rare, for both our own and the German patrols were not too willing to risk personal contacts and possibly their lives for such a purpose.

My men were old-timers and knew all the tricks of the game. When any member of a patrol thought he heard an enemy patrol, it was incumbent upon the officer in command to await confirmation and developments. The pros and cons of the least suspicion had to be weighed with infinite care. My men knew how to make use of this situation, and my patrols spent much time speculating on the possible appearance of these enemy ghosts! After an hour or so we returned to our lines and I wrote my report.

Some of these reports were based on fact, but most of them were pure fiction. As I remember them now, many of them were masterpieces of invention; inconclusive, yet always suggesting that every effort had been made by our patrol to garner information and/or make contact with the enemy. Under such circumstances one's imagination was often sorely tried in supplying acceptable "news items" that could be examined at Battalion H.Q. and then confidently filed away under the heading of "Intelligence." For many years after the war I kept my copies of these reports in an old theatrical basket that I had in storage and which, alas, was lost in a fire.

I cannot say that the changed conditions of June 1918 made an entirely new man of me, but I began to cast about for a new and more sure way to gain information on patrol. I went to Colonel Monroe, my commanding officer, and reasoned as follows: After "stand down" at dawn, sentry discipline relaxed to some extent. The possibility of a German daylight patrol seemed so remote that, had I warned our sentries to maintain close watch, I might have found myself recommended for sick leave. If our minds were so closed to this contingency, how much more blind would be the Germans, who followed the book implicitly and used little imagination.

I proposed to Colonel Monroe that Corporal Tanner, my sniper, and I go out into no-man's-land just before dawn and lay up until full daylight. At night it was always most difficult to judge objects and distances. In daylight these difficulties would be obviated. I further suggested we use camouflage, a theatrical device which I had first learned under very different, though not always more peaceful circumstances, and which would compensate us somewhat for the loss of anonymity afforded by darkness. The "ham" in me had suddenly become stronger than my sense of survival. Colonel Monroe seemed intrigued and gave his consent.

The following morning I was awakened by my batman at 3:30 A.M. Camouflage suits had been made for us to resemble trees. On our heads we wore wreaths of freshly plucked foliage; our faces and hands were blackened with burnt cork. About 5:00 A.M. we crawled through our wire and lay up in no-man's-land. All sentries had been alerted to our movements. The German trenches were some two hundred yards distant.

For several days we tested our adventure, and it soon became evident that the enemy had no suspicions whatsoever of our presence. We were able accurately to locate German machine-gun positions, which were later phoned back to artillery and put out of action. We also noted a sparseness of enemy front-line positions, supporting High Command's contention that something was up.

One day Colonel Monroe said, "Rathbone, we must have a prisoner or some positive identification—can you handle this, or shall we make a raid?"

"I can handle it, sir," I said.

I was supremely confident that the shock of our appearance in German trenches during daylight would sufficiently disorganize the enemy, thus enabling us to accomplish our purpose, and make our get-away.

And so the following morning we went out as usual and lay up until full daylight. Suddenly out of an empty sky a squadron of German airplanes dived down on us. Each airplane was painted a different color. The leading plane was black—and its pilot was the famous Baron von Richthofen—the second plane was painted red and its pilot was Hermann Goering. The other planes were painted blue, green, yellow, etc., but their pilots, as far as I know, never became as famous as their leaders. The squadron passed over us not more than 100 feet up, strafing the British, who returned their fire, while from the German lines there were cheers upon cheers. What event could top a thrilling visit from the famous "Richthofen Circus"? It had disrupted the monotony of the daily routine and given it an almost festive atmosphere. In a very few minutes the planes were gone, but an aura of unreality prevailed. We remained motionless, listening to the sounds of talking and laughter and casual movement from behind both our lines. Richthofen's arrival had served our purpose well. The enemy had let his guard drop. I whispered to Tanner, "Let's go."

We crawled so slowly that it must have taken us almost an hour to reach the German wire. I had picked a spot between two machine-gun posts. Reaching their wire I stood up and waited. Receiving no sign of recognition from enemy sentries, I ordered Tanner to follow me. Very carefully—like hunters —piece by piece we cut our way through the wire, reached their parapet, and rolled over into the German front lines. We remained there motionless for several minutes. The only sound now to be heard was a skylark climbing up into a cloudless blue sky, as the opposing armies took their midday siesta. We rose and proceeded slowly and with the utmost care along the German trench. We made our way around a traverse—then another stretch of empty trench—and proceeded further. Suddenly there were footsteps and a German soldier came into view behind the next traverse. He stopped suddenly, struck dumb, no doubt, by our strange appearance. Capturing him was out of the question; we were too far away from home. But before he could pull himself together and spread the alarm, I shot him twice with my revolver—he fell dead. Tanner tore the identification tags off his uniform and I rifled his pockets, stuffing a diary and some papers into my camouflage suit. (What a mania the Germans have always had for keeping detailed records.) Now things happened fast. There were sounds of movement on both sides of us, so we scaled the parapet, forced our way through the barbed wire —I have the scars on my right leg to this day—and ran for the nearest shell hole. We had hardly reached it when two machine guns opened a cross fire on us. We lay on the near lip of the crater, which was so close to their lines that it gave us cover. The machine-gun bullets pitted the rear of the crater.

Now what to do, with almost two hundred yards to go to make home base? Again I decided to gamble on German psychology. I told Tanner I would up-and-run to my left to the next shell hole; as soon as I was on my way he was to do the same thing, going to his right. It worked! As we dropped by turns into shell holes, the German machine gunners failed to make up their minds which of us to stay with, and their indecision unquestionably saved both our lives. Tanner and I arrived back in our trenches at approximately the same time —and at about one-half mile distant from each other. The information we had brought back was of much value. There seemed no doubt that a German retreat all along the line was imminent.

On my way back to headquarters to report—somebody said, "Gosh, but you stink!"

And now at last I could smell it myself—it was on my left boot. In one of the shell holes on my way back I had stepped into a decomposing body. For a moment I thought I was going to faint. Right there I removed the boot, and someone stuck a bayonet through it and heaved it back into no-man's-land. Up to that moment, I had felt no fear, sustained and driven by the bravura of the mission and with the image of Richthofen's bright circus dancing in my brain. With one shoe off and one shoe on, the reality and horror of war came rushing in on me.

Shortly after the incident just related, our division was taken out of the line. There were no orders on the board for our first day of rest—other than to clean up and sleep. I was billeted in a farmhouse. It was a beautiful day—bright sunshine and a clear sky. How quickly one's mood changed on these occasions. It was a little debilitating, at first, and one had to be careful to hold onto one's morale. The urgency of self-discipline being somewhat relaxed, one fell into a pattern of mild indulgences.

My room overlooked the farmyard, and my bed faced a window that looked into the yard—a high-mattressed, heavy old bed, in which I had floated through the night in a dreamless sleep. My batman, Private Isles, brought me my breakfast—steaming black hot tea, bacon and eggs, toast and marmalade. Then he picked up my tunic and kilt—my belt and my puttees and boots, and left. They would need a lot of elbow grease to get them cleaned and polished and bright for battalion inspection next morning. But I had nothing to worry about since Isles was the most meticulous batman in the regiment, and his pride in me was a matter of pride in himself and his work. As a civilian, Isles had sold hats in Liverpool, in all probability to members of my family. But he never took advantage of our being fellow-Liverpudlians, and even on the day he was demobilized he saluted me as smartly as on the first day we had met.

I was enjoying my breakfast and dreaming optimistically of going home on leave, when from the farmyard I heard the most terrifying squeals. Looking through the window, I saw the farmer lugging a pig out of a pen. The wretched animal was struggling violently. Suddenly the squeals turned into diminishing gurgles—the farmer had cut the pig's throat. A moment later I threw up my breakfast. Yes, one certainly must watch out for diminishing returns in one's morale.

That evening I met the farmer's daughter and promptly fell in love with her. There was something so gentle, wide-eyed, and sweet about her—she reminded me of A. P. Herbert's poem:

> "I like them fluffy," I gently replied.
> Not huffy, or stuffy, or puffy with pride.
> With downy soft eyebrows and artful blue eyes,
> The kind that the highbrows pretend to despise.
> With fluffy complexions like plums on the wall,
> With fluffy opinions and no brains at all!

She was the first pretty girl I had seen for a long time—and the results were disastrous. I couldn't sleep and all the next day I waited for that moment when I would see her again. Her mother never left us alone—her mother, who sat at the other end of the kitchen table—watching and listening and breathing heavy garlic fumes over us both.

I shall never know what Marie thought and felt about me,
as she could not understand English, and I was afraid to speak
to her in French in case her mother should understand my
intentions. I recited Rupert Brooke to her, and Shakespeare's
sonnets:

> Shall I compare thee to a Summer's day?
> Thou art more lovely and more temperate:

I had no idea whether Marie was inclined to be temperate
or not, and under the circumstances still less inclined to try
and find out. Inevitably, in due course, we were joined by her
pig-sticking father, a morose, suspicious-looking man. Not
that one could blame him—my intentions were definitely not
honorable—and he didn't have to be a particularly shrewd
man to notice it in my voice and in my manner. I made violent
love to Marie without once even touching her—while she
would sit looking at me, smiling with those limpid eyes, and
the drumming on the table with her fingers being intermin-
gled with periods of nibbling on something that looked like
salami. From time to time she would glance toward her
mother and meet that expressionless stare with an enigmatical
stare of her own. After about an hour of this sort of thing,
Marie was ordered to bed. Oh! the miserable frustration of it
all!

In desperation I managed to find out where her bedroom
was situated. Fortunately there was a tree quite close to her
bedroom window, whose branches gave promise that I might
make a surreptitious entrance to her room. One night I decided to proceed upon my evil purposes. It was a pitch-black
night and I had difficulty in finding my way. Eventually I
found the tree and scaled it. I balanced myself precariously on
a branch and edged myself slowly toward her window. I gently tapped on it once—twice—three times. Suddenly I heard
a startled voice. "Qui est là?" It was her mother's voice.
Wrong tree—wrong room. The branch broke and I fell with
a thud to the ground. As I picked my way back in the dark-

ness, I heard a window open and a male voice this time, inquiring, "Qui est là?"—the pig-sticker, ye gods!

Fortunately, the next day, there was a phone call from my brother, John. His regiment, The Dorsets, was stationed close by, and he had leave to come over and spend the night with me. This, at least temporarily, put an end to my budding romance. Colonel Monroe obligingly gave his consent and John and I spent a glorious day together. John had an infectious sense of humor and a personality that made friends for him everywhere he went. In our Mess on that night he made himself as well-liked as in his own regiment. We retired late, full of good food and Scotch whisky. We shared my bed and were soon sound asleep. It was still dark when I awakened from a nightmare. I had just seen John killed. I lit the candle beside my bed and held it to my brother's face—for some moments I could not persuade myself that he was not indeed dead. At last I heard his regular gentle breathing. I kissed him and blew out the candle and lay back on my pillow again. But further sleep was impossible. A tremulous premonition haunted me—a premonition which even the dawn failed to dispel.

Some weeks later, at one o'clock on June 4, 1918, I was sitting in my dugout in the front line. Suddenly I thought of John, and for some inexplicable reason I wanted to cry, and did. Immediately, I wrote him a letter to which he never replied, and in due course I received the news of his death in action at exactly one o'clock on June the fourth. We had always been very close to one another.

More weeks passed by and once again my battalion was out of the line, resting. I heard by chance that the area around Marie's farmhouse had been heavily shelled. The farmhouse was not far distant, and come what may, I had to see for myself what might have happened to her. I borrowed the Colonel's horse. It was raining cats-and-dogs, and I was soon soaked to the skin. Precariously I found my way to the farmhouse. It was a heaped-up pile of rubble and the ground all around it pitted with shell holes. Other houses nearby had been badly damaged, too. A stray dog hunted for food—he was the only living thing in sight.

Making my way slowly back, I stopped at a house and made some inquiries. There was no news of my little Marie and her family—my little Marie with her "downy soft eyebrows and artful blue eyes . . ." When I eventually reached headquarters I apologized for the condition of the Colonel's horse, but I offered no excuses. I called Private Isles and asked him to have my uniform dried out. Then I sent word to Colonel Monroe asking to be excused from Mess that night—I was not well and had gone to bed. Mercifully, very soon, we returned to our trenches. And mercifully, very soon, the war-to-end-all-wars, the war that was to make the world safe for democracy, was over. The Fifty-seventh Division was sent to Le Havre awaiting transport to England and demobilization. A miserable town, Le Havre. At least it seemed so to me in those days. There was little to do but to get into trouble. And there was plenty of trouble almost anywhere you cared to look for it. However, the Liverpool Scottish left town with a fine reputation for their courteous and gentlemanly behavior. This was given personal recognition by a certain "Madam" of a certain "House of Flowers." She and the "girls" decided to throw a farewell party for "the boys."

I think it was the most unique party I have ever attended. "Madam" was gorgeously resplendent in an outrageously decolleté evening gown—while the "girls" were all dressed in their Sunday best. A large central room was charmingly decorated with flowers, and there was a sumptuous supper, at which nothing but champagne was served. An elderly, rather superior-looking woman thumped out dance music of the period on an upright piano that had definitely seen better days. The style and the decorum were magnificent. We danced with the "girls"—but conversation was difficult as they spoke little English—and most of us spoke less French.

The whole affair had an almost "classic" dignity, and woe to the Scot who might dare to get out of hand. The party was over about 10:00 P.M. and some of the men took their "girls" for a drink to a local hotel; a sentimental reminder, no doubt, of where they had first met. Later, they may have returned and with "Madam's" consent lingered on for a while, bidding one another a more intimate and final adieu—Vive la France!

EPILOGUE

In the summer of 1934 I was in Toledo, Ohio, with Miss Katharine Cornell, preparing *Romeo and Juliet* for our opening in New York. The Sunday we arrived there, Arturo Toscanini was on the radio with his famous Symphony of the Air Orchestra. I was listening intently, in my hotel room, when suddenly the telephone bell rang; my wife answered. "Someone for you," she said, handing me the phone. I knew no one in Toledo; who could it be?

"Hello, yes, who is it?"

A very English voice answered, "Corporal Tanner, here." I could hardly believe my ears.

"Corporal Tanner! What on earth are you doing in the United States?"

"I'm a citizen," he answered. "I'm a cop, here in Toledo."

Needless to say, we enjoyed a somewhat emotional reunion, which my wife Ouida helped us celebrate well into the early hours of the following morning. Some of the ghosts in my life have come back to haunt me, and some of them have been astonishingly real.

2

The Great Illusion

——Vive la France! Vive l'Angleterre! Vive l'Ecosse!
Ypres, Festubert, Mademoiselle from Armentières, "pinky,
pinky parlez-vous," Colonel Monroe, Private Isles, Corporal
Tanner—it was a whole and complete life that quite plausibly
might have been spent on some other planet. As real as anything I should ever know in my life and yet, with each succeeding dawn of each succeeding day in each succeeding year,
I was to be left with an ever-increasing sense of its unreality.
How in the name of all the saints had this thing happened to
me? In August of 1914 I would not have believed it possible
that I could eventually become a competent and reasonably
well-adjusted soldier. But that was just what *had* happened.

When England declared war on Germany, I had been very
young, and dreaming of prodigious accomplishments for myself in my chosen profession. But by the middle of September
in that year the end of my dream world as a promising young
actor appeared ominously on the periphery of my life. I felt
physically sick to my stomach as I saw or heard or read of the
avalanche of brave young men rushing to join "the colors";
and if needs-be to give their lives for God and King and
Country (for King and Country maybe—but for God! What
utter blasphemy so casually to inform God which side he was
on). Was I "pigeon-livered" that I felt no such call to duty
(or did I, and just refuse to accept it?), that I was pondering
how long I could delay "joining up?" The very idea of sol-
diering appalled me—and to think of it, there were men who

did these things of their own free choice, and some of them had become great generals and admirals and had statues erected to them, like the one to Lord Nelson in Trafalgar Square in London. All this I had always accepted as I had accepted fairy tales and stories about explorers and wild-game hunters, but only through the medium of books and in paintings. As a boy I was an avid reader of G. A. Henty, and stories about the glory of the Empire by Rudyard Kipling. The nursery walls featured reproductions of Lord Kitchener, *The Charge of the Light Brigade*, and *The Thin Red Line* (the Guards Brigade at Waterloo). But now these things were become an inescapable reality for me personally—

> Theirs not to reason why,
> Theirs but to do and die.

What a shambles such nonsense made of all good common sense. Most probably somewhere in Germany there was a young man, with much the same ideas as I had, and one of us was quite possibly destined to shoot and kill the other. The whole thing was monstrous, utterly and unbelievably monstrous—irrational, pitiable, ugly, and sordid.

But in due course (and in spite of myself!) I eventually became a soldier; and as Private Rathbone I was trained at a camp at Richmond Park, just outside London, to kill Germans. I learned to hate them, to call them Boche and Huns, to believe them capable of all kinds of barbarous atrocities including bayoneting babies. I learned to kill them with a Lewis gun, a rifle, and a bayonet. Of all my training I loathed bayonet practice most—rushing frantically at a sackful of wet straw and thrusting my bayonet into it—turn the blade sharply so as to increase the size of the wound—then withdraw the cold steel and proceed on to another dummy figure and give it some of the same medicine. The bayonet and the boot. How these images crowd in on me.

By the grace of God a hiatus saved me from what looked like being an early baptism of fire on the battlefields of northern France. I purposely and with grim intent applied for a commission and was accepted. The officers training camp I was sent to was at Gailes in Scotland (the famous golf course at Gailes is one of the most difficult in the world). There I met and became close friends with a young man by the name of Macdonald, a Scottish International Rugby footballer. Between us we took over the camp and organized it into "the Reds" and "the Blues!" We played Rugby and soccer and held all manner of track meets against each other. We were enormously efficient and uncompromisingly competitive. Very soon Macdonald and I became and were accepted as a couple of arrogant little heroes, both by the cadets and the officers in charge of the training camp. But one day the commandant, Captain Smith, sent for us and coldly advised us that our term of training had but three more weeks to go and he saw little chance of our passing our exams and receiving our commissions, since our classroom work was of an extremely low caliber! Having scared the living daylights out of us he rose from behind his desk and offered us both a cigarette, which we miserably accepted. Then he returned to his desk and sat looking at us grimly. At last he could bear it no longer and his handsome face broke into an easy smile.

"Look," he said, "I've been watching you fellows very closely ever since you arrived here and it didn't take me long to realize that you both have unusual qualities of leadership. The army in France needs young men like you and I am going to see to it that you get your commissions—but on one condition."

On any condition as far as we were concerned! Captain Smith continued, lighting another cigarette.

"You fellows are going to 'swat' like dogs for these next three weeks and come up with creditable exam papers. It's up to you, so get going and don't you let me down. And I don't give a damn who wins the football final. Dismissed!"

We both got our commissions and "the Blues" (my team) won the football final, Captain Smith presenting the cup!

I was sent to the Liverpool Scottish (as per my request).

Here again luck was with me, but this time not of my wangling! The Liverpool Scottish, Second Battalion, was attached to the Fifty-seventh Division, a division which for reasons best known to the War Office was held in England for several months.

This considerable period of adjustment had worked miracles for me. The companionship with my fellow men of the British Expeditionary Force, *their* feelings, *their* needs, and *their* problems were a challenge and a great responsibility that I could not refuse to accept. As Private Rathbone I cannot be certain what might have been my fate as a man, "pigeon-livered" or not. But as Second Lieutenant Rathbone I was no longer in a position to consider myself. I was in command of a platoon of men who were almost completely dependent on me in every possible way, and who looked to me for example and leadership, whatever the circumstances. I became very fond of my men and I like to think that they were fond of me.

By the time I reached France I was completely adjusted. There was a job to be done and it had to be finished before I could start dreaming again. Saying "good-by" to Mother and "Daddie" at Victoria Station in London was nothing like so bad as I had anticipated it might be. Somehow or other they didn't seem quite like the same people I had known a few months ago. I could find in them no signs of any deep emotion, and for myself I can honestly say I disclosed none either. We had conditioned ourselves severely for this moment, and now we were being impelled, by the splendor of the uniform I wore for King and Country, toward that destiny that might mean we should never see one another again (a thought we had learned to ignore)—or a reunion in distant years to come (a thought to which none of us could afford to give consideration).

"It's like seeing Basil off to school in the old days isn't it, Edgar?" My mother was speaking.

"Yes . . . write as soon and as often as you can, son, won't you?" My father's emotions were nearer the surface.

There was a train whistle, some wry smiles, and a final "good-by dear"—I was never to see my mother again.

As the troop train sped on its way to the troopship at Folkestone I thought of Rupert Brooke and shared his sentiments.

> If I should die, think only this of me:
> That there's some corner of a foreign field
> That is for ever England.

* * * * * * * * * * * * * * * * *

> And think, this heart, all evil shed away,
> A pulse in the eternal mind, no less
> Gives somewhere back the thoughts by England given;
> Her sights and sounds; dreams happy as her day;
> And laughter, learnt of friends; and gentleness,
> In hearts at peace, under an English heaven.

It was a curiously silent group of men that stood on an upper deck watching the coast line of England come into focus on that morning of our return home for demobilization. As I remember it now we had boarded the ship in high spirits. We were still very young and memories fade with merciful ease at that age. The war was already a long way behind us, and much of the fear and the filth and the smell were drifting into a healthy forgetfulness. Why then had we suddenly grown so silent? Because there were some memories that could not so easily be erased. There were those who should, but could not come back with us, who rested forever silent and forever still in graves of French soil that they had made "for ever England"—my brother John being one of them. Years ago it seemed, and years ago it was, that on one's way overseas for the first time, on that troop train from London to Folkestone, one had shared with Rupert Brooke his thoughts in *The Soldier*—and now there were those last thoughts in his poem that our hearts would say in prayer, but could not say as he had said it.

If sentiment there be in this then be it so, but no sentimentality. In sentiment there is truth; in sentimentality there is an element of self-pity, and of this latter there was none, I hope and believe, in any of us. And as I look back on it now I am glad of the sentiment aroused in us on that day upon that ship. And I am equally glad I do not share with so many young people of my later years the ridicule and scorn they so freely express for this heartwarming feeling of true affection.

In time all this and much else would pass silently by, soon to be replaced by the reality of things as they were. There was a tinge of fear about one's heart and mind as the readjustment to civilian life took shape. For so long there had been but one single purpose to one's life, a life completely disciplined and organized from "up top." This hard-earned routine was not going to be easy to escape from. So much would never be the same again. So much must be changed within myself and in relation to others and there would be no superior officer to turn to for help and guidance. *I was completely on my own for the first time in my life.* Of course there were my father and my sister. But my father had aged considerably, I thought, since I had last seen him. He seemed completely lost without my mother, and to the day of his death he was to cling to me desperately, loving me more and more in his uncertain loneliness. My sister was lost to us both. Her spirit had been deeply wounded by my mother's and brother's death during the war, and year after year after year even to this very day she mourns them in an ever-increasing solitude of prayer and contemplation. And so each one of us lived alone in our own particular form of loneliness. Together our memories of the past would unquestionably have been shattered by our individual and peculiar forms of selfishness. In all this I was the most selfish, for a strong sense of moving forward was already trembling within me, while they had decided to live in the past. Then there were my wife and son. He was now nearly four years old.

Marion Foreman had been on the stage for some time before I met her at Stratford on Avon in August 1913. She was an excellent actress with a beautiful speaking and singing voice. We were cast opposite one another in "second leads," such as Lorenzo and Jessica in *The Merchant of Venice*, and Silvius and Phoebe in *As You Like It*. Both on and off the stage we saw much of each other for many months. We were married in October 1914 and in July 1915 our son was born. Shortly afterward I went to war. We were separated in August 1919 and Marion divorced me in 1926. There is nothing more of this that I wish to remember. The colors here are gray and often black, and regrets and hurts leave scars that can never permanently be erased. Even after so many years I do not trust myself to be completely objective. There are too many elusive temptations in facing up to or avoiding the truth. But certain it is that broken marriages, particularly where children are involved, inevitably lead to hurtful and sometimes tragic consequences.

Added to this considerable disruption in my family life there was also a disturbing period of waiting upon events that would lead me back to the theater. During this time I experienced hours of deep despondency, even fear. There were now two homes to keep up (however simple my one room in Kensington might be), and my money was running out. I borrowed a hundred pounds from my cousin Rosalind Paget and later another hundred pounds from an old friend. It was essential that the decision I had made should not affect my wife and child in their way of living. I had much time for reflection and self-analysis. Self-condemnation fought bitterly with self-justification, and there was no one to turn to and talk with about such intimate personal matters. My father was hurt and my sister was shocked by the break up of my marriage. Marion refused to believe that we would not in due course come together again, and my son was missing his father. In search of some answer to the voice of my insistent conscience, and as a sop to my self-imposed loneliness, I would often allow myself to drift back into the past and relive much of it again in daydreams, and in dreams of my restless sleeping.

* * *

The night was black as pitch; this I remember. I was too sleepy to know if the stars looked down on me. In later years I was to learn that one could reach up and almost touch the sky on such a cold, clear night; on such a night as this, at six thousand feet above sea level, just outside Johannesburg, South Africa, where I had been born, a brief three and a half years before.

We were enveloped in darkness, my mother and I, as she held me gently but firmly against her breast and picked her way carefully through the night toward The Sisters of Nazareth Home, where we were to seek sanctuary. A few paces behind, my father followed carrying my sister, aged two. The blackness surrounding us, and strange unfamiliar sounds are now my only memories of this eventful night—indefinite recollections, without that taint of terror which might so easily have tormented me had not the steady beat of my mother's heart lulled me back to sleep again.

There was a price on my father's head. He was accused by the Boers of being a British spy. Whether he was or not I shall never know. I never asked him about it, and he never gave the slightest indication at any time that he would be interested in satisfying my curiosity! The rest of the story I must relate to you as my mother told it to me, many years later, and many years ago.

The Jameson Raid was an abortive venture, and my father had been a friend of Dr. Jameson, and also of Cecil Rhodes, who was "the power behind the throne" in South Africa at the close of the twentieth century.

The Jameson Raid into the Boer colony of the Transvaal began on December 29, 1895, and it was upon this day, or rather night (or a night later perhaps—my mother was not quite sure on this point), that it became necessary for my father and his family to seek sanctuary. Heaven alone knows what further complications to all our lives might have ensued had my father been captured by the Boer forces, who had turned back Dr. Jameson and effected his capture three days after the abortive venture started.

It was of course not possible to stay with the Sisters of Nazareth very long, and a couple of nights later the four of us left for the railroad yards, intent upon making our way to Durban, Natal, a British Crown Colony. We had been forced to leave our home and everything in it the instant news of the failure of the raid came through, and we were able to take with us only the clothes we wore and a bundle of hastily gathered accessories.

There was a considerable exodus from Johannesburg early in January, 1896. Many British subjects were alarmed by the failure of the raid and fearful of its consequences. Somewhat hysterically, they ran for cover until they could see from a safe distance which way the wind might blow in regard to their own individual and personal interests. My father's interests were perfectly clear—to head for Durban, Natal, and the first boat back to England! It would seem that he had had all he wanted of the newly developed gold fields, President Paul Kruger, and Her Majesty's unofficial representative, Mr. Cecil Rhodes.

Once again, under cover of darkness, we left our sanctuary. Upon arrival at the railroad station we found that train service had been considerably disrupted. There was however a freight train leaving in a couple of hours. The situation was too urgent to wait for a passenger train in the morning. So we boarded a freight car and prepared for the long haul to Durban. It is some three hundred odd miles from Johannesburg to Durban, one hundred and twenty miles of which would be consumed in reaching the Natal Border—one hundred and twenty miles—and every mile fraught with danger to us all. We were fortunate in finding a car not too heavily loaded, in which there appeared to be adequate room for brief exercising should circumstances allow such a luxury. At one end of the car there was a small wooden seat. There my mother sat with her two children in her arms, while underneath it crouched my father, well hidden by the voluminous folds of my mother's skirt. Intermittently could be heard the sounds of voices and the coupling and uncoupling of cars as the freight train was made up. Every start held the promise that we were on our way, and the hope that my father could take a brief respite from his cramped hiding place. At one moment we were left for an interminable period on a siding. My father was enjoying a cigarette, and looking out into the cold, dark, starlit night. Suddenly his body tensed. He was about to throw his cigarette out of the car, but thought better of it and stamped it out slowly and deliberately with his foot. Without a word he motioned to my mother and returned to his place under the seat. She was immediately alert to his action, and before long she could hear the measured tread of men approaching. Then my father's voice, "Can you hear me Barbara?" Her heart beat a little faster as she answered him, "Yes."

"Boers—they're armed—be careful," he continued. "Wake the children and if necessary make them cry."

The sound of the measured tread of feet came slowly closer and closer. Then it stopped in front of the open freight-car door, and someone looked in. He was a huge man with a beard, no hat, and a captured British rifle slung over his shoulder. Mother always said that he looked like General Botha. His eyes rapidly took in the contents of the freight car, and finally came to rest on us.

"What are you doing here?"

"I must go to Durban with my children."

"Why?"

"My husband is in Durban—he is ill—he needs me."

"Your name?"

"George—Barbara George," she replied, using her maiden name.

"You English?"

"Yes!"

"And your husband is English too?"

"Yes."

"And what is your English husband doing in Durban?"

"He works there."

He looked at her quizzically. "He works there—he is ill—and you are in Johannesburg?"

"We have been visiting the children's grandfather."

At this moment, my mother, who had been pinching me vigorously, obtained the results she had been anxiously waiting for. I let forth a hideous scream, and could by no means be consoled! The desired effect was accomplished—the big man at the door sagged visibly and slumped out of sight. Then his voice was heard saying, "All right, lady, all right—be on your way and may the good Lord protect you." To the Boers the Bible and the precepts of family life were a religion they not only professed, but practiced.

A moment later the freight-car door was closed. Far in the distance at first, and then coming closer and closer, the sharp contact of couplings could be heard. At last a sudden jolt as our coupling made contact, and in the darkness there was a sense of movement. My father emerged from his hiding place. He kissed my mother, and took up his duties as sentry until we should arrive at the Natal Border. The journey to Durban was uneventful, except for the fact that my mother showed symptoms of sickness, which worried my father very much. Upon arrival in Durban it was to be proven that his fears were not unfounded. In a Durban hospital it was diagnosed that my mother had typhoid fever. A day or so later both my sister and I joined her in the hospital, patients of the same dread disease. Typhoid fever! All three of us lay at death's door for many days.

After several weeks we were well enough to sail on a Union Castle liner for England. However, my mother begged my father to postpone our sailing for a week because of a dream she had had. Though he was anxious to return home, my mother's "hallucination," as he called it, concerned him deeply and he canceled our passage, and we sailed a week later.

"There are more things in heaven and earth . . . than are

dreamt of in your philosophy." So often in one's life a situation or a circumstance can best be epitomized by turning to Mr. Shakespeare, who seems to have said more things for more people than any other writer who ever lived. I do not ask you to accept, without questioning, what I am about to tell you, only to believe me when I say that my mother was incapable of being untruthful and that her story was substantiated by my father. The dream which my mother experienced in such detail, and which caused our delay in sailing, was as follows: She dreamed we had sailed and were experiencing heavy seas in the Bay of Biscay. Suddenly terrifying sounds indicated that something very serious had happened. A steward entered our cabin and informed us that all passengers were ordered on deck immediately, and to take such warm clothing as might be at hand. Once again in my mother's arms, my father carrying my sister, my parents found themselves on the main deck. A tremendous storm was at the height of its fury, and it was evident that the lifeboats were useless, several already having been washed away. There was no question in my mother's mind but that we should all be drowned. The ship was listing badly and was powerless to keep her course. Wave after wave battered her helpless hulk. This agonizing experience was momentarily alleviated by a parade on deck, in full-dress uniform, of a band of the Seaforth Highlanders. A command rang out and their pipe band began playing "Flowers of the Forest," as the ship started to sink. At this moment my mother awakened.

The ship on which we had canceled passage sailed on schedule and all on board enjoyed a pleasant uneventful trip, until they reached the Bay of Biscay. There, in one of the worst storms ever recorded, the ship sank with all hands, including a band of the Seaforth Highlanders, who played themselves into a watery grave with "Flowers of the Forest." The Union Castle Line can verify these facts. My mother's strange participation in this terrifying story you must accept, and bring to it such answer as you may.

We reached England aboard the *Walmer Castle,* unaware of the fate that had been in store for us. And so as a boy of four, I had already defied the stars three times.

* * *

Childhood was sweet—very sweet. The days were long, but not nearly long enough for all the dreams and adventures we envisioned and planned and experienced—my brother, my sister, and I. I had a little brother now, and the family was as complete as it would ever be.

The woods at the bottom of our garden were a magic forest peopled with the strange beings of our imaginations. The nursery was warm and friendly with games of an infinite variety. In our bedroom the firelight flickered fitfully and lulled us to sleep, but not before Mother and Daddy had brought us an assurance of security beyond measure—"Gentle Jesus meek and mild, look upon a little child . . ." "Our Father, who art in Heaven . . ." said together, kneeling beside our beds.

Distant voices downstairs—guests to dinner. The night that Mother came into our bedroom and lit the candle beside my bed—tears in her eyes. . . . "Wake up my darlings, wake up —the Queen is dead." Queen Victoria. Little did we realize that for all of us this was the beginning of the end of an Empire upon which the sun never sets. . . .

The first tremulous stirrings of puberty with Esther—little Esther with her amorous odor of hay—the hay loft was at the farmhouse at the bend in the road, where we met wide-eyed, expectant, fearful, as we paused in a kiss . . . loving and longing . . . Esther's hair caressing my face . . . my hands trembling with the willful impulse to explore the divine mystery of her being. . . . She wore sneakers—dirty little white sneakers and she turned her toes inward as she walked . . . holding my hand, and the appleblossom flecking her wayward hair.

Sneakers—pumps—cricket boots—football boots—track shoes

—theatrical boots and shoes—army boots and "civvies"—each stir up memories that linger indelibly.

Pumps—that pair of black patent-leather shoes with the little black bows on them—worn at one's first dance, where Cynthia was dressed as a fairy queen—and one learned that to love carries no guarantee of being loved in return.

The disturbing perfume of new-mown grass on a cricket field—the exciting stimulating odor of "dubbin" rubbed affectionately into the leather of one's football boots—that firm sympathetic response of the soil as one dug one's spiked shoes into it at the beginning of a race—that sick-sweet smell of decomposing flesh on army boots—theatrical boots and shoes that required one to move with an ease and grace and a style, lost long ago to man's modern utilitarian mode of dress—"civvies" that felt like a bedroom slipper when exchanged for that army boot.

The family Christmas at Greenbank Cottage with Grandmama and Grandpapa—the cuckoo clock in the hall—making butterscotch in the nursery on a rainy day—my first introduction to the theater, the pantomime. Producing and directing a play I had written in which I, of course, played the leading role. The improvisation and imagination that went into the costumes, the scenery, and the props. The squabbles during rehearsals, caused mainly by the fact that no one in the cast had a part comparable to the one I had written for myself. Then at last, it was curtain time. Some old drapes of Grandmama's from the attic—incredibly insecure—however did they hold up? Our audience? "The grownups" of course, silent, submissive, and sartorially resplendent in full evening dress. All else but my own personal triumph was soon forgotten, except the determination to one day play a leading role in a professional pantomime—in a real theater.

During the last week of the Christmas holidays there was a wonderful party at Great-Uncle William's when I wore my patent-leather pumps. We traveled the breadth of England to get there. *Oh, if only I could tell you. . . .*

The train left London for Liverpool at midday. It was
December 21 of that year in which, on June 13, I had
proudly turned ten. The magic of childhood and the growing pains of each succeeding year on the road toward adolescence mingled disturbingly this Christmas. But approaching
adolescence held a slight advantage and, as the long train
pulled out of Paddington Station, the mystery of childhood
clung desperately to the fringe of my memories . . . Grandmama's two-horsed carriage, pungent with the odor of Russian leather, with which it was fitted. A very special treat it
was to go driving with the old lady; to have tea at Great-
Uncle William's at Greenbank, where the two white swans
sailed majestically on the lake; and "Rags," an ancient fox
terrier, who sat and watched them for hours. Rags was a
philosopher now. Years ago he had chased the swans, and
once they had caught him and nearly killed him. Since that
day he had been content to watch them, planning for the
moment when he would take his revenge! But the day never
came. So he had to be content to kill them both in his
dreams, which he did very often. . . . And then to return
home with Grandmama after it was dark! The carriage
lamps shining like beacons, and chasing away the little shadows that came too close and were frightened, which took
one look at those wonderful carriage lamps and fled precipi-
tously into the protecting arms of the larger and more distant night. And Granny's black bonnet, tied in a neat bow
under her chin, serenely adorning her little old face, as she
snoozed, and the carriage jogged on. . . .

Memories of a near and yet, at ten years old, so distant a
yesterday! . . . The gun-metal watch in one's pocket. Oh,
the wonder of it but a year ago! . . . A present from Mother
last Christmas, it had now become little more than an accustomed utility. . . . The small blade of one's pocketknife
(Father's present the Christmas before last) had lost its point
last summer, whittling an old walking stick of Uncle Alfred's. (There had been trouble about this!) The large blade

had rusted easily in London's damp fogs, and needed cleaning constantly. How fiercely those two blades had gleamed on Christmas morning but two years ago!

Our train to Liverpool hurled itself through the countryside with that ever-insistent rhythm so conducive to sleep. I dozed off and was awakened by the station noises at Crewe Junction. With what incredible speed one travels that unknown distance between sleeping and waking. I had been watching the telegraph poles pass by, each one equidistant from the next, and the Carter's Little Liver Pills advertisements, which gave one the ever-increasing number of miles from London. Distant objects stood still; those nearer passed by like figures on a merry-go-round. Tickety-tack, tickety-tack, tickety-tack, I slept again as mile after mile we sped on our way to Liverpool.

Russian leather! Granny's carriage was there at the station to meet us. There had been snow and Greenbank Cottage was draped in white, with glistening icicles hanging from the eaves. The windows radiated the warmth from inside, and Christmas decorations peeked promisingly from between drawn curtains. The old cuckoo clock stood there in the hall where it had always stood, as impersonal and imperious as ever, in spite of the little bird's hourly efforts to brighten up the proceedings. My room opened onto a balcony overlooking the hall; and my windows looked onto the rose garden with its high, red brick wall.

The moonlight filtered through my drawn blinds. The cuckoo sang his hourly song in the hall. I was overexcited and could not sleep—ten o'clock—eleven—midnight. What strange event awaited me on some approaching tomorrow? I always knew when "something" was going to happen. Good or bad, I could always sense its coming. I wanted to cry, and buried my face in my pillow with my arms tightly about it. Everything was so very very still. Only the cuckoo's voice and the tick tock, tick tock of the clock in the hall—I fell asleep.

"Where do you live?" I asked.

"In Wavertree. Next door to your grandmother's house," she replied, without looking at me.

Her light brown hair framed her piquant little face, with its dark brown eyes, and a full warm mouth. Her whole being radiated an impertinent charm. I loved her as I was sure I would never love anyone else again in my life!

"That's a very pretty dress."

"It's not a dress, it's a costume," she corrected me disdainfully.

Her crown of the Fairy Queen had been cut out of cardboard and painted gold. She carried a wand with a silver star at the top of it. The bodice to her costume was made of satin, studded with sequins. The skirt, to just above her knees, was layer upon layer of white and pink tulle that stood out from her protectingly, so that it was impossible to stand very close to her!

"You had better go and sit down somewhere; the play is about to begin."

It was the voice of a "grownup"—Aunt Alice of course! She always "managed" the children's Christmas party at Great-Uncle William's. There was a smile in her eyes, a smile of sympathetic understanding; that look that "grownups" always assume when they think they recognize "first love." (Aunt Alice was a spinster and was therefore most curious about such things.)

The room was dark as the play ran its course, many children participating. I have no recollection as to what the play was about. I only knew that in it there was the most beautiful Fairy Queen that had ever been seen.

"In Wavertree. Next to your grandmother's house," she had said.

I must see her again, I must, I must!

But the Christmas holiday would end one day—what would I do then!

The frightening thought quite overwhelmed me for a moment. Forget it! Forget it! There could never be an end.

Somehow, everyone must be made to understand that I could not go on living without her.

The garden wall at Granny's was high, but not too high. I would scale it some night . . . tonight! I would call to her from her garden. I would beg her to come down to me. I would hold her in my arms to keep her warm, and because I loved her so terribly! And I would *tell* her how much I loved her, and she would understand, and we would run away together!

"Say 'good night,' dear, and thank Uncle William for a lovely party." It was my mother's voice.

"Good night, Uncle William, it was such a lovely party and"—(she's so beautiful, so unbelievably beautiful I cannot live without her)—"and I will never forget how beautiful it was as long as I live."

"Button up your coat, darling, it's very cold. Say good night to Cynthia, Basil."

"Good night, Cynthia—and"—(tonight in the garden I shall be waiting. You *will* come to me, won't you? *please,* and we will go away together; somewhere, where no one will find us, forever)—"and—you were the most lovely Fairy Queen I have ever seen." There was so much more to say but not now. (I love you. Can you hear me? I can't say it here, but you know it, don't you? Please *love me,* because I can't live without you.)

The horse's hooves beat a staccato rhythm in the still cold night.

"What's the matter, darling, you're not crying, are you?"

"Of course not, Mother. I think I've got something in my eye."

"Blow your nose, dear—that's right—better?"

"Yes, thank you."

As I looked through my bedroom window the moon came out from behind a cloud, and I could swear that he winked at me. No, it had not been a dream—it had happened—last night!

The rose garden below was a carpet of snow— It must be

very cold out there, I thought; and there would be our foot-
prints to betray us; and my allowance was all used up; and
there would be no more until I returned to school next term.
I felt very sleepy, and when one is sleepy like that it's better
to wait till the morning. If it were a nice day we would go
skating on the pond, and she would be there and I would see
her again. In the morning I would write her a letter and slip
it into her muff as we skated together. Yes, we could write
to each other, and I would save every penny of my allowance next term, and then at Easter! But we never went
to Granny's at Easter, only Christmas. Oh, why was it all so
difficult! I crawled back into bed again and slipped gently
into a dreamless sleep.

I never saw Cynthia again. She left with her parents for
St. Moritz the next morning. And we never spent another
Christmas at Granny's either. Granny died in the spring.
And there remain for me now only the memories; the little
old face in a black bonnet, tied with a neat silk bow under
the chin; the scent of Russian leather; the cuckoo clock in
the hall; a garden by moonlight under a blanket of snow; and
a pain in my heart, as I think of these things, that will stay
with me as long as I live.

Many years later, in what I believe is generally referred to
as one's declining years, I was to revisit Liverpool for the
first time since my childhood. I took a taxi and drove out to
Wavertree— The windows of Greenbank Cottage were shut-
tered, and a sign spelled out two ominous words "For Sale."
As I lit a cigarette, I felt something rubbing softly against
my legs—a slight movement and the cat fled, jumping up
onto the garden wall. From which point of vantage it eyed
me, with some hostility I thought, as if daring me to follow. Behind that wall was the rose garden, and looking up, I
saw the windows of my room. One of the shutters was loose
and moved slowly back and forth as if determined to attract
my attention. I turned and walked away.

The road to Greenbank was heavily shaded by the new
foliage of spring—there it stood!—the iron gates with the

family insignia, MENS SANA IN CORPORE SANO—the broad driveway—the long sloping lawn to the lake.

Suddenly I heard myself ask, "But where are the swans?"

"There was swans here once I'm told," a voice replied.

I turned and standing beside me was a little old man, in a cloth cap, tweed coat, corduroy breeches, and gaiters, smoking a blackened clay pipe.

"Who are *you?*" he asked.

"I came here often when I was a child." And then, "Who lives here now?"

"I do," he said. "I'm the caretaker. The folks is all dead. Fine people I'm told they was, with plenty o' money. But it's all different hereabouts now." He paused for a moment, pulling on his pipe, which had gone out. "This place here's been taken over for some sort of social service work." He seemed pleased and surprised at what he had said!

"Is that your dog over there?" I asked.

"Beg pardon, sir?"

"Rags! Rags!" I called to the animal, who was approaching us cautiously.

"His name ain't Rags," said the old man, relighting his pipe from a match held protectingly in a wonderfully gnarled old hand that looked like the withered branch of a tree. "I calls 'im Snotty. 'E's not much to look at, but 'e's a good watcher. Don't go too near him, sir—'e'll be apt to bite."

I looked at my watch. There was a lump in my throat, and I just managed to say, "I think I ought to be going."

We walked together in silence down the driveway to the gates. He closed them behind me, then doffing his cap and almost as if to himself, "Must 'ave been a nice place once."

"It was—if only I could tell you," and I walked quickly away.

At last I knew, and forever, that memories are like forgotten melodies that are best left to sing their songs in the silent places of one's heart.

3

Repton School 1906-10

So very male—the football boot, beside which the cricket boot takes on a somewhat feminine texture, despite its metal nails in the soles—carefully whitened with blanco before every cricket match—with little green smudges here and there, where the grass's green juice has irreparably marked the right toe as it dragged across the crease when one bowled that ball that was to be the dismissal of one's opponent at bat—a fast bowler with a natural swing-in from the leg side —pitch the ball a few feet short of the batsman so that it rose sharply from the turf and turned in onto his off-stump. (A curve ball from the outside, to you baseball fans.) Larwood and Voce for England, Gregory and MacDonald for Australia—what a ruckus there was to be about "body bowling" in years to come in the test matches in Australia.

Yet a tall spindly kid was doing it in 1910 in house matches at Repton School. He never got his cricket colors, and he would have sacrificed all the best of his prowess in the field of sport to gain this honor. Such disappointments loom large in a youngster's life—but his character develops along those lines so earnestly sought after at English public schools. He must learn to lose and show no emotion in losing.

Football boots—well soaked in "dubbin" against the invariably inclement weather—football boots with their masculine leather thongs . . . on the notice board outside Pears' Hall—that magic word—"Hopefuls" . . . one day my name on that board . . . the first step toward one's colors. Days when one had played badly . . . inspired days when one played with the thought of some day playing for England! Then, at last that cold, wet afternoon when I. P. F. Campbell, our captain, walked slowly toward me and took my hand on the football field. I had won my colors! A roar of young voices approving his choice, and a moment later one was lifted onto the shoulders of one's friends and carried in triumph from the field of play. Later, one was to hear such applause again—many times, but no first night in any theater anywhere held such an ecstasy of accomplishment as that moment when one received one's colors at Repton School.

Strolling up to the starting line, trembling with excitement . . . the half mile for boys under sixteen . . . digging the spikes of one's track shoes into the soil . . . standing there, waiting, bent slightly forward, taut, intense . . . and then at last the crack of the gun—what a release! Instinctively one's body coordinates perfectly and we are literally flying toward the finish line—Gillies is level with me step for step—I can feel Carr's breath on my neck—a few yards from home Carr has pulled level and the three of us come home together—a final plunge and I fall rolling over on my back. I lie there breathing heavily, my eyes closed. I hear someone approach. "You all right, Rathbone?" "Yes, thank you, sir, I'm just blown—who won?" "You did." And like the child I was I turned over on my face and cried.

My father and mother had been somewhat at a loss to know why I was so insistent upon going to Repton School. My reasons were lame—but never lost their insistence. I had private reasons, which, if they became known, I felt would cast some doubts upon my intent to work hard like a good boy and pass my exams.

Repton School in 1906 was possibly the most renowed public school in England for its accomplishment in the field of sports. Not that we didn't turn out our renowned scholars —but I can assure you I had no intention of competing for these honors. I enjoyed essay writing, Greek, Latin, and history—but I had little time for "swatting" (study) owing to my concentration on sports.

I scraped through my exams, remaining pretty much at the bottom of my classes except for Carr and Vatchell, my bosom friends, whom I could rely upon to keep me out of last place. But I made one serious mistake. I won first prize for an essay on "Was Shylock the Villain of a Melodrama or the Hero of a Tragedy?" The Reverend Arthur Catley, my housemaster, was somewhat shocked by this sudden display of cerebral ability, and from that time onward I was suspect of being a slacker.

To my friends it was a fluke that "Ratters" had won a first prize, but they couldn't have cared less, since I continued to bring glory to my house on the field of sport. Little did the Reverend Arthur Catley and my friends realize that, during homework in the dining room after supper, I was working on my first play, *King Arthur*. To both Catley and my friends this would undoubtedly have indicated that I was not quite the "he-man" they thought me to be. Repton was not a school that prided itself in the arts, and any boy so interested would definitely be suspect of being a "queer one." And so I kept my love of the theater to myself.

In the Pavillion were engraved for posterity the names of Repton's "greats." C. B. Fry, Jack Crawford, Bill Greswell, who all played for England in the test matches against Australia, and Bunny Austin, who helped England win and retain the Davis Cup for several years, to name but a few. And then there was dear Mr. Chips, that beloved character of James Hilton's. Years, many years later, when I saw the motion picture *Goodbye, Mr. Chips*, I wept unashamedly during those portions shot at Repton School itself.

They build an *esprit de corps* in English schools, a deep sense of pride in the accomplishments of those who come after—as well as those who have gone before. One has a sense of belonging that neither time nor space can erase.

My father, who was suffering from a severe financial setback, and my mother had made considerable sacrifices to send me to Repton; sacrifices which my brother and sister shared, in that they received, materially, a little less all around in order to enable me to have the maximum of opportunity. They knew this and gave their tithe willingly and affectionately. And so at times I could not help but feel an uneasiness in the face of my meager academic accomplishments.

Even my modest and unassuming entrance into this world had been heralded as an event of considerable significance (the first-born son to the eldest of my grandfather's children—my father—Edgar Philip Rathbone). Grandfather had heralded the event in a poem dedicated to me, which whenever I read it frightens me! It was beautifully inscrolled on a card and mailed to every member of his considerable family.

To
PHILIP ST. JOHN BASIL RATHBONE
(My Grandson)

Welcome my lad, to a world of fight:
A world of battle, life long, my boy.
Let the struggle be ever for Truth and Right:
Then, a winning fight is a lasting joy.

You have blood in your veins, boy, of those who fought:
Fought without rancour, and yet hit hard.
With unflinching pluck, with no selfish thought
For the triumph of Right was their reward.

Love while you fight, boy, keep ever free
From petty, ignoble, self-seeking strife;
And your crowning comfort in death shall be
The thought you have lived a noble life.

P. H. Rathbone.

Dear, distant Grandfather, I wonder so often if I have let you down. Your poem suggests that there is so much in one's heritage to be proud of and I am constantly aware, and sometimes a little afraid, that I have not lived up to all your high hopes of me—a Rathbone fought with "the South" in the American Civil War (I have his cavalry sword)—a

Major Rathbone was with President Lincoln in his box at Ford's Theatre the night Mr. Lincoln was murdered. Major Rathbone was severely wounded on this occasion and later died of his wounds—Cousin Eleanor Rathbone was the first woman ever to be elected to the British Parliament. At her death Cousin Eleanor received a personal eulogy from the floor of "the House" from Prime Minister Churchill himself —Uncle Herbert was Lord Mayor of Liverpool. There were poets of distinction in the family, Stephen Phillips, Laurence Binyon, and an outstanding actor-manager, Sir Frank Benson—and my father himself was not without note in his own profession of mining engineering. He was one of the first three to reach the Klondike in search of its gold. The Rathbones were also the Liverpool, London and Globe Insurance Co.; Holt and Company, shipping; and Rathbone Brothers, cotton. No wonder then, when young Basil was born, the first male grandchild, high hopes were held that he might eventually uphold certain family traditions.

Old, very old Great-Uncle William, of Greenbank, and Grandfather Rathbone of Greenbank Cottage also followed another family tradition, that of sponsoring and subsidizing the arts.

That great actor, at the turn of the century, Sir Henry Irving, was a constant visitor to Greenbank Cottage when he was playing in Liverpool. And it is said that one night after dinner, on a Sunday, Grandfather fell asleep while Sir Henry was talking. They were alone in Grandfather's study after the other guests, including Sir Henry's co-star, Miss Ellen Terry, had gone home.

Sir Henry, like my grandfather, was a night owl—and on this particular occasion had probably launched into some lengthy dissertation of some new production he was planning. Grandfather, who enjoyed his port—and had chronic gout—was motionlessly attentive, at least so it appeared. Actually, he was sleeping soundly. He was rudely awakened by the gaunt figure of Sir Henry standing over him and saying, "Dammit, sir, you are the first man who has ever dared to fall asleep while I was talking." To which my grandfather is reported to have replied, "Dammit, sir, you are the first man who has dared to put me to sleep with your confounded dissertation on why I should invest in one of your bloody booby traps."

With such a background Basil's future seemed somewhat optional. Add to this a very beautiful Irish mother, who was a talented violinist, and a mercurial and adventure-loving father, who was a mining engineer with frustrations as an actor, singer, and writer, and it became an odds on bet that Basil's choice, whatever it might be, would meet with opposition.

When I left Repton School I told my father that I wanted to make the theater my profession. The theater had recently taken its rightful place among the arts, following upon the knighthoods of Sir Henry Irving, Sir Herbert Tree, and my cousin, Sir Frank Benson. My father asked me to compromise by going into business for one year, at the end of which time I might do as I pleased. It was a generous compromise. And so I became a junior clerk in the main office in London of the Liverpool, London and Globe Insurance Co.

Mr. Lewis was the general manager—and from my first interview with him it was made clear that I was due for early promotion, provided I worked hard. I was given special instruction and attended lectures after hours, and within a few months I was moved to the accounting department of the West End Branch at Charing Cross, under the local management of E. Preston Hytch—a bald-headed, hard-working Dickensian, with very little discipline over his staff. During this period, I was elected to play cricket and football, every Saturday afternoon for the L, L & G's first team. I was also invited to spend a weekend with Mr. and Mrs. Lewis and their eligible daughter. It was all so obvious and made no impression on me, except to increase my determination to be rid of them all at the end of the one year.

During my stay at the West End office, my father unknowingly lost considerable ground in his hopes for my business career. The office cashier, a Mr. Howell, was a devotee of classical music. Mr. Howell introduced me to the promenade concerts at Queen's Hall under Sir Henry Wood, and together we went to the gallery for my first *Meistersinger* at Covent Garden. We would lunch together at Lyons' Corner House, where we were served by a waitress we nicknamed "ten-past-ten"—she stood with her feet denoting that exact time on the clock. On those occasions that I did not lunch with Mr. Howell, I used my lunch period to learn poems and pieces of Shakespeare. This study period was accomplished in a dusty old attic over the office, filled with ancient account books and stack upon stack of old reference papers and letters. Nobody knew about this except Mr. Howell, whom I had made my confidant and who alone was aware of my aspirations and intentions.

At lunch time of my last day at the office, I kept an appointment with my cousin, Mr. Frank Benson, at his office in Henrietta Street, Covent Garden. I had written to him asking for an interview and informing him of my intention to become an actor. I went well prepared and without the slightest doubt that the theater was about to receive into its arms one of the future's truly "greats." Such is the sublime confidence of inexperience.

Mr. Benson received me, and after some preliminary inquiries as to my father's health, his regards to my mother, etc., and their position in this matter, he asked me if I had anything prepared that I could recite to him. *Anything prepared!* now the time had come to prove that those long hours of study and rehearsal in the attic at the office had not been wasted.

I chose a scene between Shylock, Salarnio, and Salerino, from *The Merchant of Venice*—shades of Repton! Mr. Benson listened attentively as I colored each role with what I considered to be brilliant characterizations. When I had finished, there was a long pause as he looked at me quizzically.

At last he said, "A young actor is like a horse. As a yearling or even as a two-year-old it is not easy to estimate his future capabilities. But if his breeding and conformation are good, one is inclined to go along with him, for a while at least. So I'm going to give you a chance with my No. 2 Company, and then we'll see what you look like at the end of a year."

At the end of a year I had toured all over England, Scotland, and Ireland, playing in a repertory of Shakespearean plays; small parts, but an invaluable experience. Add to this, instruction in diction, the use of swords, period dancing, deportment, and make-up.

In the summer of 1913 Mr. Benson promoted me to his own company, where I played all the juvenile leads, such as Lorenzo, Silvius, Paris, etc., etc. On joining his company, Mr. Benson made it clear to me that I had won my spurs legitimately, and that I must continue to do so if I looked for further advancement. He assured me I would benefit in no way from our family relationship. He always referred to me as "Mr. Rathbone" and I always addressed him as "sir," as did all the other members of his company. Company discipline was almost military. The senior members were always courteous to us youngsters, but never familiar. Competition between us was fierce, and a casual comment from Mr. Benson at the end of a play, such as "Nice performance tonight, greatly improved," or "That was an interesting make-up you put on in the last act—try a little more color next time," would send the recipient down to our dressing room to have his leg well pulled—and might even lead to a not-so-gentle wrestling match. Then on the way back to our "digs," fish 'n' chips and a bottle of beer all around. The host?—the recipient of Mr. Benson's approval that night, a dubious honor in times when one's salary was thirty shillings a week, the equivalent of about four dollars and fifty cents today.

4

First Flush of Success

Some cynic has said of women that you can't live with them and you can't live without them. As far as I am concerned this quip is far more applicable to the telephone. The one in my room in Kensington in 1919 never rang. It was there to consume avidly my calls to everyone I could think of, and that was all.

Then one morning it spoke for the first time in weeks. It rang clearly and incisively. I looked at it with contempt. So the damned thing had learned to speak again! "Yes who is it?—Bill Savery!—Bill!—How are you?" It was W. H. Savery, who had been Sir Frank Benson's general manager and was now managing the Stratford Festival for the autumn season of 1919. Was I at liberty? Was I at liberty!

"Yes—I have just been demobilized—Arrived back home a few weeks ago!—Stratford in August?—Romeo and Cassius in Julius Caesar—Fine, Bill—I should love to—Five pounds a week—Thanks, Bill—Shall I call in at the office tomorrow?—Sometime next week?—Thanks, Bill—Oh, Bill, that's a firm offer I presume, because if anyone else calls up—All right Bill, that's fine. I'm all yours—Oh, Bill, how did you find me?"—But he had hung up.

I sat in the chair at my desk for a moment or so just looking at that telephone, so coldly impersonal again. But however great its indifference to my future I would remember this one with deep affection all the days of my life. And I leaned over and kissed it! Then I let out a wild yell and grabbing my Shakespeare from the bookshelf I kissed it too! It was true—it was true—I was not dreaming. The long period of waiting, the looking back and the depression were gone. I was definitely engaged to play leading roles at Stratford-on-Avon Memorial Theatre, where in August of 1914 I had thought my career as an up and coming actor might be finished—and from Stratford to London *with my talent!* It was but a hop and a skip and a jump! I was deliriously happy! That night I went to the Carlton Grill to celebrate; I had a minute steak, a bottle of wine, crepes suzette, and a brandy.

There was however one feature of my return to Stratford that disturbed me deeply. Sir Frank Benson was no longer the festival director and its star. Many rumors were abroad as to the cause of this change—he was too old—new blood was needed to stimulate the organization he had created and developed over the years, and there were the usual local politics involving the mayor and council of Stratford and the vicar of Trinity Church. It may be, too, that Sir Frank had refused to accept The Stratford Festival Company in place of the F. R. Benson Shakespearean Company. However, Sir Frank had had a fabulous career—and there comes a time, no doubt, when we must all give way to a brave new world.

Sir Frank had been the first among the so-called "upper classes" in England to make acting a profession. As a young man he was a prominent member of Sir Henry Irving's Lyceum Company. Sir Henry presented him with all necessary scenery and effects when young Benson started out on his lifelong venture with a repertory of Shakespearean plays. On tour in England he traveled eight plays—a different play every performance, six evenings and two matinees. There was a short London season once a year. He was more responsible for popularizing Shakespeare in England than any other man before him—or since. His students were paid for "walk-ons," or playing bit parts, while receiving daily instruction in diction, deportment, fencing, and period dancing. No wonder when we graduated from his company we were highly sought after by London managements.

Sir Frank was knighted at Drury Lane Theatre on Tuesday, May 2, 1916, at a special Royal Command performance of Julius Caesar in which every part, even "walk-ons," were played by stars or well-known actors. After his death as Julius Caesar, Mr. Benson was commanded to the royal box. There, with all eyes on him, in his toga, dripping with blood, he knelt before King George V and received the accolade. There was an amusing moment when King George asked for a sword. There was a considerable pause—no word was spoken between the King and Mr. Benson, who remained kneeling. Then at last a jewelled-handled sword was produced from somewhere and the naked blade rested first on Mr. Benson's left shoulder then on his right, as King George spoke the magic words, "Rise, Sir Frank Benson."

There was a roar of applause from the audience as King George shook Sir Frank's hand warmly.

At his death Sir Frank left me that sword and all else of his worldly possessions. Sir Frank and Lady Benson both had money, as also did his brother Lord Charnwood, who invested liberally in Sir Frank's ventures. The last time I saw Sir Frank he was lying on an iron cot in a rooming house in the Holland Road, London. He was dying—alone—except for a few visitors like myself, and he was penniless, except for a government grant of a hundred pounds a year. His marriage had broken up, and after his "dismissal" from Stratford-on-Avon, he never had any further success. No businessman, he gradually fell into poverty, and then into virtual penury. He looked up at me from his deathbed for a long time without recognizing me. I tried to talk to him. At last he reached up and touched my face with an emaciated hand —he was eighty-nine years old. There was the shadow of a smile in his eyes as he said just one word, "Basil." Then once again he relapsed into semiconsciousness. A passionately dedicated young man—winner of the coveted three-mile race at Oxford University (a painting of him in his running shorts and his university colors still hangs to this day in the foyer of the Stratford Memorial Theatre). A "successful" marriage—

a fortune—nay, three—his own, his wife's, and his brother's —were poured into his beloved theatrical ventures. Could it have been that the death of his son, in France, during the war, had seriously affected his mind in some way? He seemed never quite to recover from this blow. He rarely spoke of it. And not until after his death did I know that I was to inherit all that was left of his worldly possessions—the sword with which he was knighted—a flowered costume vest—and a book of press clippings.

> Blow, blow thou winter wind!
> Thou art not so unkind
> As man's ingratiude.

Warwich   Castle—Leamington—Shottery—Stratford-on-Avon—The Shakespeare Hotel—Trinity Church, where Shakespeare is buried—the Memorial Theatre—and The Dirty Duck (the Black Swan Inn, to you)—willows that weep down into the river like Ophelia's tresses—proud white swans with their families of signets—rowboats, canoes, and punts—the skylark and the nightingale—and Romeo!

How could a still impressionable young man not fall in love with his Juliet? To me she *was* Juliet. And many who saw us perform maintain we more perfectly represented these star-crossed lovers than any other couple on the stage in living memory.

It is generally conceded, professionally, that it is impossible to give a good performance if you are in real life in love with your Juliet, and vice versa. Generally speaking I agree with this, and can only assume that we were the exception that proved the rule. To tell your loved one how much you love her in Shakespeare's words is an experience that beggars description.

After the play, Juliet and I would sail away up the Avon in a punt and partake of supper under the weeping willow trees—or walk through the fields and woods of Shakespeare's country until the early hours of the morning. The same moon that looked down upon us had looked down upon him—and the nightingale sang to us just as it had sung to Mr. Shakespeare and his Ann Hathaway some three hundred years before. Sleep was bathed in the magic of the moment and tomorrow's dawn held the promise of endless good nights. "Good night, good night! parting is such sweet sorrow, That I shall say good night till it be morrow."

The dream lingered on when the season finished and we returned to London, where I hoped to be engaged to play with Miss Constance Collier in *Peter Ibbetson*.

There is an amusing incident in connection with my engagement for this role. There was a bar in the Haymarket, just opposite His Majesty's Theatre. This bar, around lunch time, was much frequented by actors, those with jobs—and those wishing to advertise the fact that they were "at liberty." The day after I had seen Miss Collier at her home I tucked the script of *Peter Ibbetson* under my arm and made my way to the bar in the Haymarket. I entered, looked around, and ordered a drink. A few moments later, Henry Daniell sauntered in, unobtrusively carrying a manuscript under his arm. He joined me and ordered a drink—*he* looked at my script and *I* looked at his, and cold fear struck both our hearts. But neither of us uttered a word. We were just about to go when young George Ralph walked into the bar full of beans—he too was carrying a script under his arm. He offered us both a drink to celebrate a new job he was about to sign up for. Drinks were served and we toasted George's good fortune.

"By the by," said Henry Daniell, "what's the play?"

"*Peter Ibbetson*," George replied innocently.

"But I'm going to do that," said Henry and I in angry unison.

We looked at each other in puzzled bewilderment, and then at the scripts that each of us carried. Each script was identical:

PETER IBBETSON
An adaptation
of George Du Maurier's Book of that name
by Samuel Raphaelson.

We tossed off our drinks and ordered another. When the drinks arrived, George said, "All right, now, I'll tell you who's going to pay for this round—whoever quoted Miss Collier the lowest salary will get the part—I asked for twenty-five pounds a week—Henry?"

"Twenty pounds."

"Basil?"

"Ten pounds."

"You bastard," said Henry.

"Well, I'll be damned," muttered George to himself.

Nobody laughed and I paid for the drinks—and felt as if I'd been caught cheating. I had, in fact, been awarded the role.

The forced separations from my Juliet during rehearsals were torment. But as the pressure and excitement of the opening night of *Peter Ibbetson* at the Savoy Theatre approached, I was temporarily reobsessed by an ever-recurring "love"—her face was a mask—"drama." This "loved one" makes consuming demands upon an actor that cannot be denied.

The opening was a great success and in one night I was launched from obscurity into the limelight of unlimited adulation. Sir Johnston Forbes Robertson and Sir John Hare came backstage to congratulate me—also Sir Gerald Du Maurier, whose father had written the original story of Peter Ibbeston. Society, titles, statesmen, authors, and actors presented themselves at my dressing room. For the moment I was the toast of the town. For all this I have to thank the late Miss Constance Collier, who had played the play in New York with Jack and Lionel Barrymore. She had seen me play Romeo at Stratford.

And my Juliet? There were the beginnings of a separation between us. She, too, was in a play—and opportunities to see one another became less frequent. The theater is a hard life for lovers, and harder still for those who would make a successful marriage. "Absence makes the heart grow fonder?" —I don't think so, and I know of no case where it has proven to be true.

The success of *Peter Ibbetson* was also linked with the years to come. The authoress of the silent picture version of the story was one day to become my wife. But at this moment neither of us had heard of one another. However, destiny was working patiently on her magic loom, and two silken threads would one day come together to be tied in an irrevocable knot "until death us do part."

It was at one of those wonderful parties given by Ivor Novello that I met "Kitten." Henry Ainley was there and George Grossmith, Eddie Marsh, Winston Churchill's secretary, Mr. Anthony Eden, and a galaxy of beauty and talent and fame—both male and female.

Kitten was sitting in the pantry. I was bored with the party, and there was nowhere to sit down—it was about 2:00 A.M. Kitten looked up as I walked in and purred like a cat. I think she was a little tight. The resemblance was startling . . . Marie! . . . with her "downy soft eyebrows and artful blue eyes." I sat down beside her on a kitchen chair.

"Hello, Marie darling," I said. "I thought you were dead!"

"Don't talk silly," she replied. "My name is Madge. Who are you?"

Who was I! This came as a bit of a shock. I told her I made blankets to keep fleas warm in the winter—and she laughed like a rippling brook. Then she said, "This party's a crashing bore . . . want to take me home?"

I paused, and she rose to her feet.

"Well, do you or don't you?" she said.

"Of course I do," and I took little Marie in my arms and kissed her passionately, as I had always wanted to do.

We walked back to her flat, a delightful custom that Londoners have, weather permitting. We held hands all the way, stopping at street corners to kiss again, and again, and again. Each time after I kissed her she would purr like a cat, and that is why I rechristened her "Kitten." We stopped at one of those wonderful taxicab nightstands and had tea with bacon and eggs. Almost any time after midnight, if you stopped at one of those stands you would find "toffs" and their girls in full evening dress seated beside cabbies—and an occasional bum having a snack. It was 4:00 A.M. when we reached her flat. She made no motion to denote that I was not to follow her. . . .

Kitten had a divine sense of humor—she slept all day and was up all night. A short while after we had met, I was engaged to play Iago in *Othello* at the Royal Court Theatre for James Bernard Fagan. Godfrey Tearle was the best Othello I had ever seen. The opening was one of those glamorous nights when just about everybody who was anybody was there. My dear friend the late Sir George Arthur, Kitchener's secretary, had put up a thousand pounds toward the venture. And on this opening night he had as his guests Mr. and Mrs. Asquith, Mr. Lloyd George, Lord Balfour, Mr. Anthony Eden, Lady Cunard, Lady Colefax, and heaven knows who else.

This production of *Othello* helped me to learn an important lesson, i.e., that you are not necessarily as good or as bad as a critic may say you are. On the opening night the play seemed to be going very well, and there were but two or three scenes left for me. One of them was that scene between Othello and Desdemona in which he rages at her, calling her "an impudent strumpet." Upon Othello's exit, Desdemona sends for her dear "friend" Iago. Some few seconds before my entrance in this scene, I developed an uncontrollable attack of hiccups. I was deeply concerned—in fact downright frightened that the effect of my affliction on the audience might produce laughs that are certainly not called for in this scene. I made my entrance and hiccuped my way through the scene. No laughs . . . warm applause greeted my exit. On the following morning I received excellent reviews from the press. One leading London newspaper picked out, in particular, the scene with Desdemona I have just mentioned. For this scene I received special praise for my brilliant conception in playing Iago, drunk!

After the play Lady Colefax gave a party. Kitten seemed out of sorts. I asked her if she was feeling all right. "Of course," she said, "but let's go pretty soon, shall we?" On the way home she was distant and "funny," staying away from me in the taxi. At last I said, "What did you think of the play?" She hadn't said a word about it. She turned and looked at me and there was a bewildered look in her eyes.

"How can you play a part like that, and not *be* something like it yourself?"

"Oh, come now, Kitten . . ."

"No, I mean it. . . . You frighten me."

Could any actor ask for a finer review!

But I shall always believe it was the beginning of the end for me with Kitten. And the end came sooner than I expected. Gilbert Miller engaged me to play opposite Doris Keane in *The Czarina* at the Empire Theatre in New York.

Just a line, before crossing the Atlantic, about my good friend Sir George Arthur. He was a real devotee of the theater. He was a little mousey man with gray hair and a military mustache. An aristocrat by birth and by nature— and there was nothing he would not do to befriend and promote promising young actors. Beside myself, I know of his generous interest in Brian Aherne, Ralph Forbes, and John Gielgud. He was a member of the elite Marlborough Club and a confidant of Queen Mary. Queen Mary loved the outside world and the theater. King George did not.

Many were the charming tales he would regale me with at luncheon at the Marlborough Club, of his weekly visits to tea with Queen Mary, every Thursday.

On one occasion Sir George arrived at Marlborough House to find the young princesses, Elizabeth and Margaret, playing on the drawing-room floor with their dolls. A short while later His Grace, The Archbishop of Canterbury, was announced. His Grace entered, and on his way across the room, to pay his respects to Queen Mary, he patted the Princess Elizabeth on the head, saying, ". . . and how is my little lady today?" Elizabeth jumped to her feet, a doll in her arms. "I'm not your little lady," she replied. "I'm a princess." After Queen Mary had greeted His Grace, she turned to Elizabeth and said, "Elizabeth, His Grace knows you are a princess, we both hope that one day you will learn to be a little lady . . . leave the room."

There was another story Sir George told me. Prince John was going to an English public school for the first time in the history of the Royal Family I believe. His father, King George, told him he would receive no special favors, and gave him two pounds pocket money, an amount he had carefully inquired was no more and no less than the other boys received from their fathers.

It was not long before Prince John, hoping to prove himself a good fellow, found himself penniless. There were still many weeks to go at school and John was desperate. Then an idea occurred to him. He would write to Grandmama, the Dowager Queen Alexandria. A day or so went by and at last the fateful letter from her arrived, but in it there was no enclosure. The letter said, in effect, that as much as she would like to help, the Dowager Queen was much afraid of her son, King George, and could not go against his wishes.

Now, quite desperate, Prince John decided to write to his mother, Queen Mary, who replied vigorously that come what may he must abide by his father's decision. What could the little Prince do now . . . kill himself? And then the darkness was shattered by a blinding flash of light. . . . He would not only be safe—he'd be rich. He sold both his mother's and grandmother's letters to school friends for five pounds apiece!

These and many other stories will always remind me of a thoughtful and generous friend who was already finding it difficult, even in the early 1920s, to adjust himself to changes he was not prepared to make. He once quoted me the following; "God grant me the security to accept things I cannot change, courage to change things I can and wisdom to know the difference."

He never changed his habit of wearing white gloves when he went to the theater . . . God bless him. . . .

5

Ouida

I sailed on the S.S. *Olympic* on December 21, 1921. The White Star steamship rolled like a barrel, and since I felt we were in for a rough trip, I promptly went to bed and, but for a time spent over a few cups of tea, slept for forty-eight hours. Kitten could be pretty exhausting, and I had hopes of resuming a more normal way of life in the United States.

On the third day out, Gilbert Miller asked me if I would like to play racquets with him. This we did daily until our arrival in New York. I did my best to let Gilbert win every game. It seemed to me good personal relations, in view of the fact that he was one of the most successful producers in both London and New York. Gilbert has always had impeccable taste in both his choice of plays and their production. Most of his productions were translations of European plays of the period, and as far as I was concerned he was exactly what the doctor had ordered for me! So consistently losing to him at racquets was a pleasure.

We spent Christmas Day at sea. I was not familiar with most of the guests Gilbert had invited to a small party on board—except at one table, where after formal introductions, I settled down for an eventful evening. The table was composed of Bill Tilden, Bill Johnston, Mrs. Molla Mallory, and Eleanor Sears. I shall always remain most grateful to Mrs. Mallory for her graciousness to me that evening. I had seen her play in the finals at Wimbledon against the famous

French woman Suzanne Lenglen; and Bill Tilden had long been a hero of mine.

In the early hours of the following morning the New York sky line rose majestically with the dawn, like a drawing by Arthur Rackham. I was emotionally stunned by its beauty, and every time since that I have left or returned to New York by sea, I have had this same reaction.

In London I had been advised to stay at the Algonquin Hotel. I held a letter, signed by Frank Case, confirming a reservation for me at his hotel. Upon arrival, I went to the desk and registered. While so doing, I heard a voice say, "Hello, Mr. Rathbone, I'm Frank Case," and I turned to shake hands with one of the most charming men I have ever met—and one of the theater's best friends. He asked me to lunch with him, rehearsals permitting. I told him I was not due at the Lyceum Theatre until two o'clock.

"Good," he said, "I have asked a fellow countryman of yours to lunch with us—Edmund Goulding." Many years later Eddie was to direct me in *Dawn Patrol* with Errol Flynn and David Niven. Lunch was most pleasant, and I quickly found myself completely at home.

After lunch I was introduced to one of the most beautiful women I have ever met, Tallulah Bankhead. Later that week, with Edwin Knopf, brother of Alfred Knopf, the publisher, we went "slumming" together. Tallulah had tremendous vitality and vivacity—and a sparkling sense of humor . . . Dear Tallulah . . . you were ever such fun . . . remember me?

There is nothing much to relate about *The Czarina*, which was only a modest success. Doris Keane kept much to herself, barely acknowledging her company. Basil Sydney, her husband, would frequently sit with me in my dressing room, which was slightly embarrassing, as I was reasonably sure he would have liked to play my part opposite his wife. I came to know Doris Keane very well in later years, and she became a great friend of mine and my wife's. . . . Oh yes, my wife. She tells me that she saw me in *The Czarina*, and that during the performance she turned to her escort and said, "One day I'm going to marry that man." I ask you . . . what chance do we men have!

At the conclusion of the run of *The Czarina*, Gilbert Miller loaned me out to Grossmith and Malone for their production of Somerset Maugham's *East of Suez* at His Majesty's Theatre in London, under the direction of Basil Dean. The play ran for almost a year. Immediately following it I was engaged by Mr. Dean to play in his production of *R.U.R.*, by the Kapek Brothers at the St. Martin's Theatre. Basil Dean was a sort of English Jed Harris in that both were "boy wonders" in the early twenties. Of the brilliant, mercurial, and unpredictable Mr. Harris, at a later time. Of Mr. Dean, be it said that he had a way of treating his actors as if they were trained animals. He cracked the whip and when he so did we were expected to jump. His was hardly an endearing personality. But he produced successful plays—and this was a factor no actor could afford to ignore.

In the fall of 1923 Gilbert Miller brought me back to America. *The Swan* by Ferenc Molnar is probably the most memorable play of my life. I loved it passionately—and it made me a star in America. But above all, it was during *The Swan* that I met Ouida. That was in November 1923, and we are still happily married in 1962.

The Swan, with Eva Le Gallienne, Phillip Merrivale, and myself was a dismal failure in its tryout weeks in Detroit and Toronto. Gilbert was all for closing the play in Toronto. However, fate ruled otherwise, and we opened at the Cort Theatre in New York on October 23, 1923. The day had been heavy with moisture and as curtain time approached a veritable cloudburst poured from the heavens. We played the first act to a house that slowly filled up, having struggled to get to the theater, and which was mostly in understandably bad humor. At the end of the first act we received a mild reception. Going back to our dressing rooms, Philip Merrivale said, "Well, I guess Gilbert was right, we're a flop."

The second act, however, went well, and at the final curtain we received a standing ovation. I saw a man about fourth row center throw his hat in the air. I learned later that it was Alexander Woollcott. The next day we had a matinee, and there was a queue at the box office a block long—we were a tremendous success.

Late in November, I met Clifton Webb on the street.

"Hello," he said. "Want to go to a party tonight?"

"What party?" I inquired.

"Ouida Bergere's, she's divine, you'll love her, she's a darling . . . come on, everyone will be there . . . I'll take you . . . Ouida won't mind . . . anyway the place will be like Grand Central Station . . . you'll be lucky if you get to meet her."

"Okay, I'll go if I can bring June. We're supposed to do something together after the play tonight."

"Okay, bring June," said Clifton. "I adore her . . . the more the merrier . . . you'll love it . . . I'll call for you after the play."

Nothing is very distinct about the occasion, because afterward it had seemed to me like just another big party, and I have never liked big parties very much, especially with a lot of people I don't know. But I'll remember as much as I can. Clifton called for me after the play and we picked up June.

There was a large curving stairway that led up from the hall to Ouida's apartment on the first floor at Fifty-third and Madison. It was a beautiful old house, which has long since given place to the CBS studios. At the top of the stairs stood Edmund Goulding, a self-appointed bartender! Eddie was lavishly dispensing drinks.

"Where's Ouida?" asked Clifton.

"Damned if I know," replied Eddie. "Have a drink?"

Clifton went off in search of Ouida, but he did not return. It seems that Ouida was having supper with the Italian ambassador and some friends in another room. June and I had a drink and some supper, and then settled down in a bay window. . . . Nobody bothered us.

It was from June I learned that Ouida was Paramount's top script writer. (Paramount was then known as Famous Players Lasky.) Young, petite, strongly opinionated—and very successful. . . . June's description of Ouida had a touch of vinegar to it.

Some time later there was a hustle and bustle as a door opened somewhere and Ouida and her friends came out to rejoin the party. We were introduced and she kissed June. She was indeed young and petite, with the most beautiful natural red hair I have ever seen . . . eyes that danced with the joy of living, and a skin texture like alabaster. She wore a low-cut yellow organdie evening dress that flared at the waist. She was the perfect Renoir. A moment later she was gone, but not before she had said, smiling sweetly, "Enjoy yourselves, won't you."

So this was the bold Cossack from the Czarina that she had said she would one day marry! At least I imagined this was what she was thinking, and I may have been right, because a few days later I was invited, with June, to spend the weekend at Ouida's place on Long Island.

On Saturday night, after the curtain had come down on our respective plays, Richard Bennet, Clifton Webb, June, and I met at Pennsylvania Station and took the last train to Great Neck, Long Island. We were met by Ouida's Rolls Royce and driven out to her place on the Sound. Supper awaited us and conversation was general. I was particularly interested in another week-end guest who had arrived earlier, an extremely alert and vigorous Irishman. He had a thin aesthetic face, fine textured sandy gray hair, and the figure of a man in his twenties. He said very little, but all the while, as he listened, he tapped out a rhythmic beat with his right foot. Behind his blue eyes one sensed a quick temper. He was a prominent New York actor, an anglophile, and he had made and lost a fortune on the market. I thought then, and shall always believe, that he was in love with Ouida. But the

difference in their ages precluded his ever mentioning it to
her or anyone else. He was a man of strong principles and
unquestionable integrity. In my imagination I associated him
with Robert Browning's poem *Evelyn Hope*.

> And just because I was thrice as old
> And our paths in the world diverged so wide,
> Each was naught to each, must I be told?
> We were fellow mortals, naught beside?

Dear Jack Miltern . . . he was to become my foster father.
And in years to come I was to see him killed on Los Felez
Boulevard in Los Angeles, as the sun was setting one clear
spring evening in 1938.

I felt a little self-conscious that night at supper . . . that
self-consciousness that comes when suddenly contact is made
without a word being spoken. . . . Ouida and I were both
thinking aloud, I believe.

I shared a bedroom with Dick Bennet and slept soundly.
The following morning I awakened late, and without moving I opened my eyes to look straight into a pair of large
brown eyes that looked fiercely back into mine. A huge,
furry head rested on my bed, motionless. . . . The hound of
the Baskervilles, without any question of doubt!

Without moving, I murmured softly, "Dick," and then
again, "Dick . . . Dick."

From the other bed a sleepy voice answered me.

"If you want breakfast ring the bell beside your bed."

"Okay, Dick, but what the hell do I do with this dog?"

"What dog . . . what's the matter with you . . . are you
dreaming?"

"No, Dick, I'm not dreaming, just call off this damned
dog, will you?"

Dick turned abruptly, tousled and foggy with sleep. Then
he saw Lutz. "Lutz," he shouted. "Lutz, get out of here,
you stinker!"

Lutz lifted his head, turned slowly, and moved over to

Dick's bed, where he lay that enormous head in the same recumbent position as he had done with me. Now, at last, I could see what had menaced me. It was the largest police dog I have ever seen, or shall ever see in my life. I rang the bell for my breakfast. Dick just turned over and went to sleep again, and Lutz returned to his watch over me. It was not until the butler came in to ask what I wanted for breakfast that I was able to get rid of the dog. Quite amiably he followed the butler out, hoping, no doubt, to partake of some tidbits in the pantry.

Later in the morning we all donned riding habits and went for a canter across the Whitney estate. In November of 1923 you could ride for miles through the lovely countryside of Long Island—broken only here and there by a house or a farm. It was a beautiful morning, crisp and clear. June was lagging behind, scared to death. Whosoever's idea it was, this was certainly not her "cup of tea."

"You seem at home on that horse. Do you enjoy riding?" It was Ouida, in an extremely trim riding habit, her cheeks flushed, but not a hair out of place!

"Love it," I replied.

"If you don't mind leaving June, let's canter, shall we?" she asked, and we did.

I took a quick glance back at poor June. She was having her troubles and looked like a rag doll tied to an obstreperous donkey.

Ouida's house was utterly charming, overlooking the Sound, with a beach and a pier to dive from. Gardens of flowers waiting for spring, and dogs . . . and ever more dogs . . . including Sans Souci, a greyhound, and Scottie, an Airedale and that monster Lutz! The house was English in taste and furnishings . . . a lived-in house . . . everything about it was comfortable, warm, and welcoming. The place was run beautifully. We lunched around two o'clock, and following lunch there was a siesta period. Tea was served about five in the living room. The firelight made strange patterns on the wall and the sun set gloriously over the sound, with the promise of a bright new day on the morrow.

The setting was perfect, and I spoke almost from the subconscious. "Show me your house, won't you?" I said.

"Would you like to . . ." and Ouida rose, and I followed. We walked rather self-consciously from room to room, politely impersonal until suddenly I heard Ouida say, "And this is my room . . . you like it? I get the sun here all day and . . ."

I turned her to me, took her in my arms, and kissed her. The embrace was disturbed by someone entering the room. Ye gods, that dog again! He came slowly toward me as if for the kill. I was scared stiff and Ouida knew it—and laughed that rippling laugh that so many others beside myself have found to be one of the most attractive things about her.

To myself, I said, "This is not the same. . . . it mustn't be. . . . There comes a time when it must be forever. . . ." This I said to myself over and over again that evening.

It was a strange dinner that night. Ouida and I trying to pretend that nothing had happened between us. If none of the other dinner guests suspected anything Jack Miltern certainly did. After dinner he became nervous and edgy and argumentative with Ouida about almost anything she might say or do, so I decided to turn in early hoping that by disappearing discreetly I might relieve the situation, if any situation there were.

There was a very late breakfast the next morning, and it was not long before we were all packing to return to town for our plays that evening. . . . June! . . . What in heck had happened to June? I was supposed to be her escort for the weekend and had behaved abominably. We were all prepared and ready to go. The taxi was at the door when I announced that I wasn't coming in until later. . . . Ouida was driving me in to town in her car. What they said about me on the way home I shall never know, but I can guess—and whatever it was I deserved it.

Granted that a chemical affinity may well prove to be a primary and overwhelming temporary attraction, there remains, however, much else that goes into a marriage that hopes for "a long run," as we say in the theater. And as in the theater no play can be allowed to drift along indeterminately without constant watchfulness over the basic constituents that get it off to a good start, so must any marriage that looks for permanence have not only certain ingredients, but an awareness that these ingredients need periodic stimulation and conservation and that "a long run" will not necessarily be a smooth run.

By the time Ouida and I met we had both lived full lives and had had much valuable experience, beyond the average, that should enable us to live together "until death us do part." I am sure we were both cognizant of the normal and obvious pitfalls. But being who we were and following our chosen professions presented added dangers. Ouida was the first to recognize this and immediately stopped writing for motion pictures. She felt strongly that two professionals in a family were one too many! If we had been able to live and work together, like Mr. and Mrs. Alfred Lunt or Katherine Cornell and Guthrie McClintic, that would have been one thing, but *our* work would have separated us. I was making a career for myself on Broadway, while Ouida would have to spend most of her time on the West Coast in the motion picture business. So Ouida asked for a release from all pending and existing contracts, one of which would have paid her $1500 a week, in order to marry an "up and coming" actor who was earning $500 a week but who had not yet actually "arrived." This may, in retrospect, sound like good sense, but it also required a courage and devotion that many of Ouida's friends considered to be considerably "beyond the call of duty!" Samuel Goldwyn was disgusted with Ouida's decision and promised to buy her a grand piano if she would give up the idea of marrying "this actor!" Jack Miltern, who knew of and had experienced Ouida's extravagance, was heartily opposed to our union, and I am sure there were many others who knew us both and who could do no more than wish us a happy if somewhat limited "fling!"

Those who knew me knew I had rather monastic tastes in living. More than once in later years Ouida was to say that I would have made a most successful monk because all I needed was a whitewashed cell to live in! But Ouida and I had many good things in common, things that were to give us great pleasure and help us on those occasions when circumstances would either draw us closer together or open a rift that could lead to a break. I think we have always shown one another tolerance, for neither of us is easy to live with! But I believe, above all, that way down we have loved deeply and that our *tastes* have had much in common. We like the same books and are impatient to pass on a book from one to the other. At times we will irritate each other very much by insisting on reading a passage aloud. "Darling, please don't," Ouida will say. "I am going to read it and you're spoiling it for me."

In the theater, motion pictures, and in music we have quite literally identical tastes. In art Ouida is most definitely my superior; her knowledge is considerable, and her appreciation is keen, incisive, and well balanced. More than all this though, we have always thought and felt alike about people, and our way of life has remained conservative in an era of much confusion, an era that has developed more rapidly than perhaps any other in history. Now, after thirty-six years of married life, I think perhaps I am prepared to adjust myself to "the times," while Ouida is inclined, here and there, to hold on to the past, almost desperately, because she is much too intelligent not to know that the past as it was has gone never to return, however much she may regret it. And when I speak of the past I mean in its relation to certain standards and niceties of human relationships such as "thank you" letters, a gift of flowers from an admirer or friend, and courtesy and respect from young men who date our daughter Cynthia.

Perhaps in our search for greater material security we have lost a spiritual security which, as much as anything, seems to me to be largely responsible for the instability of the past quarter century of revolutions, wars, and rumors of wars,

which in their turn have inevitably produced evolutions beyond our control in almost every phase of our daily lives.

But now, dear reader, I would renew my journey, *no
longer to know an insecurity in loving*, and to share all
things . . . "for better for worse . . . in sickness and in
health . . ." with a woman I know my father and mother
would have loved as dearly as I do, had they lived. And yet,
despite so much, one thing remains forever unanswered—that
inner loneliness that no one and nothing can penetrate. The
loneliness of the soul's being, that ancient spirit of so many
previous existences that has no voice except for you and you
alone, this soul that is born to life on the wings of the "Angel
of Death," the same angel that will return one day, or night,
to guide you toward the next life to come. And sometimes
when the lights are out and you are lying there beside "her,"
the image of the angel will take form—your mother, your
brother, your father, someone you love. . . . Why not? Why
should the "angel of death" be abstract? Why not a loved
one who has crossed over and knows the way that leads
from the darkness into the light? And you stretch out and
take her hand and maybe at that moment she understands,
and maybe she doesn't . . . but there have been times when
you have both understood. And rarely is a word spoken
about it, but still there are times when *your* loneliness and
her loneliness will briefly communicate with one another and
both of you will know that loving is the one sure solace we
shall ever know from the beginning of life to its end.

> —I love thee with the breath,
> Smiles, tears of all my life!—and, if God choose,
> I shall but love thee better after death.

These words from Elizabeth Barrett's sonnet were the first
I ever wrote to Ouida, immediately following my week-end
visit to her home on Long Island, when I sent her a large
box of red roses, my favorite flower. And later that night
after the theater I called her and over the phone I played her

a recording by Mischa Elman of the Preislied from *Die Meistersinger*. There was so much we had to share together, and in the beginning we were like a swollen stream in springtime, rushing upon our way to the promise of the river's timeless companionship.

We had, however, an immediate problem to face. We could not get married as Marion had refused to give me a divorce. Be it said on Marion's behalf that maybe she was waiting to see if this time I was really serious. From previous experience she had every reason to doubt it! Only my "Juliet" had so far presented a really serious problem for both of us, and even in this case Marion had been right.

When *The Swan* closed for a summer vacation I decided to return to England for a short visit. Jack Miltern was to accompany me. Ouida had preceded us and taken a charming little house on the River Thames at Pangbourne in Berkshire. I was determined that Ouida and I should be free to marry as soon as possible, and to do so I needed both legal advice and the opportunity to convince Marion that our long separation should now be legally terminated.

This visit home had another and less happy purpose. My dear father had died on my birthday, June thirteenth. He had been very ill but was well on the way to recovery, and was recuperating in the country with his sister, my Aunt Ethel. "Daddie" died as he had lived, in circumstances that I think deserve the term dramatic. It was a beautiful early summer morning and "Daddie" was seated comfortably before his bedroom window, looking out into a rose garden that was freshly in bloom. Aunt Ethel brought him his breakfast tray and a letter from Basil. She had paused while he opened my letter and read it to her. It had made him very happy. About half an hour later Aunt Ethel had returned to his room to collect his breakfast tray. His breakfast remained untouched and he appeared to be sleeping peacefully, my letter still in his hand. He was dead. I like to think that my mother was somewhere close by to meet him. It would have been good to have had Ouida know my father, who would

have loved her so much. She would have been just his "cup
of tea" . . . God bless him.

Jack and I joined Ouida later at the house on the Thames
River at Pangbourne in Berkshire. Slowly, imperceptibly,
but quite definitely, from this moment Jack was to become
my foster father. That summer of 1924 was a beautiful English summer, than which no season anywhere can be more
beautiful. The days were warm and soft and gentle, and
there was forever an invisible singing in the air as myriads of
insects busied themselves about their daily chores. The skylark paid daily tribute to us and to Shelley, and the River
Thames was framed in a profusion of foliage; the elm and
the oak and the beech and the birch; rambler roses and
honeysuckle. Ouida and I walked for miles, or would punt
together up the river to lunch at a country pub on cold
meats, Cheddar cheese, and beer.

There was a lawn from the house to the river's edge and
it was on this lawn that I thought to teach Ouida to "putt."
(I have always been an avid golfer.) The very first putt she
made she sank in one! For the next fifteen minutes, try as
she would, nothing went right for her. At last she said,
"What a stupid game," and threw my putter into the river!
I have never managed to convert Ouida to golf, but I made
of her an avid baseball and fight fan. No matter who the
fighters she always picks the underdog, who she exhorts to
kill his opponent. There is one exception; as far as Ouida is
concerned (and I agree with her) Sugar Ray Robinson can
do no wrong.

Jack, who enjoyed picking a fight almost as much as he
enjoyed going to one at "The Garden," gave me many
pointers in boxing. Jack was a boxer not a slugger, and was
incredibly fast on his feet for a man of his age. He and a
good friend of his spent a night in "the jug," one time in
Paris, for indulging in a few rounds of boxing in some night
club in Montmartre. If it hadn't been for Dudley Field
Malone, one-time Collector of the Port of New York, Jack
and his friend might still be there . . . who knows? . . . If

you know the French! . . . Dear old Dudley! You talked them out of it. The last time we saw him was at Santa Anita Race Track in 1940, and Dudley was still at it, amusing himself by sitting down with complete strangers at the Turf Club and greeting them as long-lost friends.

"Well—well—well," he would say. "Look who's here . . . and how's Auntie Molly and that scoundrel she was married to?"

And then without stopping he would invent some fantastic story about Aunt Molly, laughing uproariously the while. Suddenly, never having stopped talking, he would rise and take his leave.

"Well—well—well . . . so good to have seen you again . . . long time no see . . . we mustn't let that happen again must we?" and laughing heartily he would move on to another table, leaving his "old friends" in a frantic state of confusion and embarrassment.

At the approach of fall, Ouida, Jack, and I left our house on the Thames to return to New York. Divorce proceedings were under way. The new season recalled me to my profession and *The Swan*. *The Swan* toured the major cities of the United States from September 1924 to the spring of 1925. Ouida was with me as much as possible. Strangely enough for anyone of her temperament, a complete extrovert, she was annoyingly conservative about our situation. She would not even reserve a room in the same hotel with me. Consequently, separated by a few blocks, one of my major hotel expenses was telephoning Ouida. However, it was a lovely time for us of growing together. We heard a great deal of music and shared many books, but above all we just talked and thought, and found our coming together incredibly simple. The tour itself was comparatively uneventful except for one incident. We bought a dog under most unusual circumstances—the first of many dogs we were to share together.

It was the week before Christmas and the company was "laid off" for the week. So Ouida and I met in New York to

see some shows. It was a Saturday night that we went to
some play at the Empire Theatre. After the play we went
backstage to see an old friend, George Renevant. We were
prevented from entering his dressing room by the most beautiful black German shepherd dog I have ever seen.

"George," I said hesitantly, and remembering Lutz, "it's
Ouida and Basil."

"Oh, come in," he replied. "Moritz-platz!"

Moritz quietly retreated and lay down under George's
dressing-room table.

Greetings being over we were formally introduced to
Moritz, who was to go on trial on the Monday for his life.
Moritz had killed a sheep and the inevitable verdict would be
death. Ouida was horrified at the basic injustice of such a
verdict, and her "story" mind was immediately alerted and
quickly went to work. We would leave George and take
Moritz for a walk. She had a pocket checkbook with her
and wrote out a check for $200, the price agreed upon be-
tween George and herself. Moritz was Ouida's Christmas
present to me. He seemed puzzled by the turn of events but
followed us obediently. He understood only German and
before leaving George's dressing room I had memorized a
few words and phrases.

Moritz spent a restless night with me and the following
morning we met Ouida at Penn Station and the three of us
went to Philadelphia. I stayed at The Sylvania, one of the
lesser-known hotels where Moritz and I were to hide out
from the law for the next two weeks. Ouida stayed at The
Ritz. All day Moritz remained in my room. At night, under
cover of darkness, I took him to the theater with me where,
as with George, he lay under my dressing-room table, refusing admittance to anyone. Those two weeks were tough
for us both. Moritz had to learn English and being fully
police trained I had to help him unlearn much of his police
schooling. It was not easy for either of us. I trained him to
allow room service waiters and maids to enter the room, but
I could not train him to allow them to take anything out!

Slowly, almost imperceptibly at first we grew in understanding of one another. In the meantime George Renevant
had appeared in court and stated his case—his dog had been
stolen . . . and what's more he got away with it!

Moritz von Niklotsburgh was an aristocrat and a gentleman, far more so than many who claim these distinctions.
He was never rude or ill-mannered or ugly with me. He
accepted Ouida because he recognized her to be, as she was,
the other half of me. And Ouida respected our friendship
and rarely gave Moritz orders except through me. When
Moritz came to me he was about three years old and he
lived with us for eleven years. I never went anywhere without him. On the street he walked close to my right side. I
never used a lead on him. If I stopped to talk to a friend, he
would give me a quick look (security measures, you know!)
and then wait patiently, ears ever alert, until I moved on
again. No matter what dogs we passed he paid no attention
to them; he was as impersonal to their existence as a guards-
man on duty outside Buckingham Palace. In restaurants I
would leave him in the cloakroom. I would go to no hotel
or restaurant that would not receive him. Our friends soon
learned that an invitation to us automatically included
Moritz. When we went in to dinner, I would show him
where to wait for me and there he would sit, ears cocked,
motionless. At Mr. and Mrs. Cosmo Hamilton's he was allowed in the dining room and Cosmo insisted that Moritz
lie beside him. He never asked for food on these occasions
and never received any. His own dinner was served late,
"after the show." He preferred it that way, the ham that he
was. One night at a private recital given by an eminent artist
at a Mrs. Philip Giddens', Moritz decided he too would like
to hear the recital. So he stretched that beautiful body out
under the piano and there he remained—and I'll swear he
never missed a note. He had looked at me as he first seated
himself and I just nodded to him. Throughout the entire
concert he never took his eyes off me.

In a play entitled *The Grand Duchess and the Waiter* I

had many quick changes that required an on-stage dressing room. He had followed me down at a dress rehearsal and I had decided to let him stay. He remained motionless throughout each performance. The only indication that he was a live dog were his ears, which pricked with each line I spoke, relapsing into indifference when anyone else was talking.

He misbehaved only twice and on both occasions it was a case of mistaken identity. The first was on a hot August night and we were walking to the theater together. We paused for traffic at the corner of Forty-sixth and Seventh Avenue. Suddenly I heard a woman beside me utter a cry of alarm and astonishment. I looked quickly toward her and then followed her look down to Moritz, who was mistaking her leg for a lamppost! For a moment I was paralyzed with horror. I couldn't think, still less speak. At last she turned to me with a pained smile in her eyes. "Please don't worry," she said. "He's such a beautiful dog and I forgive you both."

A moment later she slid gracefully into a taxi, leaving me on the sidewalk red-faced and spluttering like an idiot with useless apologies.

On another occasion Ouida and I were walking one night in the Hollywood hills. Moritz was heeling as was his custom when suddenly he went off into the brush like a shot out of a gun. In those days it was perfectly safe to walk anywhere in the Hollywood hills at night. But Moritz had never behaved like this in his life. Ouida and I stood perfectly still and waited, fearing we knew not what. We called and called to Moritz, but he did not return. Quite some time later he came slinking back foaming at the mouth—had he been bitten by a snake? No, he had crossed swords with a skunk that had spat full in his face! His dejection was pitiful to look upon and he was choking himself to death, and he smelled to high heaven! We bathed him consistently and continuously day after day, week after week. But even at the end of six months there was still that faint sweet-sick odor to him, and ever after at the very mention of the word skunk he would visibly wilt and tremble.

In the late twenties Ouida and I returned to London and Moritz of course went with us. A special wooden house was built for him and he traveled on an upper deck specially reserved for dogs. Up on his private deck he was allowed much freedom and most of our time was spent with him. Arriving at Southampton was a grim experience, for it was at Southampton that we were to be separated from Moritz for the first time in our lives together. It is the law in England that all dogs brought in must spend six months in quarantine. This regulation is rigidly enforced and it must be said that since its inception there has not been one case of rabies anywhere in Britain. Eventually both owner and dog benefit greatly in that no dog need be muzzled or on a lead anywhere at any time. In Hyde Park in London it is wonderful to watch innumerable dogs running about as they please, the sole restriction upon them being obedience to their master.

Ouida was in floods of tears as Moritz was taken from us at the dock and sent on his way to some government-supervised kennel just outside London.

Our trip up to London by the boat train was a sad one. We arrived at Waterloo Station after dark, went to the flat of a friend, and before even unpacking we set out immediately to see Moritz. He was some half hour by train out in the country. The place was closed when we arrived, but the supervisor let us in and we were taken to Moritz' kennel.

This wise, intelligent dog seemed to understand what was happening. He greeted us unemotionally, wagging his tail and licking my hand. I had brought with me a pair of old trousers and a sweater. I laid these out in a corner of his quarters and Moritz sniffed them with much satisfaction. We left him a few moments later much happier.

When we arrived home we enjoyed a good supper, the first food either of us had touched since breakfast that morning. One of us visited Moritz twice a week every week of his six months' quarantine, at the end of which time he was returned to us in perfect health and condition. It was not until 1933, during a long tour with Miss Katharine Cornell, that he appeared to be ailing, and from time to time we were forced to return him to New York for veterinary examination. He had cancer. He trouped around with us bravely as long as he could, and then, at last, we had to leave him with Dr. Cohen. We shall ever be grateful to Dr. Cohen and his nurse, Miss MacDonald, for the loving care they gave him. Then one day Dr. Cohen phoned us that the end was near. I was playing with Miss Cornell in Providence, Rhode Island, at the time. Ouida and I took an early train to New York and were able to spend a couple of hours with our dear friend of so many years. He could not walk any more. He lay in a chair before an open window with a warm spring sun soothing him in his closing hours. The next day we learned he was dead.

He is buried in a little wooden casket, a silk pillow under his head, in the woods at the back of the home of our dear friends the Bartletts in Oxford, Massachusetts. There he rests with other dogs and cats and birds the Bartletts have loved and the little cemetery is tended with loving care by Mike and his mother. At Moritz' head rests a stone on which is inscribed:

MORITZ

WITH RESPECT
ADMIRATION AND
EVERLASTING LOVE
OUIDA AND BASIL

*

Come winter time and summer time,
Come sweet and cleansing rain,
Come spring time and the autumn,
Both sun and moon shall wane,
Come seed time and flowering,
And harvesting the grain,
The Earth will cease and time grow old,
But we shall meet again.

'Twas not for naught we walked the fields,
The sidewalks and the lanes,
Sharing our hopes, our fears, our doubts,
Beliefs, our joys and pains.
And though I, with human weakness,
Have not always understood,
You with your dog devotion
Blindly believed me good.

Now you will sleep a little while
And dream in peace, please God,
Then one day I shall follow you
And sleep too beneath the sod,
To rise with you and walk again
With a vague sense of remembering
That we had loved in other lives,
Before this new ascending.

On the night of his death I wrote these few words of
remembrance to Moritz. They are not included herewith as
an attempt to express myself in a medium I have had little
experience in, but as an expression of faith and hope, in a
medium I love.

6

A Gentleman's Gentleman

Before relating one of the strangest experiences to occur in our lives, I would record that Ouida and I were married on April 18, 1926, by Father Hamden of the Dutch Reformed Church in New York.

For a time we had been deeply concerned and depressed by the fact that we could find no priest who would join us together in "holy matrimony." Ouida being a Catholic and myself an Episcopalian we were faced with our churches' disapproval (nay even condemnation) because of the oath we had each taken and *broken* some years before.

I do not propose to discuss this attitude of the Christian church toward divorce except to say that I believe in its efficacy, and that without it I think the Christian church would lose much of its challenge to our moral, physical, and spiritual integrity. And this I think was much in line with Ouida's so-called "conservatism" in refusing ever "to cheapen our love" before our marriage by behavior which, even had it been accepted as "quite natural," would never have been accepted as "right." And by "right" I mean that there must always be some consideration for those unwritten laws concerning human conduct, which have come into being over hundreds, perhaps thousands of years because certain instincts within our forebears have determined a way of life into which self-respect and respect for others were born, and which have since become the very cornerstone of civilized existence in this mad world.

It was in 1929—or was it 1930 (William the Conqueror, 1066—it could have been 1065 or 1067—does it really matter? The only part of history I hated at school, and still do, is its chronology!) I was very homesick for my motherland, and Ouida, who has always been most patient with me in these moods, encouraged me to return to the London theater. But, to my surprise, I was received in London with a sort of "Oh, you're back again are you" attitude, as though I were doing something unethical! I had been away too long and my Broadway successes in *The Swan*, *The Captive*, and *The Command to Love* did not have the effect I had anticipated they would.

This visit home was made worth-while professionally by a motion picture I made of Galsworthy's play *Loyalties* in which I played de Levis, the Jew, under the direction of Mr. Basil Dean. This picture and my performance in it received considerable commendation, and I shall always consider it to be one of my most fortunate experiences.

Then there was that strange experience that I have referred to earlier. It has been said that fact may be far more surprising than fiction. Such was to be the case in our association with Dennis Poole. The story I would tell you, and which I will call "A Gentleman's Gentleman," is primarily all fact, with modest interludes of fiction where obviously I was not present to record the event and what was said on such occasions. But eventually Poole told me much in great detail I can assure you. . . .

It was a beautiful afternoon in October that we moved into the house in Connaught Square that we had rented. Ouida had "a friend" who had insisted on interviewing servants for us, so that we might settle down as quickly and as comfortably as possible. She had engaged a cook and a maid and a "tweeny." The morning following, a man named Dennis Poole called to apply for the post of butler; a position in the Englishman's home of the early 1930s that still epitomized a certain standard of living. Poole was an old-timer, and understood and appreciated all this. He approved

of class distinction as the inevitable order of things as they
were. Descended from a line of butlers, he worked very
hard to maintain the standards of the rank he now held, and
he was proud of his accomplishments. He was, in his own
category, a complete snob. "No sir," he had said when we
interviewed him, "I'm not ambitious beyond my station. I've
always wanted to be a butler. I've been in service now for a
good many years and all I ask is to be the best in my business." It would seem from his references that he had reached
his objective, for they were eulogies in praise of his work and
character.

So Poole was engaged and proceeded at once to make life
at Connaught Square extremely pleasant. He was everything
he had claimed to be, quiet, unobtrusive, polite, clean, and
extraordinarily efficient. He was also my valet, and it was
not long before my confidence in him was such that I would
leave considerable sums of money on my dressing-room
table, which Poole would find, clipping together the paper
notes and placing the coin money in an envelope with the
sum total figured on the outside—fourteen pounds, six shillings, and eight pence, signed, *Poole!* My clothes and personal
effects were scrupulously cared for and everything accomplished with a minimum of effort. It was too good to be
true! And yet there he was, day after day, fulfilling our
every need, beside being a great success in the kitchen. Cook
"adored" him; the upstairs maid giggled every time he came
near her, and the tweeny worshiped the very ground he
walked on. For Poole was extremely good-looking: tall, fair-
haired, with blue eyes and built like an athlete. He was
youngish, I thought, for a man of such wide experience
(about forty perhaps). No, he had never married; he was
afraid it might interfere with his work. He was critical of
himself in one thing only, that he did not care to stay in one
place too long. It was his fondest hope to retire one day and
travel. These little conversations over my morning tea as I
shaved amused me. Poole had all those qualities of a good
doctor's bedside manner, and he got one off to a wonderful

start each day! He was fond of poetry and, with the slightest encouragement, would recite yards of Kipling, whom he admired passionately. He reminded me somehow of Aubrey Beardsley's *Ballad of a Barber*,

> Yet with no pride his heart was moved;
> He was so modest in his ways!
> His daily task was all he loved,
> And now and then a little praise.
>
> An equal care he would bestow
> On problems simple and complex;
> And nobody has seen him show
> A preference for either sex.
>
> How came it then one Summer's day . . .

But I am getting ahead of my story. "One Summer's day" —that was many months later.

Poole was also endowed with a vivid imagination and, after dinner at night, he would regale "the kitchen" with stories of high adventure. One night my wife and I stood at the top of the stairs listening.

"Coo-er, you ain't half scared me. I shan't sleep a wink tonight." It was the tweeny who spoke.

"Don't be a silly child 'e's only makin' it up."

And then, as if in an attempt to fortify herself against her own imaginings, Cook continued, "Come on, let's all have a nice cup of hot tea."

Poole said, "Heavens, look at the time! I'd better get upstairs and see if there's anything they want."

It was an evening early in November. My wife and I were reading in the library and were disturbing each other considerably! For both of us were reading books that engrossed us completely, and still being very much in love we were anxious as usual to share any pleasurable experience one with the other. This evening we had interrupted each other constantly.

"Darling, do listen to this, it's Maugham at his best."

Resting her book momentarily, she pleaded with me. "*Please* don't read any more to me, dear, you're spoiling it for me and I want to read it myself."

It was at that moment that Poole came in.

"Yes, Poole?"

"Excuse me, madam, but if there's nothing more for tonight might I go out for a while?"

"Certainly, Poole."

"Thank you, madam." Then turning to me, "Same time in the morning, sir?"

"Yes, thank you, Poole. Good night."

"Good night, sir. Good night, madam."

I was reminded of a letter I had forgotten to write and went to my desk. Having finished it I put on my coat and walked to the corner to post it.

It was a beautiful night and Connaught Square was bathed in moonlight. The bare branches of the trees traced a pattern of lace against a cold clear sky, while the crocus bulbs, the jonquils, and tulips slept peacefully beneath the surface of well-tended flower beds. The firm step of a "bobby" on his beat was music to my ears. It was good to be home again.

Poole was just leaving as I returned and, to say the least, I found his transformation startling. He was immaculately dressed, white tie and tails, a boutonniere, fur-lined coat, a gold-topped cane—and wearing a monocle in his left eye. He casually dropped the monocle as he made way for me to pass.

I was smiling as I said, "Under the circumstances I think it is I who should say 'after you.'"

He was immediately the good servant as he explained, "It's the servants' ball tonight, sir, at Lady Carstairs'."

"Oh, I see, yes; then I mustn't detain you."

"Is there anything I can do for you before I go, sir?"

"No, thank you, Poole. Good night, and enjoy yourself."

"Thank you, sir. Good night." And he walked up the street toward the Edgeware Road and hailed a cab.

I told my wife, who seemed quite unperturbed.

"These servants' balls have quite a tradition, you know," she said. "Everyone's a snob in his own little way, and these events help burn up some of the fuel that might get trouble-some if there were no outlets. I wonder why Cook isn't going—too old, I expect. She's probably had it all and pre-fers the evening paper with a nice 'cup of joy,' before the kitchen fire. But it's quite a sight I assure you. We should go sometime. Lords and ladies of the realm dancing with cooks and butlers, and no condescension on the part of the titled folk, and the domestics like soldiers on parade!"

She laughed her adorable laugh that came from her heart.

"Yes-s-s," I said. "We are a wonderful people really, aren't we? We've been finding the answers for centuries—ever since King John. I wonder if we shall find the final one."

It was Poole's "day off" one vile night in March. Since dawn the wind had howled around the house like an injured child. Then late in the afternoon it started to rain in buckets.

"Cook tells me Poole's a fresh air fiend," I said to my wife as she returned to the study, after making sure all the win-dows were closed. "Did you look in his room?"

"No."

"Let me."

"It's all right. I'll go."

So we went together. We found Agnes, the tweeny, stand-ing as if mesmerized before Poole's dressing table. As we entered she froze and looked frightened.

"What are you doing here, Agnes?"

She turned to my wife, her eyes like two saucers.

"Cook sent me up to see if 'is window was closed."

"Well, close it quickly, the rain's coming in."

She did so and was about to go when I stopped her.

"Poole wouldn't like it you know, if he found you here."

"I know, sir, but I just couldn't 'elp it. I never did see such a thing in me life. 'E's a gentleman's gentleman if ever there was."

Poole's dressing table might well have surprised almost

anyone entering his room. I looked at my wife and she was giggling rather self-consciously. Laid out on the dresser, very neatly, were two gold-backed hair brushes and a gold-backed comb; a beautiful Swiss watch, as thin as paper; a manicure set in an ivory case, and a row of cut-glass bottles. I lifted the stopper from one of them—eau de cologne; another contained an excellent cognac. I looked at his bed, turned down for the night, silk sheets! Silk pyjamas marked Sulka, and an elaborate and expensive oriental dressing gown were laid out ready for his return!

"What on earth—" but I failed to finish the sentence.

"Seems to me I married the wrong man!" My wife giggled again, but somehow I didn't think what she had said was too funny. She was a little surprised to find me in such ill humor and I was a little surprised at myself, for I am not without a sense of the ridiculous!

The next morning, over my early cup of tea, I approached the subject, somewhat tentatively at first.

"Oh, Poole, when you go out would you mind seeing that your bedroom window is closed. At this time of the year one can't be too sure of the weather."

"I'm sorry, sir. I hope there was no damage yesterday."

"No. But you have rather nice things and they're apt to get soiled."

"Yes, sir."

A pause, and then continuing to lay out my clothes, "Some of my gentlemen have been more generous to me than I deserve."

It seemed to me there was a touch of superciliousness in his reply and, for the first time since he had come to us, I found his manner rather irritating.

"Are you insured?" I asked.

"Oh yes, sir."

"You're wise."

"Thank you, sir."

No, I didn't like him at all this morning! What was the

matter with me? I was picking on the man, and for no good reason you must admit. And yet I was reminded again of Aubrey Beardsley's barber:

> He left the room on pointed feet,
> Smiling that things had gone so well—

It was a nice little flat on the Edgeware Road within easy walking distance of Connaught Square. For so modest an address the place was furnished in very good taste: a few antiques, some good lamps, expensive carpeting, heavy green satin curtains, a large comfortable sofa, and a couple of Chinese Chippendale chairs. The only incongruity that might be noted was a large framed portrait of Rudyard Kipling over the fireplace.

It was ten o'clock on a Sunday night. A coal fire crackled and spluttered in the grate. Mildred lay stretched out on the sofa reading the *Sunday Express* and eating chocolates. Mildred was in her late twenties. Her raven black hair, green eyes, and olive skin were nicely contrasted against a rose pink negligee. She wore pink mules; and a pair of diamond earrings decorated two unusually pretty little ears, which her coiffeur was designed to show off.

She looked up as he entered.

"Hello, 'ducks.' "

"Hello, 'pusskins,' " he replied, removing his hat and coat. "I'm expecting a visitor; rather important. Do you mind?"

He bent over and kissed her.

"Who is it?" she asked.

"It's about my sister."

"Oh, that."

She rose from the sofa and stretched herself like a cat.

"When's he coming?"

"Any minute now."

"Afterwards can we go out somewhere?"

"Perhaps."

"All right, 'ducks.' Call us when he's gone."

"Here, what about a kiss."

"Later."

And she left the room, taking her chocolates with her, and still reading the *Sunday Express*, without once having looked at him.

He stood before the fire waiting. Before many minutes had passed there was a ring at the front door and he went to open it. A man entered—deliberately dressed, it would seem, to disguise the title he bore.

"May I take Your Lordship's hat and coat?"

"No, thank you."

"May I offer you a drink?"

"No, thank you."

"Cigarette?" The man shook his head.

"Won't you sit down?"

"No, thank you. I'm dining out and should be grateful if we might dispense with all preliminaries and come to the point."

The other took his time. He lit a cigarette and sat down on the sofa, looking into the fire. Then he spoke.

"My sister's baby will be born in June."

"How much do you want?"

"Let's say a couple of hundred pounds to start with, shall we?"

"Who shall I make the check out to?"

"To me."

His Lordship's face was a mask. This fellow should know nothing beyond the business on hand between them: and once an agreement had been arrived at he would leave, and never see the creature again. (His Lordship's title was hereditary and his son, now at Eton, would proudly receive it one day and swear to protect the family traditions invoked on the noble escutcheon.) The man on the sofa continued.

"A couple of hundred should take care of everything until she's up and about again."

"And then?"

"Six hundred pounds a year, paid quarterly."

"To you?"

"I think so. Then if there's any trouble about the money later on you can say I was your 'bookie!' Play the horses?"

"Sometimes."

"Good."

"Anything else?"

He thought for a moment as he looked into the fire.

"Yes-s-s-s. You're a member of Ciro's and The Embassy Club. I'd like cards to them both."

"Don't go too far. There are limits you know, even with a man in the position I find myself in."

"It's easy. You want to do a favor for a friend from Australia, home on leave. There's your answer."

He rose from the sofa and eyed his visitor coldly.

"Will that be all?" asked the other sarcastically.

"Yes, thanks. And I'll make you a promise. Keep your bargain and you'll never hear from me again."

Having showed his visitor out Poole turned back into the room and took off his jacket.

"Heigh, 'pusskins,' where are you?"

Mildred entered almost immediately! She walked slowly over to him and looked up into his face provocatively.

"How did it go, 'duckie?'"

"You 'eard. You ain't got cloth ears—as the girl said to the soldier!"

She laughed; and he took her in his arms and closed her mouth with a kiss. . . .

Connaught Square was resplendent in her new spring dress. May had arrived with unusually seasonable weather, and it was time to think of moving to our little place in the country, near Penn in Buckinghamshire. Poole was the last of our servants to take his holiday. He was to return on June the first to start packing up. And here it was June 13 and neither hide nor hair of him.

Inquiries solicited of the agency from which we had engaged him produced no results. My wife was very upset, for

Poole had been the cornerstone to our comfort all winter, and we hated the thought of losing him.

It was late in the afternoon a few days later when the maid announced, "A Miss Edith Poole to see you, Mum."

"Who?" my wife asked with some considerable surprise.

"She says she's Poole's sister."

"Oh—ask her to come in, will you."

"I hope he's not ill," I ventured.

"I'll kill him if he isn't!" and Ouida laughed a little nervously.

Miss Poole was shown in and had no sooner sat down than she burst into tears. A small woman of about thirty, in the last stages of pregnancy, she was dressed simply in a tweed coat and skirt. She carried her hat in one hand and a newspaper clipping in the other. She looked hot and uncomfortable.

"Whatever it is you must try and control yourself." My wife moved over to her and put her hand on the poor woman's shoulder. "Would you like a cup of tea or something to drink?"

"No, thank you."

She stopped crying and looked up at us, and in her eyes I saw that what she had to say was bad, very bad.

I said, "Take your time, Miss Poole, and know that if there's anything we can do to help you we will."

Her answer to me was a faint smile of gratitude that came and went as rapidly as the sun from behind storm clouds. She held out the news clipping. "You mean you know nothing about it?"

"No." It was my wife who spoke.

"They got him."

"Who got him?"

"The police."

"You mean your brother?"

"Yes."

Slowly she told us a story that resembled nothing so much as the plot of some incredible soap opera.

London had of late been troubled by a masked highway-man! (I had read something of this in the newspapers from time to time. But since my wife and I were not much for night life it had not registered with us too strongly.)

Café society was in the habit of walking part of the way home in the early hours of the morning before finally taking a cab. On any seasonable night, in the West End, they could be seen wandering along laughing and talking, with complete disregard for any possible danger that might lurk in dark corners and side streets.

Poole had been observing this human traffic for weeks before successfully making his first coup. A short distance from Ciro's he had started to follow an elderly couple. They turned momentarily without stopping as they heard footsteps behind them, and seeing a man in full evening dress strolling casually behind them they proceeded on their way. A few moments later, with a cheery "good night," the stranger passed them. He was some twenty yards up the street when he stopped, took out his cigarette case, and removed a cigarette. As the elderly couple approached he was heard to say "damn," as he felt for a match or his lighter.

"Excuse me, sir, but do you have a match?"

"I think so," the man replied. "Just a minute."

As he went to his pocket he heard Poole say, "All right, whatever you have hand it over . . . quick . . . and you," to the woman, "that necklace and earrings please." Poole pushed his revolver into the man's ribs. It was all over in a matter of seconds, and Poole darted down a nearby alley-way.

There was another night when Poole had enjoyed himself immensely! He was dining alone at the Carlton Grill, a hunting ground he had so far neglected. He had ordered whitebait, sole Colbert, salad, a Napoleon, and a bottle of Liebfrau-milch. It was during the sole Colbert that he spotted his man. He finished his cognac and coffee, paid his bill and waited, smoking a Corona cigar.

As the man left, Poole followed him. They met at the

checkroom, and as they put on their coats Poole said, "Forgive me, sir, you wouldn't by any chance be Henry Dodsworth?"

The man looked around.

"No, I'm afraid not."

"I was at school with a Henry Dodsworth," Poole continued, "and the resemblance is quite remarkable."

"Sorry to disappoint you." He tipped the girl at the checkroom, then turned to Poole again and smiled as he asked, "Where were you at school?"

Without batting an eyelash, Poole said, "Repton."

The other seemed pleased.

"Really—I'm an old Carthusian. We used to play soccer against you chaps."

"Yes, I know. I nearly made the eleven my last year."

"Good for you. I was never much at sports myself. A spot of tennis and golf to keep the weight down, you know." He laughed and Poole laughed with him, but not for the same reason. This old school-tie stuff was too good to be true! What a "setup," if everything else went as well.

They walked slowly up the Haymarket together.

"Soccer's a great game to watch, don't you think?"

"The best," Poole replied.

"Do you have any favorite?"

"The Spurs."

"Good old Tottenham Hotspurs—fine team! I've always been an Arsenal man myself."

The weather, the theater, and the coming cricket season with a visit from the Australians engrossed them completely, so much so that they found themselves still chatting amiably as they turned into Portland Place.

"You live up this way?"

"No," Poole replied. "St. John's Wood."

"I say, old man, you're a long way from home."

"It's all right, I've enjoyed it. I'll take a cab."

"Well, this is my place. Thanks so much for your company."

As he reached for his key Poole reached for his revolver.
"Come on, quick, whatever you've got, hand it over."

The man laughed until he felt the gun in his ribs. Then he
did as he was told. And a moment later Poole had disappeared.

Poole varied his hunting ground, but his technique was always the same: the well-dressed "man about town," likable,
an easy conversationalist with a clear-cut plan, which he put
into effect with great speed and assurance. It was this speed
and assurance that disarmed his victims so completely, and by
the time they had recovered there was nothing to be done except make a routine report to the police. Few of them could
even remember what he looked like!

Scotland Yard was much disturbed and it was reported
there would be a "shake-up" in its detective force if an arrest
were not made very soon!

Then a month passed without incident, to be followed by
a sudden alarm that "he" was at it again!

It was early in June when they finally caught him.

Poole had hesitated to use his cards to Ciro's and The
Embassy: he considered the contacts too risky. But to celebrate the end of his holiday, and his return to work with us,
he had taken Mildred to The Embassy to dine and dance. He
was determined that nothing should happen that night that
would embarrass and, indeed, involve Mildred should he
prove thoughtless.

However, his good intentions were sorely put on trial quite
early in the evening when he spotted a couple who looked to
him like "sitting ducks." The temptation was like a drug that
slowly worked on him as he waited for them to leave. As luck
would have it Mildred excused herself for a moment, and almost immediately after she had gone, the couple arose and
left. Poole sauntered after them, smoking a cigarette.

At the captain's desk he said, "Tell my wife I'll be back in a
moment, will you?"

The couple turned up Bond Street. There was not a soul
else in sight. His phenomenal luck was still holding!

"Excuse me," Poole said to them. "You dropped something."

As they turned he reached for his revolver. Where was it? He didn't have it, and decided to bluff.

"Come on, hand it over, whatever you've got."

The couple seized him—a policeman and a police woman —decoys!

They took him back to The Embassy, where two inspectors were stationed inside the front doors to the long passageway that led to the club. With them was a waiter holding a small silver tray on which was Poole's revolver.

"This yours, sir?" asked the waiter. "It was found in your coat in the cloak room."

Some of this we learned from Miss Poole, and the rest at his trial, which was quite a gala event. He was always impeccably dressed in court, and each time that he entered the dock he greeted the fashionable assembly with a smile and a wave of his hand. He was debonair and gallant to the last, clearing Mildred completely of any association with the criminal side of his life (which was very difficult to swallow! For surely dear Mildred could not have thought she was living in such comfort on his butler's wages, which she nevertheless insisted that she did, and so saved her not so precious skin).

"His lordship's" name was never mentioned, but I learned later from Edith that he was more than generous to her and her son.

I was of course called as a character witness. But there was nothing I could say to mitigate his sentence of two years in one of His Majesty's prisons, and nine lashes with "the cat" for carrying a firearm.

I heard from him several times while he was in prison where, during his spare time, he had taken to composing popular songs, both lyrics and music. He never mentioned his physical punishment and it was this that made me reply without fail to all his letters.

"The cat o' nine tails" has a wooden handpiece to which are attached nine leather thongs. These thongs are soaked in oil before use on a prisoner, who is allowed to receive only three lashes at any one time, and the prison doctor's presence is mandatory. The prisoner receives the lashes across his back, with results that can best be left to one's imagination. And, worse than all, the prisoner is not told when he will receive his punishment. He may wait for weeks, in an agony of suspense, before he receives the first three lashes. Then months may pass by before he is called on again for the second three; and so on to the bitter end.

During one year in the early 1920s there had been quite a number of cases of "robbery with violence." In all these cases "the cat" was included in the sentence. The following year there were virtually no cases of a similar nature, and having served its purpose "the cat" was once more discontinued.

I have heard it said that most prisoners stand up better under the death sentence than one that carries with it the additional penalty of "the cat."

I saw Poole once again, a few weeks after he had been released from prison. He looked very well and was, as usual, immaculately dressed. He told me he had learned the saxophone during the past year, and had been engaged to play with a small orchestra on Saturday nights, at a hotel in Reading. He was still composing and one of his songs had been published. "I Walk Alone in the Cool of the Night!" He had dedicated the song to me and asked me to accept the copy he had with him. I was glad to do so. He wrote on it in a bold flamboyant hand, "From your devoted servant, Dennis Poole"; and beneath he wrote out a verse of Kipling's *If!*

He said he had been tempted to go abroad, but what was the use. "There's no place like the old country, is there, sir?"

We talked of England, her quiet country lanes—the soft rolling landscapes that cradled her picturesque homesteads—her cathedrals and churches—her men and women, proud inheritors of more than a thousand years of progressive government—of the blood of the Romans, the Norsemen, the Normans—that ran in our veins. And he spoke with pride of her laws, in spite of his own experience. "Because you see, sir, it makes no difference whether it's me or 'his lordship.' We get what's coming to us."

His wife had divorced him and was living with her mother, a fact he related without bitterness. "We had a nice time while the going was good. I don't blame her."

I never found out the whys and the wherefores of his predilection for a Jekyll and Hyde existence. All I could get from him was that he had learned his technique from the movies: they had taught him what *not* to do! And he claimed, with complete sincerity, that he had never hurt anyone in his life, and had always contributed liberally to organized charity. "Anonymous, of course," he had said with a wry smile.

I had to go out and he helped me on with my coat. We walked together for a while. Then he took a bus, and I never saw him again. But years later I heard that he had lost his life in the Battle of Britain, giving all that he had, with thousands of others, to that tight little island's finest hour.

I vow to thee, my country—all earthly things above—
Entire and whole and perfect, the service of my love.*

---

* Cecil Spring-Rice. British Ambassador to the United States 1912–18.

7

The World Is Not a Stage

"All the world's a stage," said Mr. Shakespeare, "and all the men and women merely players." What a good "player" Dennis Poole was on the stage of his little world. And how often it happens with so many who have had little or no experience in the professional world of entertainment. There is a Central Park West bus driver on the No. 10 route whose comedy patter keeps his passengers in a state of surprised delight and amusement. It is all completely impromptu and varies considerably depending upon the weather, local politics, news from abroad, or some personal jocular comments between himself and a regular customer. I know of many a comedian whose material would greatly benefit by engaging my bus driver friend as a writer. Fanny Brice had a friend who could keep a roomful of guests in stitches of laughter with a whimsical and creative humor. But when she put him on the professional stage he was a complete flop. There is a Brooklyn taxicab driver who serves tea or coffee to his clients in winter and inquires if they prefer classical or jazz music during the ride. (He has a phonograph beside his driver's seat and a nice selection of recordings.) If no music is requested he delights himself and his "fare" with a sort of Bob Hope patter that is remarkable for its humor and its considerable understanding of human frailties. A real philosopher this taxi driver from Brooklyn—In many ways perhaps the best "player" alive today is Bishop Sheen; his is a consummate artistry whether on his T.V. program or in the pulpit—and Churchill or Roose-

velt could have had their names in lights outside any theater,
had they so wished! These and oh, so many others, including
Poole, have one primary asset in common, a complete self-
assurance (a quality I think almost unknown to all really good
professional actors). But Poole had something else besides his
self-assurance which was equally important to him—he did
not require an audience! And it was only when his sense of
audience participation began to intrigue him that he failed.
(This is of course a moot question, but I often wonder how
far a professional actor should indulge in audience participation.) So long as Poole was content to "perform" for the staff
in the kitchen, for me or Ouida or his "pusskins," or for himself and his eternal shadow it seems to me that he was a most
efficient "player"—And I am sure the West Side New York
bus driver and my Brooklyn taxi friend would have failed,
like Poole, on a larger canvas, as did Miss Fanny Brice's
friend. The story of Dennis Poole brings another question to
mind. Is there any essential difference between actors and entertainers? Very hesitantly I would define the actor as one
who submerges himself and becomes someone else. The near-
perfect example of this state of body and mind being Sir
Laurence Olivier. There are occasions when Sir Laurence is
unrecognizable, not only physically but in a violent transformation in his process of thinking that affects every sense of
his being. Whereas the entertainer always remains himself,
however great his talents—the classic example of this perhaps
being Victor Borge. There are rare examples of both actor
and entertainer, as an example I think first of Danny Kaye.
With Danny Kaye it is merely a question of which category
he chooses. Alas, he more often than not chooses the entertainer, and therein our theater of today loses a potentially
great actor. In our day and age there are *few* great actors and
many good entertainers and the theater is thereby a loser.
Bishop Sheen, Churchill, and Roosevelt must then be of that
category we have defined as entertainers, as most great ora-
tors throughout history have been, including Disraeli and

Marc Antony. They are *themselves* at all times whatever may be their talent and purpose.

Poole is somewhere in the middle of all this, a talented man with aspirations to be an actor; but he could not resist being an entertainer. It takes much discipline to be either, an actor or an entertainer of quality. I think the real trouble with Poole was that he had most of the failings and few of the assets of a true artist, his discipline always being the servant to his vanity.

The ability to act goes far beyond motive and constitutional adaptability, far beyond desire and daydreams. In brief moments of hallucination I have imagined myself conducting great orchestras! I like to play recordings of famous symphonies, and endeavor to find the beat, and conduct them. Incidentally I have appeared (not as conductor!) as narrator in *Peter and the Wolf* with Leopold Stokowski and his Youth Orchestra; Schumann's *Manfred* with Massino Freccia and the Baltimore Symphony Orchestra; *The Nightingale and the Rose* by Oscar Wilde, a tone poem especially composed for me by Alexander Steinert in which I appeared with Eugene Ormandy and The Philadelphia Symphony Orchestra both in Philadelphia and at Carnegie Hall, New York. And I have made many appearances in Honegger's *King David*. These experiences have only succeeded in aggravating my sense of frustration as a disappointed musician, but they have also helped to show me that one can only really "belong" to a given art through close familiarity and eventual mastery of its techniques.

Although any well-equipped modern actor should be able to adjust his technique to all four mediums of the theater, motion pictures, radio, and television, he should bear in mind that each of these mediums is distinctly individual and needs to be approached as such. A basic theater technique will serve the actor well in any of these mediums, but there will be necessary adjustments and compensations to be made in order to meet the individual limitations of all four mediums. As an obvious example, the human voice is the sole medium of communication in radio. Whereas in motion pictures it must be remembered that the screen magnifies many times over every movement of the body and the slightest facial expression. In movies and in television there should be a concentration upon economy, since every member of one's audience has, as it were, a front row seat in the theater; whereas in the live theater one must reach out, project, in order to be heard and understood in the back rows.

Only in the theater is the actor called upon to make use of his entire physical equipment. From head to foot he is visible to his audience throughout the entire play. His thinking, i.e. characterization, must not be evident only in his face but in the expression of every limb of his body, and this coordination must be sustained for a period of approximately two consecutive hours. Actually his character concept will subconsciously start developing as he sits before the mirror in his dressing room and the world outside fades into the creative being of his imagination. I never open any mail there may be for me at the theater nor will I see anyone before a performance. One hour is all too short a time to recapture nightly that dream world which must become a reality. In my early days as a young actor in London, a great old actress, Mrs. Kendal, took an interest in me. She would "command" me to tea with her at her house in Portland Place in London. There sitting bolt upright in her very Victorian home we would partake of tea sandwiches and pound cake while she "lectured" me.

"Young man," she would say.

"Yes, Mrs. Kendal?"

"I saw you again in your play. You are improving, but you are still unsure in the use of your hands. Now what did I tell you about those hands?"

And I quoted to her what she had said to me some weeks before. "By their hands ye shall know them."

"That's right. And what else have I impressed upon you?"

"To fully prepare myself in my dressing room before every performance," I obediently replied.

"Well," continued Mrs. Kendal, "whatever preparations

you had made on the night that I last saw you were entirely inadequate because your hands were certainly not coordinated with the rest of your body and with what you were saying. They were in fact a contradiction, even a denial of the words you were speaking"—and so on and so on and so on. . . . I learned much from the "command" visits to tea with Mrs. Kendal, who practiced what she preached to young actors like myself. She had impressed upon me the advantages of the utmost concentration at the moment of first closing one's dressing room door and from that moment on seeing no one and allowing oneself to think of nothing but the performance that lay ahead. And in this it is said she herself went to considerable extremes. Fifteen minutes before curtain time her dresser left the dressing room and five minutes before her entrance Mrs. Kendal would go into the wings. She would speak to no one and no one would dare speak to her! Consequently she made her entrance into a room on stage as if she had lived there all her life. One wonders what happened to her when she and Ellen Terry were playing Mistress Ford and Mistress Page to Sir Herbert Tree's Falstaff in *The Merry Wives of Windsor* at His Majesty's Theatre in London around 1910. A never to be forgotten evening in the theater. There was an almost childlike magic about Miss Terry, a physical and spiritual effervescence that many of her contemporaries greatly envied her; and it would seem that she could do all they did and more with comparatively little effort and, some said, without much self-discipline! However, there were others who held the opposite to be true; that Miss Terry's technique had reached such perfection as to become invisible.

Another great actress I was connected with during my early days in London was the extraordinarily beautiful and exceptionally gifted Mrs. Patrick Campbell. She taught me, I think, to be prepared for almost any emergency that might happen to an actor anywhere at any time! I was playing Alfred de Musset opposite her George Sand at the Duke of York's Theatre in London late in 1920. She was then in her early fifties I should say, and still devastatingly beautiful. She

had also retained to the full a wit and a devilish playfulness
that could completely demolish opponents and often confuse
her friends! She referred to an elderly and well-known American hostess to whose home she had never been invited as
"that well-kept grave on Memorial Day." She had christened
me "that young actor with a face like two profiles stuck together" . . . and then later as being like "a folded umbrella
taking elocution lessons!"

In the play *George Sand* I did not make my appearance until the second act and only then after the curtain had been up
some fifteen minutes. As de Musset I was curled up in a big
curtained double bed in nightgown and nightcap, supposedly
sleeping off the effects of the night before. Mrs. Campbell as
George Sand was playing a scene with the German poet
Heine, who is said to have been one of her lovers. From time
to time, as George Sand, she would tiptoe over to the bed and
peep through the curtains to assure herself that I was still
asleep and as Mrs. Campbell, at least once every performance,
she would stop to converse with me personally! "Darling,"
she would say in a voice audible to her audience for at least
six rows! "Did you bring your dinner jacket? You have got
to take me out to supper tonight at Mrs. Guiness'. Didn't my
secretary call you?"

I would silently indicate that all was well and she would go
back to her scene with Heine! On some other night she would
come over and peep through the curtains (how I dreaded
these moments!) and say, "Darling, are you asleep?" Getting
no reply she would continue, "You naughty boy! You
wouldn't do much sleeping if I was there would you" and
then go back to her scene with Heine. There were other
scenes in which she would look at me with those liquid laughing eyes and just nothing would happen. The stage manager
would start to prompt her, but she would pay no attention.

At last she would say to me, "Do you know what I'm
thinking, my darling . . . I'm thinking how beautiful you are
tonight . . . now tell me, my darling, what do I say?" and I
would prompt her! I can only assume that audiences must

have concluded that these extemporaneous scenes were all part of the play.

It was, on occasion, all quite mad and rather frightening to anyone with as little experience as I had had. Mrs. Campbell was not the least bit in love with me, and was always a most gracious and charming companion on the many occasions that she invited me to be her escort to some supper party given for her after the play. She always went out to these supper parties dressed in her last-act gown. After each performance there was a crowd of admirers waiting at the stage door to see her. She told me she didn't want to disillusion them by appearing to be just like anyone else. There was magic in her madness and I loved her for it. To Miss Constance Collier, to Mrs. Kendal, and to Mrs. Patrick Campbell I owe a deep debt of gratitude for those days of trial and error during which I gained such valuable experience.

These women had mastered their individual techniques, and it must not be thought that Mrs. Campbell's asides to me were in the least prejudicial to her performance. Her technique was very different from that of Mrs. Kendal, but none the less effective. The appearance of reality was at all times maintained, but the actors themselves were undeceived. The method by which real emotion is used to serve a theatrical end is most often observable in children, for whom technique is an almost unknown factor and who are not, strictly speaking, actors at all; they play-act. I should like to illustrate this point by recounting an incident which occurred, many years later, during the filming of *Anna Karenina*, in which I played Karenin, Anna's husband, and Freddie Bartholomew played our son.

There was a scene in which, after having forbidden Anna ever to see our son again, I had to tell the child that his mother had gone on a long journey (or something of that nature) and that I did not know when he would see her again. Freddie Bartholomew, as my son, was acting up all over the place and Clarence Brown, our director, suggested I might be able to help the boy since Freddie and I were such friends. I promised to try and Clarence Brown walked off the stage to get himself a cup of coffee.

"Freddie, dear boy," I said, "this scene isn't coming off as it should, you know."

"Yes, I know, Uncle Basil. What am I doing, please tell me?" Freddie replied.

"You are not listening to what I am telling you, about your mother's going away for a long time. And if you are listening you are not conveying any feeling. You are just making a lot of noise and hamming it up," and we both laughed about it.

"Now, Freddie dear," I continued, "this is one of your very best scenes and you have just got to be good in it for Cissie's sake." Cissie was Freddie's guardian and he simply worshiped her. Then like a flash it came to me. "Freddie, listen to me carefully—in this scene just forget all about my being your stern father, Karenin, telling you about your mother going away—when I come in and talk to you just imagine it's me, your Uncle Basil, and I am breaking the news to you that Cissie is dead."

Freddie looked at me, and then turned away from me as his eyes filled with tears. I went quickly to our assistant director and said to him, "Get Clarence as fast as you can. I think Freddie is about ready to make this scene."

Clarence Brown came back at once. The camera was already set up, and all there was to do was turn on the lights. I entered the room and walked over to Freddie's bed. I could tell at once that he was applying the formula. He no longer greeted me as an ogre, but the strain of what he had to do gave to his little white face a timidity that was deeply touching. As I talked to him of his mother's going away he was not listening to what I said but translating my words, as it were, into a scene in which Uncle Basil was telling him of Cissie's death. The effect was a heartbreaking scene at the conclusion of which I had to spend a considerable time comforting Freddie and getting him back to normal. Everyone on the set including Clarence Brown praised his performance extravagantly, and in self-defense Freddie had to keep our little secret and admit with us all that he was indeed truly a great actor!

"What the hell did you do to that boy?" Clarence asked me, overjoyed at the scene.

"I can't tell you, Clarence," I said. "I promised Freddie I wouldn't and I've got to keep my promise."

And Freddie Bartholomew, wherever you are, I have kept that promise until this moment.

It is very rare indeed that material written specifically for one medium transposes satisfactorily into another. Good plays are never made into better pictures. A good picture is "murdered" by a T.V. presentation. A good original M.S. for T.V. has rarely been transposed successfully to "live" theater. *The Little Moon of Alban* was a touchingly beautiful, most expertly written original manuscript for T.V. It was a failure as a play. *The Swan* was a great success on Broadway and a failure in motion pictures. I know of no attempt to transpose an original motion picture M.S. into a stage play. And most great books make better reading than viewing in motion pictures or T.V. The truly creative writer will inevitably be bound within the form and framework of his chosen medium, and prose and poetry seem only to mix well in the theater, and then only perhaps when the author happens to be Mr. William Shakespeare! Water colors do not mix with oil paints and a "miniature" technique will be of little use to an artist when broad strokes are demanded in painting a large canvas. The actor, however, must be prepared to work with oils, in water colors, in miniature as in T.V. or on a large canvas as in the theater. But alas the actor is not a creative artist. He is an artisan who works within the limitations of the framework of his particular craft. He is entirely dependent upon his author for his material and inspiration, and he is also dependent on the many other arts and crafts of the theater. Long runs, an economic necessity, hamper an actor's equipment and deprive him of opportunities to be versatile. Short runs are failures and he cannot eat and pay his rent on failures. Motion pictures and television may supplement his income to a degree, but are liable to defeat that inspiration which was the source of his initial dedication as a young and hopeful artist.

And so it is that many an actor finds himself frustrated by the limitations of his craft and turns to other work that gives him the opportunity to be more creative. John Barrymore was an artist long before he became an actor, and despite his phenomenal successes he always considered acting a constricting occupation and at times could be quite violent about its limitations. Lionel, Jack's brother, was a good painter and a composer. At least one of his compositions I know was performed by the Los Angeles Symphony Orchestra. Sir John Gielgud, one of England's finest contemporary actors has, in the past few years, devoted much of his time to direction. Sir Laurence Olivier's considerable creative talent long ago refused to be confined within the actor's limited opportunities. Alfred Lunt, Sir Cedric Hardwicke, Margaret Webster, Eva Le Gallienne, Cyril Ritchard, and Elia Kazan (to name but a few) are all actors who have felt and responded to the urge to express themselves more creatively, as did two actors of many years ago named Molière and William Shakespeare!

I myself have relieved my tensions by impecunious writings and by fiddling on the fringes of great music! But there have been times when one has been seduced by this *pâté de foie gras* we call acting, and I am not forgetting that *pâté de foie gras* is considered a delicacy and is quite expensive! So it was with me in the beginning. I went to dancing class and ballet school and attended the Salle d'Armes of Felix Grave and Leon Bertrand. Later in Hollywood I worked with M. Fred Cavens, the greatest swordsman of them all. In all I have played fifty-two roles in twenty-three plays of Shakespeare, some forty of these in about twenty of his plays in my first three years in the theater. My apprenticeship was both

stimulating and exciting. Following upon World War I there
were appearances in *Peter Ibbetson*, *Henry IV*, Part II, *The
Merchant of Venice*, Sardou's *Fédora*, *George Sand* by
Philip Moeller, and *The Czarina* in January of 1922. Then,
when I met Ouida, and had experienced a two-year run in
The Swan, 1923–25, the urge to express myself more creatively caught up with me. Ouida's creativity was enormously
stimulating and we started to work together. In *The Command to Love* she designed the sets and upon the request of
Messrs. Wiman and Bill Brady, Jr., the producers of this play,
she turned an initial failure into a long-run success on Broadway by her skillful editing and reconstruction. She has been
"the power behind the throne" ever since, and I have rarely
done anything that has not had her complete endorsement.
However, between times I was often at my desk writing,
writing, writing, but never with any success.

The actor is so dependent on so many things—and so many
of these are variables—that his hold on the traditional securi-
ties of life is, at best, precarious. The last and perhaps most
important variable—the enveloping atmosphere within which
the actor works—is the climate of public taste and opinion,
official and unofficial. To illustrate this, I should like to tell
you the story of the life and death of a play. Unfortunately,
an actor feels his dependence on the public more surely when
something goes wrong. The play in question was *The Captive*, produced by Gilbert Miller, then acting as general
manager for Charles Frohman, Inc., at the Empire Theatre,
New York, in October of 1926.

It must have been June or July of that year that Ouida and
I, but newly wed in April, were enjoying an evening concert of recorded music of which I had a considerable library.
We had a duplex apartment on Beekman Place. Dear Moritz,
my black police dog, was lying beside me motionless, his ears
pricking and his body from time to time trembling with excitement. There was a little mouse that visited us occasionally
and could run circles around Moritz! He would appear from

I know not where and for some time he and Moritz would sit staring at one another. Then the mouse would make tentative feints and finally Moritz would leap at him. But Moritz never got anywhere near him, and I can only conclude that his little friend lived to a ripe old age and died of sheer boredom.

Suddenly, on this particular night around nine o'clock, the telephone rang. It was Gilbert Miller . . . could he come up and read us a play. No, he couldn't wait, besides it was in French and there was as yet no translation. The play, *La Prisonniere* by Edouard Bourdet, was already a tremendous success in Paris, and Gilbert wanted to produce it in the fall in New York. Gilbert arrived and started to read about 10 P.M. His translation into English was fantastic. It was as though he held in his hand the finished English translation, with such ease and fluency did he translate to us. When he had finished, both Ouida and I were drunk with excitement. It was a brilliant, brave, and tragic story, which Gilbert suggested was based on an early experience in M. Bourdet's own life. Briefly the story of the play was as follows: M. de Montcel, a widower, was anxious that his daughter Irene should make a good match, and he particularly favored the son, Jacques Vieieu, of an old friend of his family's. Jacques was much attracted to Irene and was anxious to announce their formal engagement. However, Irene, who appeared fond of Jacques, seemed reluctant to make a final decision. At the end of Act I Irene receives from a florist a very large and beautiful bouquet of violets. She tenderly raises the flowers to her lips and kisses them passionately as the curtain falls.

In Act II Jacques and Irene have formally announced their engagement. But it appears that something about this engagement is proving deeply disturbing to Jacques. Before long it becomes evident that Jacques suspects that his fiancée has a lover, and that this lover is one of his best friends, M. d'Aiguines. This suspicion is aggravated by the fact that he knows of the many visits his fiancée pays to the home of M. and Madame d'Aiguines. He also senses that his fiancée is not really in

love with him. So he sends for M. d'Aiguines, who calls on
Jacques halfway through Act II. They are old friends and
were at school together. They meet cordially and Jacques
proceeds carefully to question his friend. D'Aiguines is at
first evasive and seems to be avoiding some personal problem.
At last Jacques accuses d'Aiguine of being his fiance's lover.
D'Aiguines denies it forcefully and starts to leave. Jacques re-
strains him and pleads for his friend's help. "There must be
someone" . . . "Do you know him?" . . . "Please help me."
At last d'Aiguines breaks and tells Jacques . . . yes, Irene has
a lover and it is none other than his wife, Madame d'Aiguines! A tremendous scene follows in which M. d'Aiguines
tells of his marriage to his beautiful and most desirable wife,
only to find out that she is a Lesbian. He pleads desperately
with Jacques not to marry Irene, giving his own experience as
an example of its utter hopelessness.

AIGUINES

If she had a lover I'd say to you: Patience, my boy, patience
and courage. Your cause isn't lost. No man lasts forever in a
woman's life. You love her and she'll come back to you if you
know how to wait . . . but in this case I say: Don't wait!
There's no use. She'll never return—and if ever destiny should
cross your paths again fly from her, fly from her . . . do you
hear? Otherwise you are lost! Otherwise you'll spend your
existence pursuing a phantom which you can never overtake.
One can never overtake them! They are *shadows*. They must
be left to dwell alone among themselves in the kingdom of
shadows! Don't go near them . . . they are a menace! Above
all, never try to be anything to them, no matter how little—
that's where the danger lies. For, after all, they have some need
of us in their lives . . . it isn't always easy for a woman to get
along. So if a man offers to help her, to share with her what he
has, and to give her his name, naturally she accepts. What
difference can it make to her? So long as he doesn't exact love,
she's not concerned about the rest. Only, can you imagine the
existence of a man if he has the misfortune of love—to adore a
shadow near whom he lives? Tell me, can you imagine what

that's like? Take my word for it, old boy, it's a rotten life!
One's used up quickly by that kind of game. One gets old in
no time—and at thirty-five, look for yourself, one's hair is gray!

JACQUES

Do you mean—?

AIGUINES

Yes—and I hope you'll profit by my example. Understand this:
they are not for us. They must be shunned, left alone. Don't
make my mistake. Don't say, as I said in a situation almost like
yours, don't say, "Oh, it's nothing but a sort of ardent friendship
—an affectionate intimacy . . . nothing very serious . . . we
know all about that sort of thing!" No! We don't know *any-*
thing about it! We can't begin to know what it is. It's mysterious—terrible! Friendship, yes—that's the mask. Under cover of
friendship a woman can enter any household, whenever and
however she pleases—at any hour of the day—she can poison
and pillage everything before the man whose home she destroys
is even aware of what's happening to him. When finally he realizes things it's too late—he is alone! Alone in the face of a
secret alliance of two beings who understand one another because they're alike, because they're of the same sex, because
they're of a different planet than he, the stranger, the enemy!
Ah! at least if a man tries to steal your woman you can defend
yourself, you can fight him on even terms, you can smash his
face in. But in such a case—there's nothing to be done—but *get*
out while you still have strength to do it! And that's what
you've got to do!

JACQUES

. . . Why don't you get out yourself?

AIGUINES

Oh, with me it's different. I can't leave her now. We've been
married eight years. Where would she go? . . . Besides it's too
late. I couldn't live without her any more. What can I do—I
love her.

(Pause)

You've never seen her?

(*Jacques shakes his head*)

You'd understand better if you knew her. She has all the feminine allurements, every one. As soon as one is near her, one feels —how shall I say it—a sort of deep charm. Not only I feel it. Everyone feels it. But I more than the rest because I live near her. I really believe she is the most captivating, harmonious being that has ever breathed. . . . Sometimes when I'm away from her, I have the strength to hate her for all the harm she has done me . . . but, with her, I don't struggle. I look at her . . . I listen to her . . . I adore her. You see?

At the conclusion of this scene, on d'Aiguines' exit, I would stand at the door watching him go for a full minute of applause. Shocked, disturbed, frightened by this appalling exposé of a social sickness, not so freely discussed or accepted as it is today, audiences were, however, deeply appreciative of Mr. Arthur Wontner's restrained and dramatic performance. When their applause subsided a deathly silence overtook the house as they waited and watched for my reactions. They were not kept long in suspense. Act II ends with a terrifying scene in which Jacques tells Irene he knows about Madame d'Aiguines and Irene pleads with him to marry her and save her. He takes her in his arms, but as his lips are about to meet hers she turns her head away from him. "Irene," he says in despair. "No, no!" she replies desperately. "Pay no attention . . . it doesn't mean anything . . . it's all over . . . you will help me?" Jacques looks at her with a growing sense of helplessness and says, "I'll try." Curtain. Act III is an exposition of everything that d'Aiguines had warned Jacques would happen. As a solace to his miserable marriage Jacques renews the acquaintance of an early mistress he had had and is attempting to adjust himself to a situation we all recognize must one day come to some tragic conclusion.

The play was produced without any preproduction publicity with Helen Menken as Irene and myself as Jacques. Of course there were rumors as to what it was all about since a limited number of Americans had seen the play in Paris, but our first night audience was completely ignorant of its theme. They were stunned by its power and the persuasiveness of its argument. We were an immediate success and for seventeen weeks we played to standing room only at every performance. At no time was it ever suggested that we were salacious or sordid or seeking sensation. It was a modern Greek tragedy in the tradition of such great Greek tragedies as *Medea* and *Oedipus Rex,* and, as in Brieux's *Damaged Goods* or Ibsen's *Ghosts,* we were helping to educate a public to a better understanding of a social sickness that could not be ignored. Such matters have always been the prerogative of the theater when approached seriously and in good taste. And M. Bourdet and Mr. Miller and his company were doing just that, no more and no less. These were challenging days for us in the theater and we accepted them gladly.

There was that charming Sunday lunch that Ouida gave and prepared herself (there is no finer chef in the world than my Ouida when the inspiration moves her!) for Monsieur and Madame Bourdet and some dozen prominent guests from the world of the theater. This was M. Bourdet's second marriage—a beautiful woman who had obviously enabled him to recover from any tragic experience he may have suffered from in earlier years. No mention was made of the origin of the play and M. Bourdet offered none. Shortly after this luncheon the Bourdets returned to France and we settled down to what looked like the biggest stage success of my life.

Then one night, after seventeen weeks of playing, I went to the Empire Theatre at the usual time. Ouida had come into town with me. (We were living at Great Neck, Long Island, at the time.) There was some play that she had wanted to see. There was no suggestion that anything might be wrong. I entered my dressing room, undressed, put on my dressing gown, and proceeded to make up. Dear John Hart, my colored dresser, who had worked, and was to continue to work, with me in almost every play I ever appeared in in

America, came into my room a few minutes later. He said there were quite a lot of people gathering in the street outside and there seemed an unusual number of police around. Hardly had he said this when my dressing room telephone rang. It was James Reilly, Mr. Miller's general manager. He said, "Hello, Basil—you O.K.?—Fine—Well keep your window closed and bolted—don't worry—everything's going to be all right—just go ahead and give your usual performance." And before I could answer he had hung up. I looked through my window before bolting it and it was as John Hart had said—there were indeed an unusual number of people standing around outside and more policemen than I had ever seen anywhere at one time in New York. I went to Helen Menken's dressing room, which was next to mine. She too had just had a phone call from Jim Reilly. Yes, she had heard a rumor there might be trouble and that the play might be closed by the police department that night. I went back to my dressing room, finished making up, and John dressed me for my first scene. Just before curtain time other members of the cast walked into my dressing room and asked if I knew what was up. We had not long to wait to find out.

As we each walked out onto the stage to await our first entrances we were stopped by a plainclothes policeman who showed his badge and said, "Please don't let it disturb your performance tonight but consider yourself under arrest!" Incredible? Yes, incredible but true. It was the most agonizing performance I can ever remember experiencing. The theater was well picketed by the police and the entire audience soon became aware of their participation in something highly unusual. The performance of the play meant little to them. Quite naturally they were expecting lightning to strike at any moment. At the close of the play the cast were all ordered to dress and stand by to be escorted in police cars to a night court.

Ouida arrived from the play she had seen and, as she has always done under duress, faced the situation impassively, except to announce to the police that wherever I was going she was coming with me. Ouida can be very determined upon occasion and the police soon gave up and submitted to her request. The street outside was jammed with a crowd of people that typified that masochistic pleasure derived from other people's misfortunes. It was not easy to reach the police cars and we were individually escorted through a jeering and often abusive mob. At the night court we met with Miss Mae West and her company, who were playing in *Sex*. Also present were an assortment of streetwalkers, petty thieves, and drunkards. There too in the night court was Gilbert Miller, who had been picked up by a police car at a dinner party he was attending. One by one we were "booked," I presume on a charge of offending against some morals code, and individually released on bail, according to our "billing!" I believe Miss Menken and I were considered secure at $1000 each, whereas the other roles and the stage manager were valued at considerably less! "The Management" provided all the necessary bail. We were forbidden to re-enter the Empire Theatre and ordered to make ourselves available to appear in a downtown court, where charges would be preferred in due course.

It was a miserable ride back to Long Island, but as usual Ouida faced facts with much more courage than was at my command. She calmly wrapped up the past and with her incurable optimism looked boldly forward into the future.

I have been given to understand that what had happened was apparently this. Somebody was running for office in a local election and our arrest was considered to be a fine example of this gallant gentleman's care and consideration of New York's morals! or lack of them. Lumping us together with Mae West's play *Sex* was meant to suggest that both plays were equally guilty of a low form of moral turpitude that was considered destructive to the average family's high moral if ill-informed standards. And here I would say of Miss West that I never knew her to produce, perform, or speak an ugly or vicious thought. She has always reminded me of that certain little girl or boy in every school who

have a fund of "Oh, such naughty stories"—off-color, perhaps a little untidy at times! Yet often amusing, *and never
harmful.* How far we have departed from this inoffensive
back-fence humor over the past quarter century, during
which period there have been produced both in London and
in New York some of the filthiest, most decadent, and de-
generate plays of any period past, and one hopes of any
period yet to come.

And now to share with you the last act of this hideous
betrayal, this most infamous example of the imposition of
political censorship on a democratic society ever known in
the history of responsible creative theater; this cold-blooded
unscrupulous sabotage of an important contemporary work
of art; this cheap political expedient to gain votes by humiliating and despoiling the right of public opinion to express itself and act upon its considered judgment as respected and
respectable citizens.

A few days after the closing of the play we were ordered
to appear at a downtown court. Our predicament had now
become a *cause célèbre.* We were headline news in every
newspaper. Consequently the court was packed with hungry
sensation seekers, many of whom did not spare us their un-
favorable comments. After the judge was seated we were
lined up before him. From left to right facing the judge
there were Max Steuer, one of the most famous criminal
advocates of his time, Mr. Gilbert Miller, Mr. Kondorf, the
company manager, Miss Helen Menken, myself, Mr. Arthur
Wontner, Miss Ann Andrews, and the balance of our small
cast including Mr. Percy Shostac, our stage manager. Addressing Mr. Steuer, the judge asked this eminent attorney
if he had been engaged to represent "all these ladies and
gentlemen." To which Mr. Steuer replied, "No"—he had
only been engaged to represent the interests of Charles Frohman, Inc., Mr. Miller, and Mr. Kondorf. The judge appeared
as much taken aback as were we. He continued, in effect,
"Am I to understand that these ladies and gentlemen are
here in court without legal representation?" To which Mr.

Steuer replied that he had not been instructed to represent us. We were bewildered at receiving this information—nay, it would not be an exaggeration to say we were stunned. At this moment there was a disturbance in the court as a man pushed his way forward and vaulted the barrier that separated us from our "audience!" It is not easy to recollect exactly the dialogue that followed, but I will endeavor to give its substance.

MR. HORACE LIVERIGHT: Your honor! Your honor! I object.

THE JUDGE: (*in astonishment at this unseemly procedure!*) And who are you?

MR. LIVERIGHT: I am Horace Liveright, publisher, your honor, and I object not only to the inhuman treatment of these fine artists but also to the infamous charges brought against them.

The court buzzed with excitement. They were indeed getting their "money's worth!"

THE JUDGE: Please leave this court immediately.

MR. LIVERIGHT: Your honor. I have with me Mr. T. Hayes Hunter—(another famous attorney of that time).

THE JUDGE: Leave the court, Mr. Liveright, before I prefer charges against you personally. I will hear you in due course when these matters at hand are disposed of.

MR. LIVERIGHT: Thank you, your honor.

As Mr. Liveright withdrew I felt we had found the champion we had all so dearly hoped for in our extremity.

Now the ugly betrayal continued. The judge asked Mr. Steuer if Charles Frohman, Inc., Mr. Miller, and Mr. Kondorf were prepared to renounce any further association with the play *The Captive* and the production thereof anywhere at any time in the future.

The answer was "Yes." And Mr. Steuer, Mr. Miller, and Mr. Kondorf proceeded to leave the court. The judge then turned to us and asked if we were prepared to follow our management's decision.

It was then that little Ann Trevor spoke up, and with tears in her eyes she said, "My lord, Mr. Miller brought me from London to play in this play. I think it is a very beautiful and important play. I love it and I am proud to have been a part of it."

His honor was obviously touched by this genuine and most appealing outburst, which was followed immediately by a cold and most incisive statement of his case by our stage manager, Percy Shostac. "Your honor," he said, in effect, "I will not betray the principles by which I endeavor to live. This is not an evil play, it is not even a harmful play. It is a great play which is saying something extremely important to our present-day society. Something they need to know about, recognize and act upon. I will under no circumstances desert this production of Monseiur Bourdet's *The Captive*, even if it should mean that I spend the rest of my life in prison!"

Ann Trevor and Percy Shostac—two gallant "little people" unafraid to stand up in defense of their considered judgments and convictions—worthy descendants of the forefathers of this great country.

It was then that Mr. Horace Liveright sought permission to speak again. He asked the court for time to consider our situation. Such time was granted. From the court we went to Mr. Liveright's apartment, where we met with Mr. T. Hayes Hunter. There we sat for many hours considering every possibility and every legal aspect. Finally it was Mr. Hunter's considered judgment that we should reappear in court and accept the situation *under protest*. This we did at a later date; with the exception of Mr. Percy Shostac, who refused to abide by the court's decision and received a suspended sentence. God bless him. Horace Liveright was disappointed in the eventual outcome; a fighter, he had looked for a "battle royal," but was persuaded by Mr. Hunter that we would all be pursuing a hopeless cause since by this time it would seem that the public and the newspapers were hopelessly prejudiced against us. But at least we had gone down fighting for our right to stand up for our convictions and our belief in our personal integrity. We were only forced to surrender when it became evident there was no other course open to us. *Sic transit gloria mundi.*

Throughout all this Ouida was a great comfort and inspiration to me. She was as angry as I was with this experience of flagrant injustice. But once it was over she would not dwell upon it. She had no thought but for the future.

The summer of 1927 was a very happy one for Ouida and myself, Jack Miltern, and my black police dog Moritz. We were the guests of our dear friends Dr. and Mrs. Bierhoff at their charming summer home in Blue Hills, Maine. We walked and talked and fished and played golf and ate prodigiously. The countryside was a garland of flowers, the air tasted of fine wine, and our host and hostess were generous to us beyond measure.

The Command to Love became my next important adventure in the fall of 1927, a delicious, most delectable play in the vein of the best French bedroom comedy, the success of which was so much due to Ouida's unlimited talents in the reconstruction of this play and her designs for its décor. But here once again we were to encounter the uncertain hand of local censorship, which, however, expressed itself this time without viciousness, only to expose the pathetic immaturity of "the guardian of the public's morals." As with *The Captive* we had already run on Broadway for several months before someone's "sensitivities" became suspicious of our innocuous fun. We were severely "edited" but continued our successful stay at the Longacre Theatre for a year, to be followed by another year on tour during which time we put back much that had offended New York!

8
Judas

I think I was still in my teens when the relationship between Jesus of Nazareth and Judas-ish-Kerioth first troubled me. At first I was frightened at myself, for "the devil hath power to assume a pleasing shape" and was perhaps "abusing me to damn me." And yet over the years the thought pursued me and eventually became an obsession. I felt I *must* think it through and try to arrive at some conclusion. If Judas was the mean, despicable betrayer he is said to have been, why did Jesus choose him to be one of his disciples? At what time in his life did Jesus become aware of his divine mission here on earth? Certainly by the time he made his choice of the twelve.

Both as man and Son of God did Jesus choose Judas for his eventual betrayal? And if so, why this so obvious a "villain," as Judas is portrayed to have been both in writings and in art? From time to time and particularly at Easter, these and other thoughts, consistent with my growing pains, persisted.

After some years my original guilt complex diminished and I gave my thinking unlimited scope for development. Slowly but surely I released myself from the self-accusation of irreverence and even blasphemy. Picking my opportunities carefully I attempted to discuss the subject with friends I hoped might be sympathetic listeners. But I got little response. I talked with Ouida and found her interested but extremely skeptical of a play based on such subject matter.

It was not alone that she felt the play might fail, but she was also fearful there might be considerable adverse criticism from churches, the press, and public opinion. However, I talked with a few people of the Jewish faith and found them intrigued by my idea. Encouraged by these contacts I decided to make a preliminary study of the Jewish faith and customs. I also read Renan's *Life of Jesus*, *The Life and Times of Jesus, the Messiah* by Edershem, and *The Unknown Years of Jesus* by Humphreys. Then around 1927 there appeared a small piece in a New York newspaper about a book by a German, just published in Germany, the theme of which was identical in almost every detail with the idea I had had for so long of the Jesus-Judas relationship. A coincidence, but to me a significant coincidence. I found it provocative that two people separated by many thousands of miles, who spoke different languages and who had never met, should be stimulated by an identical process of thinking in respect to this subject.

About this time, while playing on Broadway in *The Command to Love*, I met with a man by the name of Walter Ferris. A Yale graduate, he had studied for the priesthood but had decided against the Church before his ordination. Having a little money, he made teaching his chosen profession and instituted a private school somewhere in Connecticut, which turned into a modestly successful venture. When I met Walter he was very much at a loose end. The school provided him with an income, but he wanted to write, which was quite obviously his vocation. He had a fine, flexible, inquisitive mind and a beautiful, poetic command of the English language. To Walter I talked of my idea and he caught fire immediately. In my mind I had had the play completely constructed for a long time; but I knew that its writing required a very special quality; a complete simplicity with a poetic feeling, but not poetry. This was a job for "a man of letters" and I was no "man of letters," and Walter Ferris was. He seemed to me the perfect collaborator.

One wet, cold afternoon I went to Walter's apartment.

He had a fire burning and served tea. We sat there together and I outlined in detail my construction, and my conclusions as to those incidents that could be faithfully and reverently converted to fit in with one's thesis. We did not meet and talk like conspirators but as two Christians who dared, in our extreme youth and perhaps ignorance, to search for a more comprehensible meaning of this strange story of the association between the beloved Master and his fated disciple. Act by act, and scene by scene I passionately released the still waters of my imagination, which poured from me like a broken dam, while Walter sat quietly making voluminous notes, questioning me, analyzing my answers, objecting, agreeing, reserving his judgment. It was very late when we had finished; we were completely exhausted, and I had to rush to the theater, without dinner, for that evening's performance of *The Command to Love*. This performance was one of the most difficult examples of enforced concentration I had ever experienced. After the play was over I hurried home to tell Ouida of the inspirational afternoon I had spent. She listened attentively and sympathetically, but I knew I still had a long way to go to win her enthusiasm. However, Walter and I were in such complete rapport that he finished writing the play in one month. It was exactly what I had hoped for, a most sensitive and intelligent transposal into dialogue of all we had talked about on that incredible (to me) afternoon.

Now I was literally on fire. We took the play to Messrs. Wiman and Bill Brady, Jr., (producers of *The Command to Love*). Dwight Wiman had reservations, but Bill Brady, Jr., had none. His enthusiasm was most encouraging, especially since he was a devout Roman Catholic, and it was obvious to us all that we might be in for considerable opposition from Roman Catholics. The Protestant churches we felt would offer a lesser problem. Jewish rabbis I had contacted were quite positive in their approval. Then my very dear friend Richard Boleslawski was approached to direct the play and Jo Mielziner to design the sets. Both accepted immediately. A date was set. January, 1929. Both Wiman and Brady insisted that I finish the New York run of *The Command to Love* and fulfill at least some part of my contract to tour with it the season 1928–29, particularly Chicago, where a long run was expected. We ran in Chicago for sixteen weeks and I spent a great deal of my time there with Rabbi Fox of the South Shore Temple. Rabbi Fox gave me much valuable advice and instruction in the Jewish faith and in particular on the Feast of the Passover, during which festival our first act was set. In all of this, Ouida was the quintessence of patience, understanding, and encouragement. It must have been very difficult for her to bear with my obsession, for although she acknowledged that Walter and I had written a very beautiful play, she felt the theater was not the medium in which to express our thinking and she was ever hopeful we would abandon our project and collaborate on a book. But I in particular was completely opposed to this as Walter and I had written the play with a view to my playing Judas. I think by this time I was completely irrational and "possessed" of my idea, and nothing and nobody could deter me from my purpose. In January of 1929 I left *The Command to Love* and returned to New York to go into rehearsals for *Judas*. Boleslawski, whom I trusted implicitly, had done a wonderful job of casting, particularly the disciples, who were all comparatively unknown actors but essentially very simple men and dedicated to our project. The costumes were all created by Boleslawski, and he, with Madam Karinska's help, had personally hand-dyed them in the simplest materials. Only with the Romans and Joseph of Arimathaea was there a sense of color and richness. Judas, though simply gowned, stood out among the Twelve in that he wore his robes with a certain arrogant pride and they were of a better quality than the other disciples. I had learned from Rabbi Fox that the Judean of the period considered himself superior to others of his race, both in education and manner of living. From the very beginning I had conceived of Judas as highly intelligent, intolerant, and a dedicated

patriot. At first Walter and I had considered titling the play
The Patriot.

What was this man doing on the banks of the Jordan
watching John baptize? He was only interested in one thing,
a leader who could successfully head a revolt against the
Romans. It was some hundred miles from his home in Kerioth
to the River Jordan and he had probably walked most of the
way to see for himself if this John the Baptist might be the
potential leader. He watched the submersions in the river
with growing disinterest and disappointment—no, this was
not his man. Then one day from the opposite bank there
walked into the river a man who filled him with an inexplicable confusion and he trembled from head to foot with a
wild excitement and expectancy. As Jesus walked out of the
water he passed by very close to Judas. Not a word was
spoken and there was no visible sign of recognition on either
part. But Judas rose immediately and followed this man. Together they walked in absolute silence until they had reached
some higher ground, where they stopped and stood standing
together. Here it was, as related by Judas in the first scene
of our play, that he, Judas, felt instinctively drawn to the
leader he had so long sought for. Probing and questioning
Jesus, Judas had at last poured out to Him his revolutionary
plans. And could it not have been that at this moment the
Master became aware of an important cog in the wheel of
His Father's intent and purpose. I was aiming to indicate in
the play that the devil, who it is said had tempted Our Lord
on a high place, was none other than Judas himself. I do not
believe in a hell of fire and brimstone and human misery as
in Dante's *Inferno* any more than I believe in the devil, in
either the Mephistophelean form or the one with the long
tail and eyes of fire. As we are born in the grace of God so
are we born in original sin and our hell is within us. Judas'
hell was his destiny in being born into this world to betray
his leader. Some one hundred years previously his namesake
Judas Maccabeus' glorious career had come to an end in an
abortive attempt against the Romans. Add to this the ever-

present expectancy of the Messiah's coming, and surely Judas had much with which to feed his patriotic passions. Like Cassius, Judas realized that he could never be the leader men would follow in blind obedience and with unquestioning confidence and love. Judas was looking for his Brutus and here on the banks of the Jordan he believed he had found him.

To Jesus he expounded his hopes and plans for an uprising that would release his beloved homeland from Roman domination. And though Jesus had turned sadly away from him, Judas' mind was made up. This was his leader and Judas would be to him, as it were, his chief of staff. Miracles there must be to attain his purpose, and miracles there were, but not of the kind that Judas sought after. He was contemptuous of his fellow disciples and was deeply troubled by the Master's choice of such simple, ignorant fellows. But he would bide his time, and he could well afford to since there was much to encourage him. People loved his leader; great crowds were drawn to see and hear Him. Much of what the Master said and did was highly provocative and Jewish religious leaders in Jerusalem were much concerned by His teachings and His success with the people.

Pontius Pilate and his Roman legions could afford to ignore the situation. There had been Jewish radicals before and there would be others in days to come and a disturbed and disunited people were easier to handle than a united nation. This Jewish radical from Galilee would come and go as others had done before Him.

Then came that day when Jesus and His disciples came down to Jerusalem to celebrate the Passover. The Master had ridden upon an ass escorted by an immense crowd that strewed palm leaves in His way and cheered Him like a king. Why had He chosen to ride upon an ass? Surely this was an unnecessary overemphasis of His appeal to the common man. For many months past Judas had grown tired and impatient of Jesus' inevitable reply to his continual questionings, "My time is not yet come."

But now at last the time was approaching! Surely, without saying a word in confirmation, Jesus understood Judas' purpose and was preparing to meet it. At the Last Supper Jesus' intent was made even clearer. How could his eleven naïve, illiterate Galilean friends understand that positive acknowledgment that Jesus had given to Judas in accepting him as the one chosen to betray Him. And betrayal in a sense, as far as Judas was concerned, it might well have to be in order to force a situation which might not ever come again and, if misused, might lead to disaster.

Judas' appearance before the Sanhedrin was a desperate move. To betray his Master without accepting "blood money" would incur the suspicions of this already suspicious and worried council. So Judas accepted the money offered him. Twenty pieces of silver! A puny sum for so great a service—the equivalent of some eight dollars today.

To the Garden of Gethsemane he led Jesus' enemies and a large crowd went with them. It was now or never—at last His time *had come* and there could be no turning back. The great miracle of the Master's life must now be accomplished. Perhaps it might even be that the Messiah would at this moment make Himself known. But come what may, frustration and a burning uncontrollable impulse to fulfill his destiny could no longer be contained.

The fanatic now walks up to his Master and kisses Him. But there is no miracle, no Messiah, just a complete and humiliating acceptance of the course of the inevitable. Is it not possible that besides Peter and John there was also Judas that followed Him now. In dark places might he not have been found watching and listening, desperately hoping for some sign that all was not lost. Peter's denial would not have surprised him. The desertion of the eleven was typical of their fair-weather friendships.

Only when He was crucified was Judas completely shattered and broken . . . oh, the pity of it, the useless waste of a great dream, the utter humiliation of it all. And so Judas went off and hanged himself. What else was there left for him to do. "Father forgive them for they know not what they do." Surely this must also include Judas.

This brief thesis of the play is as much as may be recorded here. Further development in detail would require considerably more space and time. The play remained on Broadway for three weeks. It received mixed reviews, which did not hesitate to remind Mr. Ferris and myself of our impertinence in trespassing on the Gospel story. We felt no sense of trespassing then and, speaking for myself, nor do I now. My belief was and still is that divine providence chose Judas for the part he was ordained to play in the birth of Christianity, and that a mean, despicable "little" man had no place within the might, majesty, dominion, and power of Our Lord Jesus Christ, whose compassion and understanding are beyond all human conception.

Failure refers to box office receipts. Within this context then we were a failure. But many Catholics and Protestants and Jews wrote letters and came backstage to see me. Some were much moved by our play, others were disturbed, and a few were offended.

I think one reasonable explanation of our "failure" was given to us that is both valid and understandable. A Catholic priest, a good friend of mine, said to me when I asked him why we had met with such opposition from virtually all denominations of the Christian Church, "My dear Basil, it is all right for you and Mr. Ferris to have made this journey because it seems perfectly evident that you know the road back home. But to many others such questionings can be deeply disturbing. These people entering upon such a journey might be unable to find their way home again and their peace of mind could be permanently affected. It is *our* duty to see that they are not exposed to such a possibility."

After thirty-three years the play is all but forgotten, except by a few of us who played in it and some of our audience who remember it, not alone in their minds but in their hearts. I myself have never been able to escape the ethical and religious problems posed. But why should they pursue me in my professional life as well?

In the summer of 1961, I was filmed in the role of Caiphas, the High Priest of the Temple, in an Italian motion picture entitled *Pontius Pilate*. Here again the question of Judas' relationship to Jesus is in question, and it would appear that the authors of this motion picture and I, as co-author of the Broadway play *Judas*, have much in common in our approach to this subject. It is interesting, to me at least, how insistently this moment in history has repeated itself in my life—from early childhood to the writing of my own play *Judas*—my portrayal of Pontius Pilate in the film *The Last Days of Pompeii*—a play I now hold and hope to do called *Spark in Judea* in which I shall play Pilate—and last but not least this picture made in Rome.

In a scene with Judas before the Sanhedrin, when as Caiphas I obviously find Judas' attitude distasteful but strive to keep an open mind, my last line to him is, "Judas—can it be that you truly love this man?" Is it a question or a statement of fact? I have endeavored to read this line without making it either. The choice lies with each individual member of one's audience; and in every case I say to you, "So be it."

Is it not reasonable to speculate upon the possibility that so wise an old man as Caiphas was perhaps the most deeply troubled human being in this whole story?

"Why could not this man of Nazareth be the Son of David despite tradition? And if so—could it not be that Judas really loved Him without ever understanding for one moment who He really was?" Caiphas' last words in this picture indicate to me an almost desperate man. As the Temple falls about him he kisses the Torah with moving devotion and says, "Help me now Lord God of Israel. Give me a sign, O Holy One, and show to me that the path I have taken leads to Thy eternal sanctuary." Is this in Caiphas fear—or doubt—perhaps even remorse? This, my final scene in the picture, will always remain for me an enigma. As forever will much else in this haunting story of the Son of Man's relationship to His disciple Judas, and the attitudes of the Roman Procurator Pilate and the chief Rabbi of his peoples faith, Caiphas, toward Jesus.

9

Katharine Cornell

It was in the autumn of 1932 that I received an offer in London from Miss Katharine Cornell to tour with her in the United States in her "tryout" of *Romeo and Juliet,* which was to be presented on Broadway the following season. This tour was to include *The Barretts of Wimpole Street* and Shaw's *Candida.* I was to play Romeo, Robert Browning, and Morrell.

Miss Cornell invited Ouida and Moritz and I to visit with her at her chalet near Garmisch, Bavaria, so that I might work with her, in particular on *Romeo and Juliet.* And so it was in the shadow of the Jungfrau and of Adolf Hitler that I restudied Romeo for the last time. A gentle people these Bavarians, with a smile and a warm greeting of welcome for any stranger to their spacious valley, rich in feed for the cattle wandering peacefully about it. And the symphony of little bells, each animal with a different toned bell about its neck, invoked a wonder in my heart that the devil himself should be abroad in full daylight in Munich, only a few miles distant; and that the whole world was heedlessly wandering toward a vortex, from which there is still no escape in sight.

Returning from Garmisch, Bavaria, with "Kit" we immediately plunged into rehearsals of *Romeo and Juliet* and *The Barretts. Candida* was to come later when these first two productions were well established. And when I say "we," it includes Ouida and Moritz! Ouida has always been my most constructive and faithful critic and fellow worker in all I have done since we have known one another; and Moritz was my constant guard and companion whether at work or at play! Rehearsals were stimulating and rewarding under the direction of Guthrie McClintic, Miss Cornell's husband. My Romeo seemed to meet with their approval, as later it was to do with every critic throughout the country. Robert Browning in *The Barretts* I approached a little fearfully. I wanted it to be an original performance and not an imitation of Brian Aherne's striking impersonation in the original Broadway production. It required at least a month of concentrated playing to arrive at my own performance without Brian's help! (Dear Brian, you were so good as Robert Browning and you were such a hazard to me at first!)

One very cold day late in October of 1933 we entrained for Buffalo, New York, Kit's home town, where we were to have several dress rehearsals and open with *Romeo and Juliet* to be followed the next night by *The Barretts*. No sooner had we arrived in Buffalo than I promptly lost my voice. I had a throat infection that was to persist throughout this arduous, seven month tour and was to cause me considerable physical and mental distress. Thanks to Ouida's tender and selfless attention I recovered sufficiently to open in both plays, and we were off in a blaze of glory. We played eighty-six cities, twenty-four of which were consecutive one-night stands and as far as I know there was never a seat to be had at any performance. The sign outside the theater was always Standing Room Only! Miss Cornell has contributed as much to the theater of her time as any living actor or actress, and it seems to me to be a most grievous oversight that a theater in New York has not as yet been named after her to honor her as other worthy stars of her generation have so been honored. Her Elizabeth Barrett was not only the greatest performance of her life, it was also one of the greatest performances by an actress that I have ever seen.

It was said by Miss Ellen Terry, Sir Henry Irving's co-

star at the turn of the century, that no actress could play
Juliet until she was thirty and at thirty she would be too old!
Miss Cornell and I were both over thirty, and Miss Cornell
proved Miss Terry to be wrong. The illusion was complete.
Miss Cornell *was* a young Italian girl in her teens. She was
radiantly beautiful, and later as Candida she was so exotically
desirable that she threw the play completely off balance!

I have always disliked Shaw's *Candida*. It is such a pomp-
ous, ultra women's-rights play, with both Morrell and
Marchbanks unnecessarily sacrificed to Candida's annoying
self-righteousness and her smug sense of superiority. But with
Miss Cornell all this simply didn't matter! She was so beautiful and so deirable that had she murdered Morrell and
married Marchbanks we would have forgiven her—or almost
—because in this production Marchbanks was played by
Orson Welles, whose performance was so fatuously unpleasant that Morrell became, by contrast, a deeply sympathetic
character, which most certainly was not Mr. Shaw's intention. Orson Welles had come to our company via Dublin,
Ireland, Thornton Wilder, and Alexander Woollcott and was
supposed to be a boy wonder verging on the phenomenon of
genius. With this type of advance publicity much should be
forgiven him, especially since he was only nineteen years old
at the time he came to us—so I was told. But these early
impressions mean little today for Mr. Welles has proven himself an actor of considerable talent, and a creative artist who
we would certainly like to hear from more often.

As the tour progressed I was increasingly handicapped by
my throat infection. That I never missed a performance was
chiefly due to the fact that Ouida was ever beside me caring
for my every need. Second only to Ouida was that ever-
present jar of honey. I must have consumed gallons of honey
during those months, which was most helpful to my throat
condition and was a tremendous source of energy. (Being
predigested, honey goes directly into the blood stream.)
Where stop-offs did not allow of time to send out laundry,
Ouida did both mine and her own and she was both my

secretary and my banker; and it was certainly not her fault
that on two consecutive weeks in Texas my week's salary
was stolen, putting a considerable crimp in Ouida's well-
thought-out and carefully guarded budget.

On the first occasion our hotel suite was entered in the
dead of night and my week's salary stolen, while Ouida and
I and Moritz all slept soundly! This was unquestionably an
inside job. The following week Ouida was on her way to
the post office—my salary was in her handbag. She stopped
at the hotel newsstand and put her bag down as she turned
over the pages of the latest *Vogue* or *Vanity Fair*. In a
flash a hand grabbed her bag and as she turned and shouted
"Stop that man," he was through the revolving doors and
out into the street. This moment of the unexpected is so
often what this type of thief relies on to make his get-away.
Before those in the lobby of the hotel realized what Ouida
was saying and what had happened, maybe fifteen valuable
seconds had passed. There was no time for details of identification and once in the street the thief could swiftly get lost—
and did!

Kit too was concerned for my health and insisted on giving
up her drawing room on her special coach to us while she
occupied the adjoining compartment. This was a typical example of her consideration for the members of her company.

There were two particularly memorable performances of
The Barretts of Wimpole Street. One at Waco, Texas, where
there is one of the finest collections in the world of items
pertaining to Robert Browning and Elizabeth Barrett. At
our evening performance there, I was allowed to wear
Robert Browning's signet ring, while Kit wore a necklace
of garnets that had belonged to Elizabeth Barrett.

The other was our opening performance in Seattle, Washington, on Christmas Eve of 1933. A couple of days before
we had left Duluth, Minnesota, by train in a terrific snow
storm. The weather all the way across the country was very
bad and our train was considerably delayed. It soon became

evident that it would be impossible to arrive in Seattle to take the curtain up at 8:30 P.M. for our opening performance. However, we rolled into Seattle about 8 P.M. to be met by a considerable crowd of people, the manager of the theater, and several theatrical moving vans! The manager of the theater advised us our audience had been offered their money back but had refused, and if we were willing the curtain would go up whenever we were ready no matter what the time! The crowd at the station were some of our audience and they cheered the announcement we would play, come what may. Back they went to the theater, which was jammed to the rafters when we arrived. Guthrie McClintic, Miss Cornell's husband, had joined us in Duluth and was greeted with an ear-splitting ovation as he walked out onto the empty stage and introduced himself. Then he introduced each one of us in turn, and we went to our dressing rooms. We helped unpack our costumes and iron out those that needed attention. Then we made up and dressed and waited. The scenery arrived and was applauded! As it was unloaded and set up and lighted, Guthrie acted as master of ceremonies, explaining to the audience how it was done, and asking for and answering questions. At 12:03 A.M. on Christmas morning the curtain went up on *The Barretts of Wimpole Street* and as we went to our dressing rooms, after the final "call" was over, it was past three o'clock. I understand that the entire audience remained for the performance with the exception of seven who for personal reasons were unable to stay.

In San Francisco there was an amusing incident—Outside the theater the neon lights read KATHARINE CORNELL in THREE PLAYS. When I went down to the theater on the last Saturday night there, I noticed a number of people in the street standing and looking up at the theater and laughing. I laughed myself when I saw what had happened. The letter P in PLAYS had gone out!

In May of 1934 our tour closed at the Brooklyn Academy of Music, and Miss Cornell presented every member of her company with an extra week's salary as a token of her appreciation. Miss Cornell is perhaps the last of those great lovers of the theater who were known in dear, but dead, bygone days as actor or actress managers. Those men and women such as Miss Cornell and Southern and Marlow (and in England too many to enumerate, from Sir Henry Irving, Sir Herbert Tree, Sir Frank Benson, Cyril Maude through to Sir Gerald du Maurier and Miss Gladys Cooper, to name but a few) gave a human and personal touch to their work and those who worked with them. Today, with rare exceptions, the theater is just another job where the management may be in real estate or the garment industry and also where, not infrequently, success may be an ugly experience.

Ouida and I were completely exhausted by the tour and were missing our Moritz dreadfully. This very dear friend of ours had died, as I have previously related, the preceding April. (A significant month for me is April. My mother was born on April 9—Cynthia our daughter, was born on April 13—Ouida and I were married on April 18—I went to France in World War I and returned from it in the month of April. And I went on the stage on April 22, 1912, missing Shakespeare's birthday and the day of his death, by twenty-four hours, on April 23.) So we asked Kit if we might take care of "Flush" for the summer. Flush was Elizabeth Barrett's dog in the play, a beautiful little cocker spaniel and an excellent actor. Kit and Flush were both willing. We had been good friends for some months (as had Flush and Moritz); now we were to become great friends.

Early in June of 1934 I went into St. Luke's Hospital in New York and had my tonsils removed. Not a simple operation in my case because of complications that had developed. However, I recovered rapidly and put on several much-needed pounds in weight. My normal weight for as long as I can remember has been around 172 pounds. During the tour I had slipped to 158 pounds. When I came out of the hospital Ouida and I took a little cottage on a golf course at Great Neck, Long Island. Here I played much golf and in the evenings Ouida and Flush and I would take long walks together. These were gentle weeks and sweet to us, and we were both in need of such rest. However, this kindly and loving companionship was not for long. In July, it must have been, I was asked for by David Selznick to go to the coast to play Mr. Murdstone in his picture *David Copperfield* . . . of this venture in more detail in a following chapter dealing with some of the highlights of my experiences in motion pictures. Suffice it to say here that it was odd to anticipate playing Romeo next winter at the Martin Beck Theatre in New York while portraying the cold, cruel, feelingless Mr. Murdstone at some motion picture house a few blocks away! I think it troubled Ouida considerably. I had been her Romeo for so many years and she was loath to give me up!

As the fall approached I became edgy and restless. I would play Romeo again for the last time. It would in fact be the last time that I would ever dare to appear as so young a man! Yes, I must say "good-by" now; "good-by" to a whole phase of my professional life, starting with Mr. Benson in April of 1912 and ending on the stage of the Martin Beck in November of 1934. I was not afraid of what was to come, it was just that I had never been very good about saying "good-bys," and in this case to so many beautiful memories. From "juveniles" and "juvenile-characters" to *real* "character" roles—I was ready—I was a skilled swordsman, I could sing, I could dance—I was a well-trained actor with considerable experience. I was bound to admit that, in fact, all my professional life I had been earnestly building to this moment. It was only that the passing of the years had for the first time in my life become an undeniable reality; and I mused with a tempting thought that perhaps at this moment the shadow of death had gently touched me, as she smilingly passed me by—my mother?

Kit made two major changes in casting for her New York opening of *Romeo and Juliet*. Brian Aherne played Mercutio, while Orson Welles took over Tybalt (Orson had played Mercutio on tour), and Edith Evans was brought from London to play the nurse. The critics were as one in their praise of the whole production and particularly of Miss Cornell's Juliet. Once again, in a matter of days, there was not a seat to be had for any performance of the play's limited run of twelve weeks. Why this time limit was placed on this presentation I do not know, since it seemed unquestionable that it could have run for a year or more.

And so, early in 1935, Ouida and I returned for the second time in less than a year to the Coast, where I was to play Karenin in David Selznick's picture of *Anna Karenina* with Greta Garbo and Fredric March. I had crossed the Rubicon! From Romeo to Murdstone, back to Romeo, and now to Karenin with Garbo. Thank you dear Kit for as memorable an adventure in the theater as I have ever known or shall ever know.

10

Motion Pictures

How readily we accept the motion picture today as a part of our entertainment and cultural inheritance just as we have accepted the railroad train and the rocket plane of tomorrow. What a fabulous half century this has been with its technological advancements and increased material advantages to the average citizen of the Western world. Before these words ever get into print a man will probably have been shot into outer space, the moon will have lost any semblance of its earlier romantic connotations, and a course around Venus will have been charted by some orbiting projectile. And yet, to slightly misquote Jack Gould of the New York *Times,* "Somebody has mislaid the magic" that once inspired us to such phenomenal creative endeavors. Perhaps we have also "mislaid" God, the originator of all creation past, present, and future, to man's ever-increasing confidence in his own accomplishment. Archibald MacLeish has written that ". . . there was never perhaps a civilization in which . . . the crime of . . . the snake-like-sin of coldness at the heart was commoner than in our technological civilization."

Those little shacks in Hollywood, where once-upon-a-time the silent motion picture was created along with most of the great names that were parent to the present industry, are much a thing of the past. Only casual recognition of a great adventure is sometimes paid to names and places that have long since become silent memories. Only Charlie Chaplin's reputation lives on to intermittently remind us that

motion pictures are but fifty years old. Charles Chaplin, one
of the greatest mimes of all time. For it was the medium of
mime that made the silent picture an individual art form.
When the silent picture became a talking picture it lost its
original art form and became a derivative of the theater. It
exploded all over the world, and a gigantic migration took
place to the West Coast, where millions upon millions of
dollars were invested, real estate boomed, enormous concrete
soundproof stages rose like mushrooms overnight—directors,
writers, actors, musicians, and technicians were at a premium,
and Broadway was invaded by an army of salesmen with
unlimited spending accounts. Slowly but surely the original
magic was being mislaid—except for a few "dreamers" who
remembered where the magic was hidden. I can only speak
of those I knew personally, and two stand out pre-eminently
—Irving Thalberg and David Selznick.

My experience in pictures before I went to the Coast under contract to MGM in 1934 was very limited. After the
failure of *Judas* in 1929 I had gone West to make a picture of
Freddie Lonsdale's comedy *The Last of Mrs. Cheyney* with
Norma Shearer.

Here I must momentarily digress before an amusing story
escapes me. Ouida and I knew Freddie Lonsdale very well
and I can assure you he was a man of very positive if sometimes misguided opinions. It is said that Freddie and a friend
were lunching one day in the Savoy Grill in London. They
had not been there long when Anna May Wong and her sister
came in and sat down at a nearby table. Freddie stared at
the newcomers fiercely. Then he said to his friend, "My dear
fellow, do you see what I see?"

"And what *do* you see, my dear fellow?" the friend replied.

"A couple of Chinks! What's happening to this place?"

"Chinks? Oh, you mean Chinese."

"My dear fellow, I mean what I say—a couple of
Chinks—"

Whereupon a hushed but somewhat violent argument ensued as to the yellow ladies' right to lunch in this white man's sanctum sanctorum. Freddie was all for having them asked to leave, at which his friend was so indignant that he threatened to leave himself.

"After all, my dear fellow, you don't seem to know who they are," said his friend.

"I couldn't care less who they are—it's an outrage," spluttered Freddie.

"But Freddie, dear boy, it's Anna May Wong and her sister!"

"I don't give a damn," replied Freddie. "Two Wongs don't make a white! Come on, let's get out of here." And they did.

Apropos of *The Last of Mrs. Cheyney*, when this play was submitted to the censor in London (Lord Cromer), Freddie Lonsdale and Sir Gerald du Maurier, who was to produce and play Lord Dilling in it, were asked to call at the censor's office. It seems that Lord Cromer had certain reservations about the desirability of his allowing this play to appear on the London stage. Both Sir Gerald and Freddie asked Lord Cromer to state his reasons, and this his lordship unsuspectingly proceeded to do. With each objection Sir Gerald would look firmly at Freddie and ask him, "Is that the intended meaning of this line, Freddie?"

"No, indeed not," Freddie replied indignantly. "No such idea ever entered my mind."

With each of Lord Cromer's objections the same procedure was followed, Freddie and Gerald looking at each other with the mock horror of injured innocence. How could the censor conceive of such things! Terribly hot and bothered, Lord Cromer soon capitulated, having been made to look as if the public censor had one of the dirtiest minds ever known. *The Last of Mrs. Cheyney* was produced in London without a single deletion and I understand Lord Cromer was not present on the first night.

Norma Shearer is one of Ouida's and my oldest and dearest friends. We were first introduced to her by a mutual

friend of ours, John Roche, who invited us to dine with him
and meet her. We picked Norma up at some swimming pool
where she gave us an exhibition of some pretty fancy swimming and diving. She was "in pictures," but her opportunity
had not yet arrived. Of course when I went out for *The Last
of Mrs. Cheyney* she was Mrs. Irving Thalberg. But this
made no difference to our friendship. In all the years we have
known her, Norma Shearer has never changed one iota. Her
charm and warm friendship and her classic beauty are as gracious and warm and classic today as on the first day we met
her. If she and I had not both been so happily married I am
quite sure I would have fallen very much in love with her!

Ouida got on with Irving like a house on fire. Between
Irving and myself there seemed to be reservations; perhaps because Irving had had to pay much too much for me!
The original contract that my agent had presented to me
Ouida had torn up, and herself had visited MGM's top representative in New York, Mr. Robert Rubin. Before she had
finished with him he had doubled my weekly salary! The
Bob Rubins curiously enough became two of our closest
friends. Perhaps Irving Thalberg admired Ouida's business
acumen and despised me for lazing behind her feminine
charms. But Ouida had a very strong argument. She didn't
want to go to Hollywood—she could hardly be said to have
been in love with her previous experiences out on the Coast,
and she threatened not to go with me if I accepted the contract as offered! She also felt I would gain stature by waiting
and not joining the crowd that was being herded into the
talking picture market. Also on her side was the fact that Mr.
Lee Shubert wanted me to star in his Broadway production
of *Death Takes a Holiday*, a fine Italian play translated and
adapted into English by my good friend and collaborator of
Judas, Mr. Walter Ferris. But at that time I was unfortunately rather an "angry young man!" I was very resentful of
the New York critics' attitude toward *Judas*. Ouida wanted
me to do *Death Takes a Holiday*, and she was right. "However," she said, "if you insist on going out to the Coast it's

going to be for one hell of a price!" And so she had gallantly gone forth and stormed the MGM battlements and come back with everything she had asked for; the result being a perfectly reasonable resentment on the part of Irving Thalberg at the exorbitant price his production of *The Last of Mrs. Cheyney* would have to pay for this young Broadway star with very little experience in pictures.

Mrs. Cheyney was, I think, the second talking picture ever to be made at MGM. It was a most interesting experience. It was directed by Sydney Franklin, one of the most sensitive and intelligent directors I have ever worked with. The whole picture was rehearsed for three weeks on the sound stage and in the sets that were eventually to be photographed. Props and furnishings were all at our disposal and "sound" and "camera" heads of department rehearsed along with us. Every minute detail was carefully planned and rehearsed over and over and over again. Consequently we "shot" the picture, a big and expensive production, in a mere three weeks. This total work period of six weeks is far less time than is acceptable for such a production today. It has never been explained to me why this most helpful procedure, for every department concerned, did not become a standard practice in the making of at least this particular type of indoor, drawing-room comedy.

On the very first day of "shooting," however, we met with a serious reversal. "Sound" being very new was naturally far from perfection. Norma's dress was very beautiful, but as she walked around in it "sound" reported that the materials used gave the impression of a heavy storm at sea! From 9 A.M. to 5 P.M. attempts were made to silence Norma's gown and we never shot a foot of film! The next day Norma had a new dress and all was well. Incidentally a minor role in this production of *Mrs. Cheyney* was played by Miss Hedda Hopper, who has since distinguished herself as a well-known and ofttimes much-feared gossip columnist.

I played in only two pictures with Norma, so our friendship was based on a more personal relationship. It mattered not at all where Ouida and I might be. On the Coast, in New York, London, or Paris, Norma would always find us and see us. The warmth of her affection was most genuine, and there was an occasion when things were not going so well with us when a visit from Norma changed the whole color of our perspective.

Irving Thalberg was one of the most sensitive men I have ever met. Slight of build, good-looking, and very intelligent, he drove himself unmercifully. It is said that he had a premonition of his early and most regrettable death, and his determination to accomplish the impossible obsessed every minute of his life. Most certainly his production of *Romeo and Juliet* in 1935 had a physical beauty, an integrity and inspiration that places it among the all-time greats. And I doubt that any picture has had or will ever have such a distinguished and memorable cast. To name but a few:

Juliet	*Norma Shearer*
Romeo	*Leslie Howard*
Mercutio	*John Barrymore*
Tybalt	*Basil Rathbone*
Nurse	*Edna May Oliver*
Capulet	*Sir C. Aubrey Smith*
Montague	*Robert Warwick*
Paris	*Ralph Forbes*
Prince of Verona	*Conway Tearle*
Peter	*Andy Devine*

When *Romeo and Juliet* was released in London I happened to be there and was asked to speak at its opening. A London newspaper of October 15, 1936, reports, "Incidentally I thought Basil Rathbone struck entirely the right note in making his speech from the stage a tribute to Irving Thalberg. The great producer has been associated with many great films, but this was entirely *his*. It was his last film; the star was his wife; and the subject is entirely true to that betterment of the screen which was his unceasing aim."

There were a couple of incidents during the making of

Romeo and Juliet relating to the great John Barrymore that I feel are worth recording. Jack and I shared the same make-up artist; his name was Brydon, and added to his artistry in make-up he was at that time perhaps the most skillful hair-piece creator in Hollywood. Both Jack's and my hairpieces had been made by Brydon and they were works of art. Jack and I also shared a dressing-room suite together, a doubtful privilege at times—such as the morning I arrived at 7:30 A.M. to find Jack asleep on the couch of our room, with a heavy growth of beard. He had not worked for a few days. Brydon was ready for me and belching his breakfast with consummate satisfaction. Brydon's breakfast was contained in a bottle he kept on his hip. It was bourbon. Midst the fumes of Brydon's breakfast I was made up and coiffeured while Jack snored peacefully on the sofa. After I was dressed in my costume a studio car picked me up and took me to the back lot where a beautiful replica of Verona had been built. The location was crowded with "principals" and "extras." The first scene was to be a big one, my meeting as Tybalt with Jack as Mercutio, a scene that would lead to our duel and Mercutio's death. We waited all morning, but no Jack. Reports were circulated that Jack was not feeling well and Brydon was having some trouble making him up. Brydon told me later that Jack had refused to get up off the sofa and that he, Brydon, had had to shave and make him up and put on his hairpieces with Jack remaining in a recumbent position. Several assistants had then engaged in dressing him, and at last, about 12 P.M., a studio car containing Jack and his "dresser" drove onto the lot. Jack looked breath-takingly beautiful as he got out of the car and walked over to our director, Mr. George Cukor. To Cukor, Jack said in a rasping whisper, "Sorry, old boy, lost me voice . . . can't speak a bloody word."

There were immediate and urgent consultations held by Mr. Cukor and his production staff and it was decided to jump the dialogue and do it another day. The scene we would shoot would be the duel itself. Cameras were set, sound was ready, principals and extras were in place when Barrymore suddenly drew his sword with a tremendous flourish and hit Leslie Howard (Romeo) a violent and accidental blow on the head. In a matter of seconds an enormous pigeon's egg appeared on Leslie's head and we were all dismissed for the day!

There was another occasion when they were shooting the scene following Romeo's meeting with Juliet at the Capulet Ball. Romeo has just scaled the wall into the Capulet garden when Mercutio and Benvolio and their attendants enter the scene calling for Romeo. There being no sight or sound of Romeo, Mercutio plays at conjuring him up, and during his conjuration speech there is a line, "He heareth not, he stirreth not, he moveth not."

I was not working this day and had come to the studio, as had many others, to hear Barrymore's rendition of this amusing comedy scene. It was just his "cup of tea." It was about 10:30 A.M. when I arrived and there was an atmosphere of dejection on the set. Things were obviously not going well. I took one look at Jack and immediately understood what was the predicament. There was that wild look in his eyes that boded no good for a successful day's work! Cukor walked over to Barrymore. "All right, Jack, let's try again, shall we?"

Barrymore rose majestically if a little unsteadily. "Why not, my friend," he replied. "And this 'take' it shall be Mr. William Shakespeare, eh?" There followed that extraordinary sound he would make, which was a mixture of a sudden violent laugh filtered by an asthmatic wheeze. "What say you my little pigeon? Dear George how I love you!" and he kissed Cukor on both cheeks.

Everything was in readiness for the next "take," about No. 6 by this time.

"All right, camera!" called George.

Barrymore and Reginald Denny (Benvolio), with attendants, made their entrance and the scene went smoothly enough until the line, "He heareth not, he stirreth not, he

[1] My father.

[2] My mother.

[3] Myself, my brother John, and my sister Beatrice.

[4] Myself at age two.

[5] My brother John in 1916.

[6] In the role of Romeo with the Stratford Players at age twenty-one. (Copyright 1940, Paramount Pictures, Inc.)

[7] As Count Alexei in *The Czarina* in 1922.

[8] Eva Le Gallienne, Halliwell Hobbes, and myself in *The Swan*, 1923.
(Photograph by Muray Associates.)

[9] With Mary Nash in *The Command to Love*, 1927.
(Copyright 1940, Paramount Pictures, Inc.)

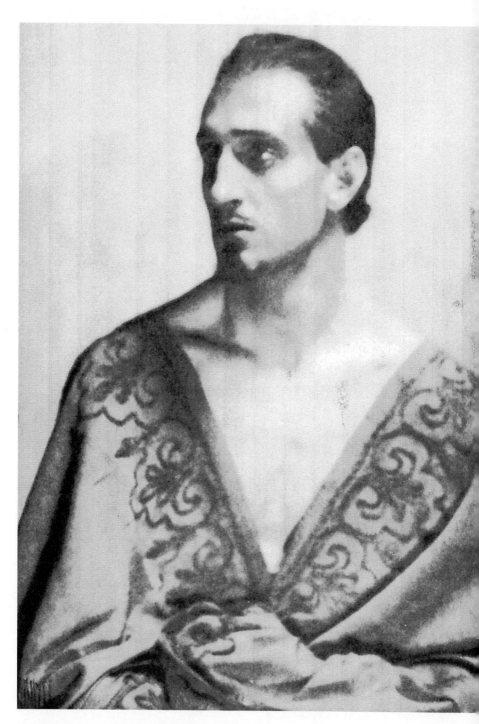

[10] Judas. *(Photograph by Hal Phyfe.)*

[11] With Katharine Cornell in *Romeo and Juliet* in 1933.
(*Copyright 1940, Paramount Pictures, Inc.*)

[12] Robert Browning in *The Barretts of Wimpole Street* in 1935.
(*Photograph by Vandamm Studio.*)

[13] As Mr. Murdstone in *David Copperfield* for M-G-M. (*Copyright 1940, Paramount Pictures, Inc.*)

[14] *Anna Karenina*, in which I played Karenin, with Greta Garbo as Anna, and Freddie Bartholomew as our son.

[15] Karenin, Anna, and Vronsky, Anna's lover, played by Fredric March. *(Acknowledgment is made to M-G-M for permission to reprint these photographs.)*

[16] The duel in *Romeo and Juliet*. This photograph is taken from the famous Irving Thalberg production, and we are, from left to right, Reginald Denny, Leslie Howard, myself, and John Barrymore (with his back to the camera).
(*Acknowledgment is made to M-G-M for permission to reprint this photograph.*)

[17] Training for the above scene with Fred Cavens, my fencing instructor.

[18] This is, I think, a truly remarkable group portrait. As you can see, the actors are costumed for *Romeo and Juliet* (opposite page). We are, from left to right, John Masefield, George Cukor, Frances Marion, Hugh Walpole, Mrs. Masefield, John Barrymore and Leslie Howard, Irving Thalberg, Mrs. James Hilton, myself, James Hilton, and Reginald Denny.

[19] Pontius Pilate in *The Last Days of Pompeii. (Copyright 1940, Paramount Pictures, Inc.)*

[20] Ahmed in *Marco Polo. (Photograph by Kahle, Paramount Pictures, Inc.)*

[21] With Marlene Dietrich in *The Garden of Allah.* *(Paramount Pictures, Inc.)*

[22, 23] There is said to be a remarkable family resemblance between my cousin, Sir Frank Benson, and myself. These pictures were taken many years apart and show us as each appeared in the role of King Richard III. *(Photograph of Sir Frank Benson — Copyright 1939, Universal Pictures Co., Inc. Photograph of Basil Rathbone — Copyright 1939, Universal Pictures Co., Inc.)*

[24] Our first Holmes film, *Sherlock Holmes*, 1939. Dr. Watson is, of course, played by Nigel Bruce. *(Copyright 1942, Universal Pictures Co., Inc.)*

[25] Holmes and Watson, out of character. *(Reprinted with the permission of the Bureau of Industrial Service, Young and Rubicam, Inc.)*

[26] As Sherlock Holmes, in one of the latter's many disguises. *(Copyright 1940, Paramount Pictures, Inc.)*

[27] Holmes, in character. *(from Robert Ullman, Bill Doll and Co.)*

[28] Frederick Worlock as Zuss and myself as Nickles in Archibald MacLeish's Pulitzer Prize play *J. B.* *(Photo by Friedman Abeles.)*

[29] A wedding photograph of Ouida and myself.

[30] Ouida and myself again.

[31] With Ouida and our daughter Cynthia.

[32] On the golf course in California with friends: David Niven, G. O. Allen (former Captain of England at cricket), Raymond Massey, and Nigel Bruce.

moveth not"; as he approached this line Barrymore took a deep breath, flexing his eyebrows and bulging his eyes. Then he said, "He heareth not, he stirreth not." Long pause, then with much relish, "He pisseth not!"

George groaned, "Jack, *please.*"

"Strange how me heritage encumbereth my speech," was Jack's reply. "Dear Mr. Shakespeare, I beg you hear me yet awhile. I am but an improvident actor [pronounced actor-r-r] and yet I would beg you to consider an undeniable fact, I have improved upon your text. 'He moveth not' is not so pertinent to the occasion as 'he pisseth not.'"

And so it went on until nearly lunch time. Thalberg was sent for and came onto the set. Very gently he pleaded with Jack to speak the line as it was written.

"Very well," rejoined Jack, "just once I will say it that thou mayest see how it stinketh." And he did, and that's the only "take" they got from him that day and of course the one that appears in the picture. Jack was furious at the trick played upon him and vowed bloody vengeance on all who had so vilely betrayed him!

We were sitting on the set one day between "shots" when Jack suddenly said out of nowhere, "Are you prone to shock, my dear friend?" I did not reply at once, so he went on, "If you are, take my advice and never go to India [pronounced India-r-r-r]." There was a slight pause and then he went rambling on. "I had an uncle once, silly old bastard, he went to India, where he developed some malignant disease and died there. They buried the old 'poop' in Calcutta [pronounced Calcutta-r-r-r-r]. Then one dissolute and oppressive day I decided to go to Calcutta to visit my uncle's grave. I would beseech his wretched stinking bones to exorcise the evil spirit that inhabiteth me. My uncle had changed his faith and had worshiped other gods who had apparently promised him an Elysium I would fain share with him . . . in due course. And so I voyaged to India, where the sacred cow has more privileges than democracy has ever offered mere man, and where mere man is a mere mouse—a brown mouse, my dear fellow, with brown thoughts that plague his impecunious existence. The first night I was in Calcutta I was much flattered by the unsolicited attention of a little female brown mouse. Have you ever found yourself enraptured by a little brown mouse, my dear Basil." (Here that sudden violent laugh filtered by an asthmatic wheeze.)

I said I had not . . . as yet.

"Sheer Elysium, my dear fellow. Together we disappeared into the black hole of Calcutta not to appear again for a week or more, while my uncle's spirit hovered threateningly between the paradise I had found and the hell of returning to my wife in America."

A distant voice on the set—"Mr. Barrymore and Mr. Rathbone please—you are in the next setup."

"Son of a bitch," said Jack despondently.

Placing neither one before the other, David Selznick as much as Irving Thalberg brought magic to the making of motion pictures in the 1930s, and it was my privilege to appear in four Selznick productions during this period, i.e., Charles Dickens' *David Copperfield*, Tolstoi's *Anna Karenina*, Charles Dickens' *Tale of Two Cities*, and Robert Hitchins' *Garden of Allah*.

Selznick, in his determination to accomplish the absolute limit of perfection in his work that was humanly possible, has always driven himself and all those who work with him with a fierce and implacable resolution. But Selznick had one great advantage over Thalberg in that he seemed to have a fathomless reservoir of vitality sustained by tremendous physical strength. He was the Richard Wagner to Thalberg's Mozart! David didn't walk toward you; he rushed at you, and what he had to say to you was said with a blinding concentration and self-confidence. There are moments I am sure when, if the heavens were to fall upon him, he would not know it! I cannot imagine his relaxing even over a game of table tennis at which he was extremely proficient. I shall never forget an evening when Charles Boyer and his charming wife, Pat, gave a dinner in honor of Eve Curie, the daughter of Monsieur and

Madame Curie, who discovered radium. There were some twenty guests including Ouida and myself—and David Selznick! During cocktails David was off in a corner with someone talking with passionate concentration about something that obviously had nothing to do with the festive occasion on hand. We sat down to dinner about 9 P.M., an epicurean meal with the finest of French wines. Naturally Eve Curie was the center of attraction. So attractive indeed was she that it appears I devoted a considerable amount of my time to her. The next morning, at breakfast, I was extolling Eve Curie's attractions to Ouida, somewhat elaborately it seems, when she quietly interrupted me, saying, "Yes, darling, I know—you have always had good taste in women, at least since I have known you! And I have already ordered a large box of flowers sent to Eve Curie in your name with a charming little note of admiration and affection.

No such amiable, ambling abstractions seemed to influence David Selznick that evening. Whatever the project was at the moment, or might be in some foreseeable future, David was carrying it around with him as if he were pregnant! I can't remember what picture he was making or preparing to make at this time. If neither were the case, which I refuse to accept even as a possibility, then I am quite sure he was turning over in his mind the story of Eve Curie's mother and father. Anyway he showed no particular personal interest in Mlle. Curie and after dinner, while the rest of us sat around under a starlit sky and talked, David fiercely removed his dinner coat and challenged Boyer to three furiously contested games of table tennis at $500 a game! Having won 2 games to 1, David promptly disappeared and went home. Or did he return to his office at the studio to sleep briefly and wake with the dawn, refreshed and ready to pursue his latest obsession? I have been told this was not infrequently his custom.

David Selznick has always surrounded himself with the finest talent available in every department of his business, regardless of cost. And so it was that the screen play of Charles Dickens' *David Copperfield* was written by the eminent

British novelist, Sir Hugh Walpole. A star-studded cast was engaged, headed by W. C. Fields as Micawber. I was to play the cold, cruel Mr. Murdstone, and one morning at MGM I thrashed the living daylights out of poor little Freddie Bartholomew as David Copperfield.

It was a most unpleasant experience, for I was directed by Mr. George Cukor to express no emotion whatsoever—merely to thrash the child to within an inch of his life! I had a vicious cane with much whip to it, but fortunately for Freddie Bartholomew and myself, under his britches and completely covering his little rump, he was protected by a sheet of foam rubber. Nevertheless Freddie howled with pain (mostly anticipatory I presume) and in his "close-ups" his face was distorted and he cried real tears most pitifully. As Mr. Murdstone I tried to make my mind a blank, thrashing Freddie as hard as I could but like a machine. From time to time George Cukor would call for another "take." "Basil," he would say, "you were thinking of something. Please don't —all right, let's try again!"

And so it went on for most of the morning. When it was over I rushed over to Freddie and took him in my arms and kissed him. We had become great friends, and he was often over to our house for a swim in the pool and dinner. This made the playing of Mr. Murdstone all the harder for me. When the picture was released I received good reviews and a very heavy fan mail—all of it abusive! Mr. Selznick, Mr. Cukor, and I had done our job well, so well that for some considerable time I was to become a victim of one of motion pictures' worst curses, "typing." I was now typed as "a heavy" or villain, a category that often did not do justice to the role it was supposed, so arbitrarily, to define, as was the case in Leo Tolstoi's *Anna Karenina* with Greta Garbo. Here again Mr. Selznick drove with a passionate intensity, drove himself and everyone else. Perfection for David was not the ultimate, but only the penultimate! The star roles were played by Miss Garbo as Anna Karenina, Basil Rathbone as Karenin (her husband), Freddie Bartholomew as our son, and Fredric March as Vronsky (Anna's lover). Here, in the making of this picture, is the almost perfect example of a loss of integrity that becomes inevitable when a single label is tabbed to a character of many dimensions. Karenin is not "a heavy," a motion picture term that Tolstoi would have shuddered to hear defined.

Anna had married Karenin of her own free will: they have a son, a boy of about ten years old. She falls in love with a very attractive young man, Vronsky, who is more of her age, Karenin being somewhat older than Anna. That she had fallen out of love with Karenin might be held much to Karenin's account. But he had not been cruel or unkind, rather he had been insensitive and possessive, and without much imagination. His faults are quite evident and Tolstoi does not spare him. That Anna should have fallen in love with Vronsky was quite understandable to all except of course Karenin. But surely this does not make him a villain!

There is one scene in Tolstoi's novel that had to be eliminated from the picture script for reasons of censorship. (Oh, the bloody, dull, plebian mediocrity of most censorship.) This scene is vital to any appreciation and understanding of the character of Karenin. It is that scene where Anna is about to give birth to her lover's child. Karenin sends for Vronsky, and quietly in his study he tells Anna's lover that his mistress is about to become the mother of his child. This is no time or place for Karenin and he leaves Vronsky alone to face the hour of his making. There is bitterness in Karenin at this moment, and who shall blame him? But there is also a pride and integrity born of his conservative and unchangeable background, and maybe a degree of compassion for the bastard child about to be born to his Anna and her lover. To eliminate this scene is to present Karenin unjustly—a dimension—several dimensions of his being are eliminated from the estimate we are asked to make of him. And in so doing Karenin is liable to fall back into a ready-made category, a category for which motion picture audiences are also largely responsible.

I first met Miss Garbo in 1928 when Ouida and I were invited to lunch with Jack Gilbert one Sunday. We were touring *The Command to Love* and were playing for a month at the Biltmore Theatre in Los Angeles. We had never met with Jack Gilbert either. During the run of *The Command to Love* in New York I had received from Gilbert a most gracious telegram of appreciation for my performance in this play. I had written him a "thank-you" note advising him of our visit to Los Angeles later and hoping then to meet him. The result was this memorable Sunday luncheon, for both Gilbert and Garbo were not only great stars at this time but Gilbert was madly in love with Garbo, a love it was said she was hesitant to reciprocate. Jack's house was high up in the Hollywood hills—a small house with a wonderful view, a tennis court, and a swimming pool. We were ushered out to the pool, where drinks were being served. Jack Gilbert greeted us warmly as if *I* were the great picture star, not *he!* He praised the play and particularly my performance in it to the assembled company that included, among others, Mr. and Mrs. Harry Eddington, Garbo's personal manager (he was later to become mine), but as yet no Garbo.

Jack Gilbert had one of the most attractive smiles a man was ever blessed with, and a laugh and eyes that were devastatingly dangerous. He was not only a woman's man he was a man's man and consequently, as with Valentino before him and Gable who followed him, his popularity and his following were enormous. After a short while we went in to lunch and sat down. The chair to the right of me remained vacant. But not for long. Miss Garbo entered and greeted us all with a radiantly impersonal smile, which included Jack! She came around the table to the chair next to me. I rose and held it for her. She seated herself without so much as looking at me, and the conversation became general except for Miss Garbo, who was interested in the food before her, and myself, who was stunned by her extraordinary beauty. Longish fair hair very simply coiffeured, she wore a simple flowered dress and no make-up. Her skin was of an exquisite texture, and her eyes were framed with the longest natural untouched eye-lashes I have ever seen. She seemed completely at her ease, occasionally laughing and talking with Jack's guests and once in a while addressing herself to me. In due course, after lunch, we played tennis and went for a swim in the pool. I was Garbo's "doubles" partner and have rarely played a worse game! Garbo was not a large woman. She was beautifully proportioned and I think could best be described as being the aesthetic-athletic type. She swam like a fish and by the time we met in the water she was very friendly and most of my inhibitions had been overcome—but only so long as I did not look into those eyes. This was a calculated risk reducing me to utter submission.

Imagine my excitement then when cast to play opposite Miss Garbo in *Anna Karenina* some six years later. I had not seen her since that Sunday at Jack Gilbert's. Our reintroduction was formal and as though we had never met before. She was just as beautiful, but something had happened. Never during the entire time of the making of the picture (some eight to ten weeks) did she give the slightest indication that we had ever met before. She remained alone in her dressing room on the set when she was not working, and never talked with anyone except Miss Constance Collier, with whom it would seem she shared the secret of some disturbance that might be troubling her. If her attitude had related to me alone I think I might have understood, for it could have been that her growing hatred for me (as Karenin) might have been made more difficult to simulate had we become good friends. It troubled me at first, but I soon dismissed it in my tremendous admiration for her consummate ability as an actress, perhaps the greatest I have ever played with. From the first day to the last we were just Anna and Karenin to one another, and I gave one of the best performances of my life, thanks largely to the inspiration I derived from Miss Garbo. On the last day that we worked together we were seated next to one another waiting to be "called." I turned ever so slightly for a last look at that beautiful face. She sat motionless, intense, there was not so much as the flicker of an eyelid. She might have been a wax figure of herself in Madame Tussaud's. Suddenly I heard myself saying desperately, but with the utmost control, "Miss Garbo, I wonder if you would grant me a very great favor. When I work with anyone I admire as much as I admire you I ask for the privilege of a signed photograph. I have one here that will help me to remember this wonderful experience in playing opposite you. Would you sign it for me?"

There was a moment's pause, and then without a movement, like the wax figure in Madame Tussaud's, she said, "I never give picture."

I was both confused and hurt, and try as I will I have never quite forgiven her. To me and to everyone else that I know who has met her, Miss Garbo remains an enigma. Perhaps it is that none of us really know her; but the most interesting aspect would seem to be, does Miss Garbo know herself?

Mr. Aldous Huxley, a very intuitive and perceptive man, once told me a most amusing story about her. She had contacted him out on the Coast, indicating she would like him to write a motion picture story for her. He was naturally very much intrigued by the idea and made a date to call on her at her home in Beverly Hills. I will try to relate it as nearly as I can in Huxley's own words. Aldous has an unusually interesting personality. Very tall with a shock of unruly hair (then!), he stoops slightly, as often men as tall as he will. He is almost blind, was completely so at one time when he learned to type by touch in his new-found darkness. But by a diligent application of some "method" he has somewhat regained his sight. While talking he rarely sits down, moving carefully and intensely about the room. Once in a while, if you ask him a question, he will stop and turn, seeming to be making an effort to focus upon the area from which the voice has reached him. His story on this particular occasion was as follows, as nearly as I can remember it. Aldous speaks in a rather high-pitched voice and somewhat hesitatingly.

"And so upon the morning previously arranged I called on

Miss Garbo. The house, a small one, was as silent as the grave. There was absolutely no indication that it might be occupied. I rang several times without receiving any response and was about to leave, thinking I had the wrong address, when the door was opened and I was ushered in by someone I presumed to be the butler. I was asked to wait in the living room, which was just off the hallway. It was a large, dark, monastic type of room sparsely furnished, with little indication that the sun was shining brightly outside. On a very large sofa sat a very small woman, a small but most exquisite woman both in features and figure and in the manner of her dress. She was beautiful, very beautiful, but her beauty seemed to me to have that decadence one had seen before in very old and renowned Italian or Spanish families. I was right at least in one respect for she introduced herself as Mercedes de Acosta. I sat opposite her and we maintained a polite conversation until Miss Garbo entered the room. She was dressed like a boy, a very beautiful boy I grant you, but I was somewhat startled by the transformation. She greeted me pleasantly and seated herself on the sofa next to Mercedes de Acosta. I was not at my ease and broached the purpose of my call immediately. I advised her that I did not purposefully write material for motion pictures, and had she any particular character in mind? She said that she had but had hoped I had given the matter some thought and would be grateful for any suggestions. I replied that I had been very busy and had had little time for such contemplation. After several uneasy minutes of conversation along these lines I pressed Miss Garbo to acquaint me with the specific character she had already indicated was in her mind. She looked toward Miss de Acosta, who returned her look intently. There was a considerable pause, neither of them spoke; but by some means of thought transference I suppose, they appeared to have agreed.

"Then Miss Garbo turned to me and said, 'I want you to write me a story about St. Francis Assisi.'

"Having absorbed the shock, I inquired, 'And do you wish to enact the part of St. Francis himself?'

" 'That is correct,' replied Miss Garbo, and Miss de Acosta added her assent with a wisp of a smile and a gentle inclination of her head. At first I was so confused that I could find no words. Then at last it came tumbling out, as much a shock to myself as it obviously was to Miss Garbo.

" 'What! . . . replete with beard?' I stammered.

"No further words were exchanged between us and a moment later I excused myself and was gone!"

After *Anna Karenina* I made one more picture for David Selznick at MGM, Charles Dickens' *The Tale of Two Cities*, starring Ronald Colman. *The Garden of Allah* was made at Pathe Studios after Selznick had left MGM and was out on his own.

Once again Selznick gave his all to *The Tale of Two Cities*, and no one could have been more romantically effective than Ronald Colman in the tragic self-sacrificing leading role of Sidney Carton. Ouida and I had known "Ronnie" for a long time, from way back when he had first come to the United States and appeared in a small part in a Broadway play. I use the word "known" advisedly, because I know of no one so genuinely shy as was the late Ronald Colman. Until he married Benita Hume he lived alone in a large house with lovely gardens and a tennis court. His closest friends were Dick Barthelmess and Bill Powell. There were also a few other cronies on the fringe of his acquaintance. He never accepted social engagements and led a bachelor life with his friends that verged on the monastic. At the same time he was playing the most romantic roles and was the secret love of millions of frustrated women all over the world. Even after his marriage he changed very little. Mrs. Boyer once told us of an occasion when Mrs. Colman persuaded Ronnie to go to New York with her and the Boyers and see some shows. On arrival in New York he was of course immediately recognized and besieged by adoring fans, not to mention an insistent press. So Ronnie shut himself up in his hotel and stayed there for two weeks, refusing to go out anywhere, while the Boyers and Mrs. Colman made it a threesome at the theater every night. It was during the making of *The Tale of Two Cities* that Ronnie was inveigled out to dinner at the house of some very close friends, Mr. and Mrs. David Torrence. Ouida was seated next to Ronnie at dinner and had a miserable night. No matter what subject matter she brought up he simply refused to be a good dinner companion. After dinner, when coffee was served, Ouida said to him, "Well, Ronnie, you have given me a wretched evening and I am glad you are going to get your head chopped off in a couple of days. It serves you right. I only wish I could be there to cheer with the old women around the guillotine when the ax falls."

At first Ronnie seemed quite shocked. Then he smilingly replied, "You're invited. I'll phone you." And a couple of days later he did!

On the appointed day, in costume, he met Ouida at the front entrance of MGM in Culver City and drove her out in a studio chauffeur-driven car to the back lot, where a huge crowd of extras and visitors were awaiting his execution. He jumped out of the car and gallantly helped Ouida to alight, showing her to a prepared seat of honor. As he left her he bowed deeply and quoted his final lines as Sidney Carton. "It is a far far better thing that I do now than I have ever done. It is a far far better rest that I go to than I have ever known."

When the gory scene was over and from an audience viewpoint on the screen his head was in the basket, Ronnie returned to Ouida bringing her a cup of tea.

"Well," he said, "dead or alive, am I forgiven?"

His charm, graciousness, and humor were overwhelming and Ouida became his slave from that moment. Finally he put Ouida back into the studio car and drove with her to the studio front entrance. There he alighted and bowing low over Ouida's hand he kissed it, and then ordered the car to drive her home.

The part that I played in *The Tale of Two Cities*, the Marquis d'Evrémonde, could rightly be called "a villain" or "a heavy." Charles Dickens purposely uses the Marquis to demonstrate the arrogance and cruelty of the French aristocracy of that time. The Marquis was a *symbol* of conditions that were a major cause in the French Revolution, but not necessarily the epitome of all French aristocrats. As at all times and in all places there are always those innocents who must suffer for the excesses of others whether they be ancient Romans, Frenchmen at the turn of the eighteenth century, or Germans or Russians in the twentieth century. As the Marquis, eventually I came by my "comeuppance" by being brutally murdered in my bed by the people I had helped so viciously to oppress.

The Garden of Allah was the last picture that I made for David Selznick. It was directed by my good friend Richard Boleslawsky (who had directed my play *Judas* for me on Broadway in 1929). Its stars were Marlene Dietrich, Charles Boyer, Joseph Schildkraut, and myself. I was looking forward to this picture as a possible break for me in getting away from "villain" roles. Count Antoni was a very sympathetic role and might prove to be of much help to my future. When I signed my contract with David Selznick I advised him I was doing so on the assumption that the role of Count Antoni would be the same in the picture as it was in the book. The picture script was still in work but David assured me there would be no change in Robert Hitchins' conception of the part, and I left his office feeling very happy about my new assignment. Also I was very thrilled to be playing opposite Marlene Dietrich, who I had admired for a long time and considered one of the world's great beauties.

Beauty such as Marlene's has always frightened me a little —It's like looking at a great work of art or listening to a symphony of Brahms. There is someone behind all this beauty—who is he or she? I am not sure to this day that Marlene has ever escaped from the dream world I created about her, in spite of her warmth and friendliness and her wonderful cooking! She is one of the best chefs in the world. I remember a dinner she gave—there were ten of us I think.

Marlene greeted us all warmly, exquisitely gowned and look-ing more beautiful than it is possible to describe. There were no cocktails, just champagne and caviar! Once the company were assembled she disappeared and half an hour or so later a butler appeared and announced that dinner was served. We went into the dining room and Marlene joined us from the kitchen, fragrant and cool and lovely as if she had just stepped out of a perfumed Roman bath. She had been in the kitchen most of the afternoon preparing our dinner and for the past half hour she had been putting the final touches to it. First we were served a soup from the *écrevisses*, which had been cooked in champagne, then came the *écrevisses* and a huge bowl of salad with French dressing, garnished with garlic; next a platter of every cheese imaginable; and to top all this off a Viennese layer cake and coffee. Nothing but imported champagne was served before, during, or after dinner. And like the princess of a fairy story Marlene en-chanted us all.

Some days she would get up very early (she had to be in the make-up department at Pathe at 7:30 A.M. at the latest, so you can imagine how early!) and prepare an elaborate lunch-eon, which was brought down to the studio in containers and to which Boyer and Boleslawsky and I were invited and sometimes David Selznick. David's acceptance of these in-vitations was important because these lunches often lasted for an hour and a half to two hours of the company's time, and the picture was a very expensive one!

Marlene is an extremely generous artist to work with and she knows her business. On occasion she would ask that a light be changed or the camera moved slightly one way or the other and I would eventually realize these changes had been made for my benefit.

"There, darling," she would say, "that's so much better for you." And this in spite of the fact that she would be playing in the scene with me.

I remember when she paid all expenses necessary to get the mother of a young actor friend of hers out of Germany, presenting her to her son one morning without his having the slightest idea his mother was in the United States, and then paying all her expenses back again to Germany when the old lady was not happy in Hollywood.

We meet less frequently now than we used to. Once in a while I will see her crossing a street in New York—"Did you ever see a dream walking? Well I did!"

I have said that *The Garden of Allah* was the last picture I made for David Selznick. Whether this has been intentional on his part or just by chance I do not know. But I *do* know that one morning while working on this picture he *did* tell me I would never work for him again and I haven't! And this is what happened:

On the morning in question I received some new pages of dialogue. The situation and dialogue were such as to suddenly put Count Antioni in a very unsympathetic situation and completely alter the course of characterization I had been developing, at the same time giving to a young actor, whose future David was interested in, a sympathy and an opportunity completely out of character with the original Robert Hitchins' novel. As one of the stars in this picture I objected strongly to this treatment. My director and friend Boleslawsky found himself in a very difficult position as it was not up to him to make a decision, and I had refused to even rehearse the scene. The production manager sent for Selznick, who came onto the set.

Selznick is not a man accustomed to arguments where he has made a prior decision, and the situation and dialogue had his O.K. He looked at me with angry contempt as he asked what the trouble was. Boleslawsky, Marlene, and the rest of the company stood around waiting for lightning to strike! I reminded David that I had signed a contract without reading a script and upon his assurance that Count Antioni would be played exactly as written in Hitchins' book, and that the new scene was a gross infringement of this understanding. This made him very angry indeed, particularly since it was said before Boleslawsky and an eagerly listening company.

David then told me I would do as I was told or he would prefer charges of insubordination against me with my union, The Screen Actors Guild. I quickly realized the consequences of such an action throughout the entire industry, and aggressively answered him. "If you think I am going to break my contract with you, you are very much mistaken. You have broken your promise to me and technically our contract but it doesn't seem to bother you. Possibly you can work it out with your conscience later. And now my dear David, let's get on with this lousy scene you have O.K.'d and I'll be a good boy and do everything you ask of me. But please understand I do so 'under protest.' "

I don't think I have ever seen anyone look as angry as David did at this moment. He was literally white with rage as he said, "You will never work for me again as long as you live," and I haven't!

I recount this episode to prove once more the old adage, "There is many a slip 'twixt the cup and the lip." And though motion pictures may be your best entertainment they are not always so entertaining in the making. It is quite possible that David doesn't even remember this incident. We have met often since and our meetings have always been most friendly. When I played Cassius in Julius Caesar "in the round" at The Edison Hotel in New York in 1950 he came with his wife to the play and sent word backstage to me that it was one of the finest performances he had ever seen.

I can only speak of those I know and for whom I have worked, and Irving Thalberg and David Selznick stand head and shoulders above any other producers of my time. I have no heart to talk of any others however excellent they may be. Having discussed a personal association with Churchill and Roosevelt it would be difficult to continue a discussion relating to a personal association with Truman and Atlee.

These pictures and associations I have related were memorable experiences. The rest one remembers but no more; and there are some "bread and butter" jobs that one would

prefer to forget! And so briefly and for the record: I made
four pictures at Warner Brothers:

Tovarich with Charles Boyer and Claudette Colbert in
which I played the Russian commissar, Gorochenko.

Captain Blood with Errol Flynn and Olivia de Havilland
in which I played Levaseur.

Robin Hood with Errol Flynn and Olivia de Havilland in
which I played Guy of Gisbourne.

Dawn Patrol with Errol Flynn and David Niven in which
I played a flight commander of the British R.F.C. in World
War I.

Tovarich was a good picture made from the very successful Broadway play of the same title. In it we were all extremely health conscious because dear Claudette Colbert,
who is married to a doctor, had a passion for administering
medicines. She would watch us all closely for symptoms—a
vagrant sneeze or a mild clearing of the throat and she was
at one's side in a moment.

"Dear Basil," she might say, "you're not well. Now don't
say that you are because you're not. I've been watching
you. Put out your tongue." And in self-defense I would do
so. "Dirty," she would continue. "It wouldn't surprise me if
you had a little temperature—let me take your temperature."
And once in a while she would win and be mortified to
find you were normal.

"Normal," she would say. "Well you don't look it. Anyway you had better take a couple of aspirin just to be on the
safe side."

She had a thermometer, aspirin, cough drops, eye wash,
iodine, and a Red Cross kit in a special bag that was always
with her on the set. Claudette is also a very accomplished
actress.

In a book published posthumously Errol Flynn has told
the public much about himself. It would be anticlimactic to
attempt to say anything more about him except very briefly.
He was one of the most beautiful male animals I have ever
met. But in retrospect, and in almost every way, he cannot

compare to Valentino, Jack Gilbert, or Clark Gable. I think his greatest handicap was that he was incapable of taking himself or anyone else seriously. I don't think he had any ambition beyond "living up" every moment of his life to the maximum of his physical capacity, and making money. He had talent but how much we shall never know; there were flashes of this talent in all the three pictures we made together. He was under contract to Warner Brothers at I believe $150 a week when he was literally propelled into his first starring role as Captain Blood, owing to an emergency, the nature of which I forget. A couple of years later he was negotiating a contract that would pay him $7000 per week. He was monstrously lazy and self-indulgent, relying on a magnificent body to keep him going, and he had an insidious flair for making trouble, mostly for himself. I believe him to have been quite fearless, and subconsciously possessed of his own self-destruction. I would say that he was fond of me, for what reasons I shall never know. It was always "dear old Bazzz," and he would flash that smile that was both defiant and cruel, but which for me always had a tinge of affection in it. We only crossed swords, never words, and he was generous and appreciative of my work. I liked him and he liked me.

Captain Blood was also Olivia de Havilland's first picture. I understand she was about eighteen or nineteen years old at the time, and a more enchantingly beautiful young girl it would be impossible to imagine. She has since developed into a very talented actress.

These four pictures I made at Warner Brothers were not great pictures, but they were very good pictures and excellent entertainment. In their category I do not see their like being as well made today.

Other pictures of quality that I made between 1934 and 1946 were:

For Samuel Goldwyn: *Marco Polo* with Gary Cooper.

For 20th Century-Fox: *The Mark of Zorro* with Tyrone Power.

For Universal: The Sherlock Holmes pictures and *The Tower of London,* a historical picture in which I starred as England's Richard III.

For RKO: *The Last Days of Pompeii* in which I played Pontius Pilate, and which was instrumental in my meeting with Amelia Earhart. The producer of this picture was Meriam Cooper, and one Sunday he invited me to lunch at his beach house at Santa Monica. There were several guests to lunch, but I can remember none of them but Amelia Earhart. To say it was love at sight would be both unseemly and utterly ridiculous. And yet with that first glance there was a tug at the heart (was it premonition?—if so it was not for the first time in my life).

Of medium height and slight of build she had those far-away eyes that travel the seas and the heavens above. Her hair was short, a mass of curls. She was wearing a trim pair of trousers and a turtle-neck sweater. She was the only woman I have ever seen of whom one can say that this mode of dress graced her sex. Her composure was sublime, her speech soft, and her manner detached yet not impersonal. I have met no traveler on this earth who was so completely ethereal.

There is one other personality-actor-entertainer whose exceptional talents have always made a deep impression on me whether viewing him "live" or on the screen or working with him, Danny Kaye. Danny's success does not lie alone in his natural, God-given talents but in a quality that few beginners seem to realize is probably a determining factor in any successful career, WORK! Danny is a prodigious worker, with an aptitude for assimilating and perfecting anything he decides to accomplish. Danny can make one cry just as readily as he can make one laugh: the mark of a truly great comedian. And he has that indefinable quality we call "class."

In *The Court Jester* we had to fight a duel together with saber. I don't care much for saber but had had instruction in this weapon during my long association with all manner of swords. Our instructor was Ralph Faulkner, a very well-known swordsman on the Coast who had specialized in saber. After a couple of weeks of instruction Danny Kaye could completely outfight me! Even granting the difference in our ages, Danny's reflexes were incredibly fast, and nothing had to be shown or explained to him a second time. I was talking to him once about this, and he told me (in effect) that his mind worked like a camera that took perfect pictures, and that he had a very keen sense of mime that could immediately translate the still picture into physical movement. Hear or see anything just once and he could imitate it without the slightest effort. One day, for instance, while "working out" together, Faulkner introduced us to France's woman's foil champion. She spoke little English and that with difficulty and a delicious accent that was adorably feminine. In a matter of minutes Danny was imitating her perfectly, or rather it was not so much an imitation as a perfect facsimile of her manner of speech *and* her adorable femininity! If such a thing be possible it might be said that Danny spoke his broken French-English better than she did!

One day, toward the end of the picture, I heard the most unearthly sounds coming from the direction of Danny's stage dressing room. I went around to see what it could be. Danny was blowing on a cornet.

"What the heck are you doing, Danny?" I asked.

"Learning to play the cornet for my next picture," he replied.

"But why? Surely you'll be 'doubled' won't you?"

"Not on your life. I am going to learn how to play this thing or I won't make the picture"—and he did! I think the picture was called *The Five Pennies.*

Danny's first love is not the world of entertainment. He wanted to be a surgeon. This is not hearsay, he told me himself. Wherever he is he manages to make contacts that enable him to sit in on major operations. It would not surprise me in the least if he had performed one himself!

In Philadelphia, on one occasion, he was invited by

Eugene Ormandy, conductor of the Philadelphia Symphony Orchestra to participate in a benefit. Here, once again, he demonstrated a facet of his extraordinary talent. It was Mr. Ormandy who told me himself that, at a rehearsal which Danny was listening to with much concentration, he suddenly asked to be allowed to conduct the opening number. The idea delighted Mr. Ormandy, and as Danny stepped up onto the podium the famous orchestra gave him a tremendous reception and prepared themselves for many a good laugh. To their surprise, however, Danny led them through the piece with incredible facility and a faultless downbeat.

Danny can also meet a caustic remark with a charming if dangerous smile, and a devastating retort. He was playing London's Palladium, where he is a great favorite. One night, after the show, a friend called on him and invited him to a very "posh" society party. Danny, who was as popular "in society" as he was with the Cockneys of Covent Garden, said he could not go as his dinner jacket was at home and all he had with him was a blue suit. His friend assured him it was of no consequence, and that his hostess would be honored to have him as a late guest, and that he (Danny's friend) would explain that he had rushed Danny over directly from the theater. It was indeed a "posh" party; not only dinner jackets but some white ties and tails, with many of the first ladies of society resplendently begowned and bejeweled. The hostess was delighted that Danny had been able to come, and so were her guests, most of whom knew him well and adored him. All but one, the Duchess of Windsor.

Introducing Danny to the Duchess, his hostess said, "You know Danny Kaye, of course?"

The Duchess eyed Danny critically from head to foot. Then she said, "Yes, of course." And then turning away from him she continued, "Still trying to be funny, Mr. Kaye?"

To which ill-mannered comment Danny replied with his sweetest, most dangerous smile, "And you too, Duchess?"

Other pictures there are that I have made, some good,

some not so good, and some just horrid. But unlike the field of music where the great works of Beethoven, Brahms, Bach, Mozart, Shubert, Debussy, Ravel, and Prokofiev are the standard of a performer's success, in the world of entertainment—theater—motion pictures—radio and television—mediocrity has always held a high place, and many a considerable reputation has been built by this monster, this insidious enemy of the human race.

II

A Home at Last

When we left New York after *Romeo and Juliet* to go West for Selznick's *Anna Karenina*, we rented a house on Los Feliz Boulevard. I signed a lease for this property for a period of three months and we lived there for three years. They were three of the happiest years of my life. I soon found out that I was much in demand and consequently had a security in continuous work that came as a very pleasant surprise to me after my life in the theater. Win, lose, or draw one is paid in the movies irrespective of the results of a picture's release. It's like getting three months' salary in advance in the theater before the play opens! Also as a picture star one's salary is at least triple that one receives as a star in the theater. Add to this for two consecutive years I was nominated for best supporting player in the Academy Awards. (Louis XI in *If I Were King*, with Ronald Colman, and Tybalt in *Romeo and Juliet*, with Miss Shearer). But above and beyond everything, Ouida and I were free to enjoy a long overdue postgraduate honeymoon. Many were the sacrifices Ouida had made for me in this journeying we had planned together and in the directing of my professional life, and we fell in love again, as it were, in this Garden of Eden. Not that we had ever fallen out of love. But our loving one another was deserving of this time we had earned together, and we were in need of the time to enjoy one another again, released as we were, at last, from the pressures and burdens that are inherent in the building of any successful career.

The house was small but extremely comfortable. It had a large and lovely garden and a kidney-shaped swimming pool. Over a four-car garage there was a spacious studio. This studio was occupied by dear Jack Miltern, who had come to live with us. Jack and I had grown to be extremely fond of each other and we both loved Ouida deeply. He was "family." Both Ouida and Jack being terrific gamblers the coming years were to be filled with intensive debates as to who would win every Saturday at Santa Anita race track! Both of them played the most ridiculous hunches, while I studied form, with the result that more often than not one or both of them always came away a winner, while I was a consistent loser! We each had our own "racing form." I would take mine to my room for serious study while they argued and "fought" downstairs as if their very lives depended on it. Glorious days and nights!

We were rarely indoors. We lived in the garden and in the pool. And what a haven it was for dogs! We bought three—"Bunty" and her brother "Cullum" Moore, two West Highland terriers, and a sad-eyed springer spaniel who had incongruously been christened "Happy." But these three soon grew to seven! One day Ouida came home with a red cocker in her coat pocket, a baby of a few weeks old—"Leo"—and that made it four. Then a friend asked us to take care of a magnificent big black poodle called "Toni," and never came back for him—that made it five. Then Ouida "just couldn't resist" buying a beautiful black German shepherd puppy, who we christened "Moritza"—and now there were six. Lastly, one afternoon Ouida heard a dog whimpering on our front doorstep. Thinking one of our dogs had got out, she went downstairs to find a white bull terrier puppy that seemed to be lost. We christened her "Judy." Advertising her presence with us in the newspapers for two weeks without any response we kept her. We had the garden completely fenced in so they couldn't get out, and in due course, as they grew older, every afternoon around four or five o'clock Jack and I took them all for a run in the open brush that covered the hill opposite our house and which led up to the planetarium. The brush was apparently full of wild life and it was a problem to teach seven dogs to heel when necessary. No dog ever caught anything and they all returned safely each day. I say "safely" because we did not know until many years later that this property was full of rattlesnakes! Jack and I had always stuck to the beaten paths.

Ouida was divinely happy. At last she had the home she had hoped for all her life. We loved each other very much and we loved our dogs and our dogs loved us and the cats— oh yes, "Gina" and "Gita," the cats!—and Ouida's canary. I was out on location one day on a picture at Malibu Lake. A woman at a house nearby was about to drown a litter of kittens. The crew and the cast saved the lot, the last two falling to me. What with the canary and the dogs even Ouida was worried about two cats. But as yet they were only kittens and by the time they grew up they had learned to avoid the dogs while we had trained the dogs to leave them alone. They were never allowed in the house of course, on account of Ouida's canary, and slept in a closed-in porch.

We deliberately made few friends and dined out rarely. There were David Niven and the Richard Boleslawskys with their two-year-old son, and Freddie Bartholomew and "Cissie," Jack and Phyllis Morgan, Mrs. Iribe, Newell Vanderhoef and John Roche and friends from New York. I think we were somewhat frowned on by "the industry" for our apparent exclusiveness and *I* was the despair of the studio's publicity department because I would not dine out with their starlets or get into some kind of trouble. But Ouida and I had waited a long time for this sort of life and no increase in salary could buy us off! All one's debts paid up (an actor without debts is not really an actor!)—living well but not luxuriously, walking and reading and talking, my new collection of classical records and the beautiful new player that Ouida had given me. Tennis with Jack Morgan —tennis lessons from B. I. C. Norton, the South African who had been match point to beat Tilden at Wimbledon, and then lost to him. Golf with David Niven and Nigel Bruce, archery with lessons from Howard Hill—a target in the garden—a bow with a sixty-pound pull, made by hand and the arrows too by Howard Hill, the official archer in *Robin Hood*. And the races! The races wore me out—the tension was too much for me. Jack on edge, vowing to make up his stock market losses—that right foot of his ever-tapping rhythmically between endless walks to the paddock and back again. Ouida, like some gypsy fortuneteller, concentrating on the next race and never speaking a word to either of us or anyone else. And then screaming her lungs out as she pleaded with her horse to come first, and either collapsing in utter dejection or practically dancing a jig if she won. And so it went for eight races from 1:30 P.M. to five o'clock. I was "runner" for Ouida, buying her bets and collecting her wins. Oh well, it was worth it as there was rarely a day when she went home a loser and, win or lose, she always bought our drinks!

We tried sleeping all seven dogs in the house, but it was just too much! So we had a beautiful kennel built in an empty room next to those occupied by "the help." It opened out onto the garden. Every dog had a separate cubicle with its name over it and a nice soft pillow to sleep on. In no time at all they each learned to know their own cubicle and went to it the moment they were put to bed. We tried to show no favoritism, but Leo, the cocker, was Jack's dog, Moritza, the police dog, was mine, and Bunty, the female West Highland, was Ouida's. It was their decision, not ours!

One day I noticed Toni, the poodle, was ailing. We tried for a couple of days to treat him, but getting no better I took him down to our vet's, Dr. Eugene Jones. Upon examining him Dr. Jones said there was some obstruction in the intestines and he must operate. He found a large piece of a rubber bone that had been in Toni's Christmas stocking the previous December. He had chewed the end off and swallowed it. He died of intestinal poisoning. Never, never, never give a young dog anything made of rubber to play with that he can chew. A lesson we learned too late. Toni was one of the most intelligent and affectionate dogs I have ever known. His death was a sad loss to us.

The months rolled by in a pattern of seemingly eternal loveliness. It was a kind time. In the summer of 1936 Ouida and I went to England, where I made a picture with Ann Harding (*Love from a Stranger*) while Jack stayed home and took care of the dogs. There were trips to Carmel and Cypress Point in northern California and to Lake Tahoe. But mostly we lived and ate and slept and dreamed and thought and talked and loved in the house and gardens on Los Feliz Boulevard. And then on January 15, 1938, the pattern of seemingly eternal loveliness was shattered by Jack Miltern's death. We had started out on this day for our usual walk with the dogs, a little later than usual. The sun was setting. It was a beautiful evening. Ouida had come running to the garden gate to call us back to go with her in the car for a drive to watch the sun set into the Pacific. But we had gone just too far to hear her calling—or had we? How much of destiny is there in events such as these? This was the day and the hour and destiny was not to be denied by anything as fragile as the human will to live. The sky was bright and clear—an eternity above us. The dogs were soon hunting and Jack and I followed the paths we had trod so often together while Ouida jumped into her car and drove off to see the sun set into the Pacific. How silent Jack and I were that day—I only remembered it afterward. We were usually a garrulous pair, but today only a few words passed between us. One was not aware of anything in particular and certainly nothing that was strange or unusual. The walk came to an end as if it had been in a dream. We put the leads on our dogs. Jack had Leo and Bunty and Cullum. I had Moritza and Happy and Judy. The traffic was heavy on Los Feliz Boulevard as we waited to cross the road to our house. Suddenly Jack walked out into it. I screamed at him to wait and a moment later he and his three dogs were hit by a passing car. I saw them, all four of them, in the air, and a few seconds later four motionless bodies lay in the road, some ten to fifteen yards distant. The cars didn't stop, they just slowed down and went round the motionless bodies. I was powerless to move. I yelled at the passing traffic for help and at last a car stopped beside Jack, who was bleeding profusely. I reached the car as the driver stepped out. He was an osteopath who had cared for me in San Francisco when I had been ill on the Katharine Cornell tour in 1934. We greeted each other briefly. Then he said, "Where do you live?"

"Across the road," I answered.

"Get a blanket as fast as you can and cover your friend with it. There's a drugstore at the corner. I'll call for a police ambulance."

On my way to the house I noticed Bunty and Cullum were missing. They were on the other side of the road waiting for me. How they made it through the traffic I shall never know. They had been momentarily stunned but were uninjured except that Bunty had lost a tooth. Leo had a broken leg and I carried him in my arms, somehow holding the other three dogs on their leashes while the doctor (how I wish I could remember his name) delayed the oncoming traffic, which paused briefly but did not stop as it passed the dying man. I carried Leo into the house and handed him to the maid.

Then I went back with a blanket to Jack. The traffic was now moving more slowly, but nobody stopped. By now Jack was lying in a pool of blood. I covered him over with a blanket and waited. I still seemed to be living in that strange dream that had started with our walk together an hour or so ago—nothing seemed real. I functioned like an automaton. The ambulance arrived. I asked, "Is he dead?"

"No, he's living." But the inflection seemed to suggest— "but not for long."

I went back to the house and waited for Ouida. It was growing dark now and I did not have long to wait for her.

"There's been an accident," I said, "Jack is badly hurt."

Ouida said nothing.

"Come on," I continued. "Let's get down to the police station as fast as we can."

We got into the car and went to the police station. Not a word passed between us. At the police station we were met by a doctor.

"Are you Mr. and Mrs. Rathbone?" he asked.

"Yes."

"I'm sorry but your friend Mr. Miltern is dead. He died a few minutes ago."

"I'll phone you," I said.

Then we just turned and walked out again. I drove Ouida home. I was still dreaming. Nothing was real. The maid had returned from the vet's with Bunty and Cullum. They had had their dinner and were with the other dogs in the garden as if nothing had happened. Dr. Jones was setting Leo's leg. He could return to us in the morning.

At dinner Ouida said, "And it was such a beautiful sunset." And then a little while later, "If only you had heard me calling you." And then after dinner she broke, crying bitterly. Holding me tightly I heard her say, "Thank God it wasn't you." Then she went to her room and to bed.

A few moments later the telephone rang and I answered it. A woman's voice spoke.

"Am I speaking to Mr. Rathbone?" she asked.

"This is he," I replied.

"You don't know me," she continued. "I am not a medium or anything like that but I have what I think you might call extrasensory perception or something. These things happen to me once in a while. I don't know why. They just happen."

"What is it?" I asked.

"Did you lose someone very dear to you a short while ago?"

"Yes. Why?" I inquired.

"Well, he has asked me to get in touch with you and tell you he's all right. He said he wouldn't be able to contact me again because he is moving on very fast, but please to tell you—and oh yes—he said to be sure and tell you there were no dogs where he is—does it make any sense?"

"It does indeed," I replied, "and I am deeply grateful to you. May I ask to whom I am talking?"

"I would rather not if you don't mind. I am not a professional or anything like that. These things just happen to me and I feel it my duty to do as I'm asked."

"But how did you get my number?"

"I called all the studios and got it at last from Warner Brothers. I told them I had urgent news for you of a dear friend who had died. I couldn't very well say *from* someone who was dead! Anyway it wouldn't have been true because you see he isn't dead, only to you, and only then for a while until you understand. You do understand, don't you?"

"Of course I do."

"And you do believe me, don't you?"

"Of course I do—and God bless you. Good night."

"Good night."

I put the telephone down gently and stood there for several minutes without moving. There was no possible way she could have heard of the accident or Jack's death. And then I remembered also that she had said she lived quite some distance away "in the Valley." Her voice was soft, well bred, intelligent, and I was convinced she was completely sincere —I believed her.

"Dear Jack," I said to myself. "Dear, dear Jack, 'bon voyage.'" I swear by all that is holy that every word of this is absolutely true. I was not dreaming.

I was sitting alone in the living room over a bright log fire. The doorbell rang. It was a representative of a local funeral parlor, sent by the police. His attitude was grotesque, almost funny. He wore his heart on his sleeve and his voice was sepulchral. He condoned our loss and would be of service. I cut him short.

"Oh cut it out," I said. "Sit down and just tell me what must be done and how much will it cost?"

He seemed relieved as he warmed his hands at the fire and supplied me with all the details, in the manner of someone trying to sell me an expensive car. I told him I was not interested in an expensive funeral and he seemed disappointed, almost bored. Shortly afterward we came to terms—*my* terms—and he left, barely remembering to say good night.

Jack's sister who lived in the East asked that his body be shipped to her for burial. Jack and his sister were Catholics. Before this was done, however, a group of ours and Jack's friends met one morning in the funeral parlor. I took the service myself. As I stood beside Jack and spoke of him to his friends I remembered the voice on the telephone and what had been said between us.

"You do understand, don't you?"

"Of course I do."

"And you do believe me, don't you?"

"Of course I do—and God bless you. Good night."

Leo, who had laid in Jack's arms in the hammock in the garden, who had gone swimming with him in the pool, who followed him wherever he went and slept in his room at night, never went to that room again.

12

The War Years

The home on Los Feliz Boulevard was never quite the same again now that Jack was no longer there and we determined to move. Besides, little Cynthia was on her way and would be with us sometime in April of 1939, and there was no room for her at Los Feliz Boulevard (or would it be a son?).

The storm clouds were gathering over Europe. We had felt them approaching at the end of 1936 when we visited Paris and Berlin and Budapest on a trip after completing *Love from a Stranger*. There were ominous evil things in the air about us, which grew more ominous and evil as King Edward VIII deserted his country in its hour of need, and Neville Chamberlain failed to understand that peace at any price had never led to anything but war. The last years of Britain as a great world power were upon us and Winston Churchill was crying like a prophet in the wilderness, only to be rebuked and rejected until those same people were to call upon him to lead them in their "finest hour." The hours of dreaming were over. There was work to be done. We too felt the changing wind and were restless. And perhaps a change would help us to put our dreams into proper perspective, gratefully remembered as long as we might live, but not to be relived until the thing that was coming was over.

And so we moved to 10728 Bellagio Road, Bel Air. A larger house with a room and bath and a kitchenette for the baby and a larger garden to care for. A garden which much of the time I was to tend myself, during the war years.

Cynthia was born on April 13, 1939, and took up residence with us some few days later. As bald as a coot, she was a beautiful, healthy child, and her coming was a great compensation for our loss of Jack. How he would have loved her and how she would have loved him. They would have had much in common—a fierce independence and that Irish trait of needling a weak spot wherever they could find one.

War was declared in Europe in August 1939, and I wrote to the War Office in London offering my services. In due course I received an official letter of interminable length in reply. It began "Dear Sir" and ended with "Your obedient servant." I waded through it and all it said was: "You are too old!" Politely but firmly.

After the swift conquest of Poland the war seemed to drift lazily along, and a number of our friends began referring to it as "the phony war," but not for long. I remember so well—it was Kentucky Derby day in May, 1940, and the German armies were pouring into Belgium and France. Things grew worse hourly and we lived constantly within hearing of the radio. Then came Dunkirk and Britain's year alone against the united Axis powers. It was then that Ouida organized her first benefit, the proceeds to be shared by the R. A. F. Benevolent Fund and the Red Cross. She organized it absolutely alone, with a secretary, at the Beverly Wilshire Hotel and netted some $10,000. It was a staggering job, attended by everyone who was anybody in the motion picture industry and was one of the most brilliant and beautiful and exciting functions I have ever attended.

By this time I had been elected president of British War Relief on the Coast, a relief agency that had its headquarters in New York and had been organized by Mr. Aldrich of the Chase National Bank and Alden Blodget, Cornelia Otis Skinner's husband. This occupied much of my spare time of which I had all too little. Jules Stein of MCA Inc. had very wisely signed me up for five years with MGM. I also started in on the Sherlock Holmes pictures and the weekly radio series. Jules Stein was one of those who believed it would be a long-drawn-out war, and he wanted to secure me with an assured annual income that would take care of me and my family under all conditions, excepting a world catastrophe. It was a most thoughtful thing to have done, for it released us from all personal worries as to the immediate future, and enabled us to throw ourselves wholeheartedly into our war work. It was not easy living with some of our American friends during this time. They were apprehensive of the United States becoming involved, and quite often it was not difficult to sense their apprehension. Talk about the war was objective and impersonal and they went about their days and nights as if something would surely happen to prevent its further expansion. We accepted this pattern of life, working quietly and carefully where and when we could. As president of British War Relief I wrote to all the top executives of MGM asking them to contribute. Not one of them so much as answered my letters. But with the Warner brothers it was very different. They were terrific Anglophiles and supported us with both their time and money. Both Harry and Jack Warner were dedicated to our cause. One's major hope for results in making requests for help at this time was not to talk of Britain's problems and needs, but to use almost everyone's tremendous admiration for Winston Churchill as a means of approach.

Meanwhile I played golf, went to the races at Santa Anita, worked in the garden and attended to one's picture making and radio work. Cynthia was growing into a beautiful child, with a mass of blond curls and a strong personality. I shall never forget the day when Cynthia's governess came blazing into our bedroom saying the child was an "ungovernable little brat," and she and Ouida had a tremendous blowup. As the storm reached its zenith I felt a little hand take hold of mine and squeeze it. I looked down into Cynthia's sparkling excited eyes. Then I heard her whisper, "Oh Dadda, how I love trouble!" She would have been about five years

old at the time, and was attending kindergarten at Mary-
mount Catholic School, a short walk across the Bel Air golf
course. On the governess's day off I would sometimes go
and pick her up and walk her home across the golf course
with her friends the McAllister boys. One day we were
walking back and the McAllister boys and she were playing
tag. They were running and shouting and laughing when
suddenly Cynthia hauled off and hit the younger boy a terrific "haymaker!" I was quickly between them, fearing the
boy might retaliate. I pointed out to Cynthia it was a disgraceful thing to have done as the little boy was also a little
gentleman (something I was none too sure of at the moment!) and couldn't hit her back. Well, that put an end to
that. But I was curious to know why she had hit him so
violently. So when I got her alone I asked her, and she told
me that he sat directly behind her in school and rubbed
chewing gum into her hair! It was all I could do not to
laugh. We didn't have chewing gum when I was a kid, but
if we had, it would have been a wonderful idea and I know
I'd have tried it. It is perhaps the fact that I have always been
able to look back at myself as a child and share some of
Cynthia's childish vagaries with her that has helped us to
have such confidence in one another. However she knew
there were limits and rarely imposed them on *me*. But it
was quite a different matter with her mother. Having disposed of all her governesses (she had several and she needled
them all till they left) she started to needle her mother, and
I have had my hands pretty full ever since! During these
years on the governess's day off, Ouida and I took it in turn
to sleep with Cynthia in the nursery.

One was usually awakened at dawn by gentle little sounds
of movement from Cynthia's cot, accompanied by pianissimo gurglings and whisperings. If I opened one sleepy eye
to look at her she seemed to sense it at once and would turn
quickly and watch my recumbent figure for signs of life.
After a couple of peeks it wasn't much use trying to fool
her, so I would rise and lift her out of her cot and she

would come into bed with me. The procedure varied each morning, but not much. She would give me a shave and a hair cut—this was rather soothing and induced a drowsiness from which one was rudely awakened to "play house"—or she would go to her little machine and play Irene Wicker's charming children's records, especially the Robert Louis Stevenson's children's poems, which Miss Wicker sings beautifully. With little or no encouragement she would dance delightfully about the room. She had invented someone called Gloria Rubenstein who danced at a place called the Gardenia Club. But this "act" more usually took place at dinner when we were required to applaud and comment (always favorably of course) on the beautiful, talented young dancer the management of the Gardenia Club had engaged for our dining pleasure. Then there were "Sally and Bet," an invention of mine. Sally was the good one and Bet the naughty one. I was only allowed to deal briefly with Sally because Bet, being a little horror, was so much more fun. It was my own private comic strip and I had always to be prepared with another adventure.

The ill-mannered waiter was a great favorite of Cynthia's. I had invented him for those meals when she was disinclined to eat. She would come in and sit down and with a napkin over my arm I would approach her. "Hello, you old bag," I would say, "and what do you want today?" She would look up at me with surprised delight.

"Have you a menu?" she would ask.

"You mean what do we have to eat here?" I would reply.

"Yes, have you anything special today?"

Then I would laugh and slap my leg and make faces and say, "Have we anything special today? Oh lady, lady, lady, just you wait."

Then I would bring her her lunch and she would say, "And what is this?"

And I would reply, "That's a nice tasty bit of cold suet wrapped up in a dirty tea cloth!"

Then she would call the manager and report me. And I

would be the manager and reproach the ill-mannered waiter and threaten to sack him. And Cynthia would say, "Oh no, please—he's really a very nice man I am sure." We couldn't sack him because we should need him again on some other day! As the ill-mannered waiter I had to think of the most horrible dishes with which to amuse Cynthia: English kippers stuffed with strawberry jam, or sardines on angel cake with whipped cream, or two poached eggs floating in olive oil, or goldfish in aspic with grated aspirin!

The manager eventually brought her the restaurant's *pièce de résistance*, her own dinner of course, and she would eat every bit of it, commenting upon how delicious it was and saying there wasn't another restaurant like it in town. It always worked. I cannot remember its ever failing and the ill-mannered waiter remains one of my favorite roles.

I was sitting one Sunday morning in my room reading a script when Ouida's niece, Ouida Branché, who was staying with us, burst into my room and said, "They are bombing Pearl Harbor!"

I thought she had gone insane.

"Who's bombing Pearl Harbor? What are you talking about?"

"The Japanese," she replied and rushed from the room.

So here it was at last, the inevitable. And thank God it could not be said that once more the United States had to pick the Allies' chestnuts out of the fire. The United States had herself been invaded. And for some time to come actual invasion became a grave possibility. One night Japanese planes were said to have been spotted over Southern California. From our home we could see antiaircraft shells bursting in the night sky, just south of Los Angeles. A Japanese submarine shelled the coast at Santa Barbara, and rapid if inadequate precautions were taken to meet an invasion. For a long time, until she was quite grown-up, Cynthia could not bear the sound of a fire alarm. Someone had told her the sirens were a warning the Japanese were coming and for years the child lived with this frightening dream.

To Mr. Churchill and the Commonwealth forces there were now added President Roosevelt and the potential might of the United States of America. The Axis forces had signed their eventual death warrant. It would take time, but the final result was now unquestionable.

Now Ouida and I were up to our necks in war work, and with no further need of inhibitions. As president of British War Relief, I was elected to the Los Angeles area War Chest Executive Committee. The British Consul asked Ouida to be unofficial hostess to the many expected "visiting firemen," and Ouida and I took over Sunday nights at the Hollywood Canteen. In our spare time! Ouida and I visited hospitals and training camps. It was a stimulating and wonderful period in our lives. We were host and hostess to Admiral Halsey and his family, Lord Halifax, four tank corps officers of General Montgomery's Eighth Army, R.A.F. pilots sent to the United States for a rest period, and innumerable others, too many to mention. Every other weekend we had as our guests in our home six air corps trainees from a camp at Lancaster, California. Ouida Branché married one of them! Such wonderful boys. They all wrote to us afterward, but very few of them came home again. They were most of them killed in the great air raids over Germany. They would eat and drink and sleep and talk and laugh and play golf and swim in our pool. Some took it all in their stride, others were moody and disturbed. Either way I think we were of much therapeutic help to them all and Ouida mothered them as if they were her own children.

During this time Ouida earned, most unjustly, the title of Hostess of Hollywood. She was even offered a radio program bearing this title. The connotation suggested extravagance and self-exploitation. Success in any field usually brings criticism from certain quarters where a dissatisfied jealousy often breeds a vicious discontent. A prominent weekly magazine attacked Ouida in the most disgraceful and unpatriotic manner. Upon the advice of good friends and legal counsel we were advised to ignore it. This sort of thing I presume comes under the heading of "the freedom of the press," but in such cases I always wonder where stands the freedom of the individual. In public life it is better not to tangle with the press. You can't win. Any denial or apology you may succeed in eliciting will be so ineffectual as to carry over the stigma of the original libel, and after all there is no news as dead as yesterday's news. Ouida employed chartered accountants. Her effort more often than not cost us money and she made huge profits for every relief organization for which she worked. There is little if anything that can damage the truth, and Ouida suffered only minor and temporary abrasions.

I think her organization at the Hollywood Canteen was her most spectacular adventure. Every Monday for two years she started to work for the following Sunday. She somehow got gallons of ice cream donated and a birthday cake containing five-dollar bills! Any member of the armed forces present in the Canteen with a birthday on that particular Sunday could come up at "the cut the birthday cake ceremony" and try his luck at cutting a piece of cake containing five bucks, and kissing the hostess, whoever the star might be on that occasion. I remember one young kid who got a hold on Joan Crawford and virtually strangled her with his kisses. Joan, wherever you are, I bet you have never been kissed like that before or since! You have no idea how many birthdays there were every Sunday! And we soon realized we had to insist on birth-date identification. During the week there was canned music, but on Sundays Ouida insisted that it be live dance music. Emil Coleman and his band were particularly helpful to us and in spite of resistance from the musicians' union we always had someone there to play for the boys. Then there was the show, and what a show—Artur Rubinstein—Lotte Lehmann with Bruno Walter at the piano—Yehudi Menuhin—*The Merry Widow*—Gertie Lawrence—Red Skelton—Eddie Cantor—We had virtually every star in the entertainment world. Sunday after Sunday after Sunday there was a star-studded program. It required tremendous organization and once again Ouida worked alone with her secretary. I have never seen such energy and determination. Behind the coffee, cakes, and ice cream counter, which ran along one complete side of the Canteen, the waiters and waitresses were all stars or featured players, such as Ronald Colman and Walter Pidgeon, the Gabor sisters, Kay Francis, Greer Garson, etc., etc., etc., and the major studios supplied us with their beautiful little starlets to dance with the boys. I shared the MC spot every Sunday with Reggie Gardiner, and in between we went backstage and helped the unseen "heroes" and "heroines" wash up. There were hundreds upon hundreds of cups and saucers and plates and spoons and knives and forks to be washed and dried continuously. Sundays became a gala day and we were always "sold out" (metaphorically speaking—there was no charge for anything) and to our regret many had to be turned away. There was room in the canteen for about eight hundred, including a roped-off area for hospital cases.

During these years of work with the Canteen, there were those who never said "no" to us. It is not really fair to single out any one person and yet his fellow artists would not mind I am sure if I said that Eddie Cantor's devotion to our needs was deeply touching. It would not matter where he was or what else he had to do or at what time he was called, he would always be with us if humanly possible. One other example of generous devotion was Bing Crosby's orchestra leader, John Scott Trotter. Bing was bringing a big show to the Canteen one Sunday and the musicians' union was making difficulties. So rather than disappoint us, John Scott Trotter paid every member of his orchestra out of his own pocket. There were some stars, a very few I am glad to say, who were unpleasant about coming to us. The complaint was often, "Don't you realize I am working in a picture and Sunday is my day off?" To which Ouida would reply, "Don't you realize that young America is fighting a war and for them there is no day off—they can be killed on Sunday just as easily as on any other day of the week." In such situations as these we really didn't care whether they came or not, because if they did, it was usually with a chip on the shoulder as if they were doing us a great favor. There were a few, a very few, who never came at all.

During the war I experienced a lot of radio both as listener and performer; and even after the war through 1947 and 1948. Television, like the atomic bomb, was still in these years only a threat, but a very definite threat to the future of mankind. For whereas the atom might one day destroy us all completely in a matter of days, television might do an equally good job, over a much longer period, by merely reducing us to a state of such impotence that our ability to distinguish what is bad from what is good could be impaired for ever and ever, Amen. Mediocrity being a state of mind in which the individual no longer knows, and therefore no longer cares, what is happening to him—if this "crime of torpor, of lethargy, of apathy, the snake-like-sin of coldness-at-the-heart" became congenital we just might one day find ourselves the slaves of some master race. Things have moved very fast these past fifty years and it seems to me that time is no longer on our side.

Whereas, not very long ago it was the creative arts and derivatives thereof that had the greatest influence over men's minds, it is now a technological civilization that rules our thinking and has virtually become an abstract form of religion. Could it be that the Western World for the past quarter century had been too dedicated to the *status quo*, and was unconsciously drifting into mediocrity? Whereas our enemies were dedicated to a form of progress, an affirmative progress regardless of how we may disapprove of their methods and philosophy.

In the New York Sunday *Times* of April 23, 1961, there appeared a piece entitled "Leningrad Report" by Seymour Topping, and I quote: "Nikolai Akimov, the celebrated avant garde director of the Comedy Theatre, does not find the didactic nature and propaganda content of Soviet plays extraordinary. 'The whole history of art demonstrates that each play should have a moral,' Mr. Akimov contended. He cited George Bernard Shaw as an example of a good theater propagandist. 'The *mission* of the artist is to shape life and bring perfection to it,' the director said. 'Every play must influence and *disturb* the audience so as to achieve results.' . . . He described [a recent play by Samuel Alyoshin] one that tries to instill a new attitude toward death. 'That is, when a person sincerely believes that he is a part of a social unit, the unpleasant prospect of death can be looked upon with more equanimity.' Asked if the play sought to help fill the spiritual vacuum of an atheistic society, Mr. Akimov remarked: 'I do not know of any society where the problem of death has been solved. It is in general an imperfection of the nature of human life. Each society has to contend with the problem in its own way.' "

Pretty heady stuff! In it there are of course undertones of the "party line." But this seems insignificant to me in the face of Mr. Akimov's affirmative thinking. If I were an actor in his company I should find much inspiration in working with Mr. Akimov; as I would with Mr. Ingmar Bergman in his theater at Malmo in Sweden, or the Berthold Brecht Theatre in East Germany, and as *I did* in my own play *Judas* with Richard Boleslawsky, an actor-director from the original Moscow Art Theatre, and with our own Jed Harris on *The Heiress*.

No art can exist, let alone progress creatively (only mechanically), through a medium that is controlled by commercials. Both radio and television have made a great contribution to information and communication and often to specific forms of education. But as art forms they simply do not exist. They could, but they don't. Can you imagine going to see a play in the theater or a motion picture, to be interrupted every fifteen minutes by someone coming out on stage or appearing on the motion picture screen to sell you a car, or a washing machine, or to suggest you may be thirsty, and to take a few minutes out to visit your local

tavern and toss off a couple of beers, always remembering
of course that the second beer tastes just as good, if not better than the first, and other such ingenuous balderdash. In
newspapers and magazines you may *choose* to look at the
ads if you so wish, but with radio and television they are
rammed down your throat whether you like it or not; and
more often than not when perhaps you might be enjoying
the development of a well-written and well-acted play, such
as Mr. Costigan's original M.S. for T.V., *The Little Moon
of Alban* with Julie Harris and Christopher Plummer.

But for the most part both radio and television are merci-
less mediums for any artist, creative or interpretive, and have
been more responsible for the growth of mass mediocrity in
our culture than anything else I can think of. Baseball sends
our youngsters out with a desire to play baseball and one
day perhaps to play in the major leagues. Did you ever hear
of a youngster having seen or listened to *David Copperfield* or *Gone With the Wind* or *Hamlet* and wanting to
read Dickens or Shakespeare or Margaret Mitchell?

Radio is unquestionably a superior medium to television
because it makes us use our imaginations. I have been told
by literally hundreds of people that when we were doing
the Sherlock Holmes series they would turn out the lights
or if they had a fire sit round it and let their imaginations go
fancy free. Many have told me that the hound in *The
Baskervilles* was far more frightening to them on radio than
it could ever be on the screen or their television sets.

In the days of radio, of The Theatre Guild of the Air
be it here said that their program was ever striving for
quality, intelligence, and good taste. I have played many
times for them and every time I was invited it was a worth-
while experience. And also it must be said that in the theater
the Theatre Guild has been an outstanding leader for over
forty years. Their record I think is unique in the annals of
the American theater. I doubt that we shall see their like
again.

In television I hope we shall one day soon have paid T.V.

so that the public may have no further excuse for not being selective. By all means let there be commercial radio and television. We have no more right to deprive a business or an industry of advertising in these mediums than they have the right to deprive us of the use of our talents as we see fit to use them. If you are interested in some toothpaste or cigarettes, a beer or an automobile or breakfast food there must of course be shows that will add this luxury to your viewing pleasure. But I know of no commercials that are other than an affront in their interruptions of such T.V. plays as *The Lark* with Julie Harris, *The Browning Story* with Sir John Gielgud, and several others of like commendable effort.

There was a radio show I did one Christmas morning during the war. The entire live audience in the studio was in uniform. It was *A Christmas Carol* by Charles Dickens, and was performed in the NBC Studios in Hollywood for the benefit of the men and women of the Armed Forces only. The format was charming. In a room, supposedly my home, I was sitting reading the Dickens story to my daughter Cynthia. There was a knock at the door and a friend dropped in to say "Happy Christmas." He apologized for interrupting, but was persuaded to stay and hear this Christmas story. I started reading again and we imperceptibly drifted into the acting version with myself as Mr. Scrooge. When the play was finished I closed the book and we all wished each other and our listening audience a very happy Christmas, and my friend left. When we went off the air there was a rush for my autograph. I signed and signed and signed for quite some while, until I became conscious there was someone else's name on each piece of paper. In firm round copybook writing there it was, CYNTHIA RATHBONE! I looked up, and there *she* was in her little starched white Christmas frock signing away as if she had been my co-star, which indeed she had certainly proved to be.

13

"Hi there, Sherlock,
how's Dr. Watson?"

This greeting might quite easily prove to be my epitaph, if not in substance at least in effect. It is a greeting that in most cases I have not welcomed, for in general it has carried with it the connotation "We too are amused and entertained by your little game of sleuthing, how goes it, pal?" I do not remember a single instance from 1939 to 1962 where an interviewer from some newspaper or magazine, or a member of an audience, or a friend has not smiled somewhat indulgently when the subject of my association with Mr. Sherlock Holmes has arisen. In the upper echelon of my very considerable following as Mr. Holmes, there has always been a somewhat patronizing, if polite, recognition of my modest achievement. In the lower echelon I have experienced nothing but embarrassment in the familiar street-corner greeting of recognition, which is inevitably followed by horrendous imitations of my speech, loud laughter, and ridiculing quotes of famous lines such as "Quick, Watson, the needle" or "Elementary, my dear Watson," followed by more laughter at my obvious discomfiture. Quite frankly and realistically, over the years I have been forced to accept the fact that my impersonation of one of the most famous fictional characters in all literature has not received that respectful recognition to which I feel Sir Arthur Conan Doyle's masterpieces entitle him. Has it been my fault? I do not think so. And certainly it is not the fault of those who were responsible for producing sixteen pictures and some two hundred weekly radio broadcasts between 1939 and 1946. Professionally it has always been conceded that both pictures and broadcasts were of an exceptionally high quality. Could it be that our efforts somewhat resembled museum pieces? Here possibly may be a clue to the problem, i.e., the word "museum." With the development in talking pictures of a mass production of murder-mystery-sleuth-horror movies our audiences have been delighted and amused by the extravagant shock technique employed. Mr. Alfred Hitchcock is perhaps the prime "spoofer" of this type of storytelling, and he has contributed more than anyone else I know of to the acceptance of the murder-mystery-sleuth-horror as one of the most acceptable "jokes" of our time. Audiences are not really frightened by such pictures. They willfully indulge in a purely synthetic hysteria, which in some perverse way seems to entertain them momentarily. They are far too intelligent to accept anything but cacophony as the chocolate sauce that disguises their poisoned ice cream!

It would seem that our *timing* was bad. Nineteen thirty-nine was far too late for a serious presentation of *The Adventures of Sherlock Holmes*. In the early years of the present century theater audiences were chilled to the marrow by William Gillette's famous portrayal of Sherlock Holmes, in a play I have read and been invited to revive. This play, believe me, is so ludicrously funny today that the only possible way to present it in the sixties would be to play it like *The Drunkard*, with Groucho Marx as Sherlock Holmes. Time marches on! I have also considered reviving other successful plays of this period, in particular *The Passing of the Third Floor Back*, in which the late Sir Johnston Forbes-Robertson made one of his most spectacular successes. Modern audiences would laugh this play off the stage. Even the witticisms of Oscar Wilde are already somewhat dated, and Mr. Shaw, despite his protestations, stands trembling on the brink! Only Mr. Shakespeare remains as modern to us as he was to audiences in the year 1600. "Dated," that's the word. The Sherlock Holmes stories are dated and their pattern and style, generally speaking, unacceptable to an age where science has proven that science fiction is another outdated joke (and turning out to be a most unpleasant one). The only possible medium still available to an acceptable present-day presentation of Sir Arthur Conan Doyle's stories would be a full-length Disney cartoon.

I was also deeply concerned with the problem of being "typed," more completely "typed" than any other classic actor has ever been or ever will be again. My fifty-two roles in twenty-three plays of Shakespeare, my years in the London and New York theater, my scores of motion pictures, including my two Academy Award nominations, were slowly but surely sinking into oblivion: and there was nothing I could do about it, except to stop playing Mr. Holmes, which I could not do owing to the existence of a long-term contract.

I sincerely hope that this objective and unprejudiced analysis of a problem I had had to live with for so many years may not offend those who are still truly dedicated to Sherlockiana, many of whom are close personal friends of mine and have unquestionably been not only entertained, but have found our performances in these pictures and broadcasts rewarding. I say "our" because there were so many who contributed to our little niche in the hall of fame. There was first our director-producer-writer, the late Roy Neil, endearingly known to his company as "Mousie." There was a nominal producer and some writers also, but Roy Neil was the master and final hand in all these departments. Then there was Dennis Hoey, our Lestrade in every picture we made. And Henry Daniel's masterly Moriarty. There were other Moriartys, but none so delectably dangerous as was that of Henry Daniel. There was Allan Mowbray's charmingly villainous Colonel Moran, and oh so many other skillfully cast and skillfully acted smaller roles. And lastly, there is no question in my mind that Nigel Bruce was the ideal Dr. Watson, not only of his time but possibly of and for all time. There was an endearing quality to his performance that to a very large extent, I believe, humanized the relationship between Dr. Watson and Mr. Holmes. It has always seemed to me to be more than possible that our "adventures" might have met with a less kindly public acceptance had they been recorded by a less lovable companion to Holmes than was Nigel's Dr. Watson, and a less engaging friend to me than was "Willy" Bruce. We had been close personal friends for many years, and his sudden death in 1953 was a painful shock to all of us who had experienced with him his great joy in Elizabethan humor. As an example of this latter quality, his unique definition of ballet was preposterously funny. Over cocktails one evening, after a hard day's work at the studio, I was trying to persuade "Willy" to join his wife, "Bunny," and Ouida and myself in a visit to some ballet that was performing in Los Angeles over the weekend. He spluttered and grunted and mumbled his unqualified refusal in that form of speech indigenous to himself alone, and which was often quite untranslatable! At last, pouring himself another drink (like Falstaff, all drinks were disposed of by him in one enormous gulp—bottoms up!) he finally refused to accompany us, giving as his reason that . . . "I will not spend good money to watch bugger's jump!"

Had I made but the one Holmes picture, my first, *The Hound of the Baskervilles*, I should probably not be as well known as I am today. But within myself, as an artist, I should have been well content. Of all the "adventures" *The Hound* is my favorite story, and it was in this picture that I had the stimulating experience of creating, within my own limited framework, a character that has intrigued me as much as any I have ever played. But the continuous repetition of story after story after story left me virtually repeating myself each time in a character I had already conceived and developed. The stories varied but I was always the same character merely repeating myself in different situations. My first picture was, as it were, a negative from which I merely continued to produce endless positives of the same photograph.

In due course, and not unreasonably I think, these endless repetitions forced me into a critical analysis of Holmes that was often disturbing and sometimes destructive. For instance, toward the end of my life with him I came to the conclusion (as one may in living too closely and too long in seclusion with any one rather unique and difficult personality) that there was nothing lovable about Holmes. He himself seemed capable of transcending the weakness of mere mortals such as myself . . . understanding us perhaps, accepting us and even pitying us, but only and purely objectively. It would be impossible for such a man to know loneliness or love or sorrow because he was completely sufficient unto himself. His perpetual seeming assumption of infallibility; his interminable success; (could he not fail just once and prove himself a human being like the rest of us!) his ego that seemed at times to verge on the superman complex, while his "Elementary, my dear Watson," with its seeming condescension for the pupil by the master must have been a very trying experience at times for even so devoted a friend as was Dr. Watson.

One was jealous of Holmes of course. Yes, of course, that was it. One was jealous. Jealous of his mastery in all things, both material and mystical . . . he was a sort of god in his way, seated on some Anglo-Saxon Olympus of his own design and making! Yes, there was no question about it, he had given me an acute inferiority complex!

221 B Baker Street

Here dwell together still two men of note
Who never lived and so can never die:
How very near they seem, yet how remote
That age before the world went all awry.
But still the game's afoot for those with ears

Attuned to catch the distant view-halloo:
England is England yet, for all our fears
Only those things the heart *believes* are true.

A yellow fog swirls past the window-pane
As night descends upon this fabled street:
A lonely hansom splashes through the rain,
The ghostly gas lamps fail at twenty feet.
Here, though the world explode, these two survive,
And it is always eighteen ninety-five.

March, 1942.

This poem by my good friend Vincent Starrett, poet, novelist, mystery writer, and book reviewer on the Chicago *Tribune* causes me to wonder why some sculptor has not been inspired to carve such thoughts out in stone. London owes itself and many millions more of us all over the world a statue to these two men "who never lived and so can never die," and who have done so much to perpetuate a colorful fragment of history at the turn of the century in dear old Londontown.

In John Dickson Carr's excellent biography of Sir Arthur Conan Doyle, he relates that Sir Arthur felt at one time that he had created a sort of Frankenstein that he could not escape from. And so he decided to kill Mr. Sherlock Holmes at the Reichenbach Falls and be done with him. Public outrage at this callous murder of Mr. Holmes by Sir Arthur was so great that Sir Arthur was literally forced to bring him back from the dead and continue the adventures.

I frankly admit that in 1946 I was placed in a somewhat similar predicament—but *I* could not kill Mr. Holmes. So I decided to run away from him. However, to all intents and purposes I might just as well have killed him. My friends excoriated me for my dastardly behavior, and for a while my long-time friendship with Nigel Bruce suffered severe and recurring shocks. The Music Corporation of America, who represented me at that time, treated me as if I were "sick-sick-sick."

My "sickness" was treated by Mr. Jules Stein, head of MCA, and by my friends as a temporary affliction—I was to be "babied" along until I had recovered my senses. It was in August, 1946, that Jules phoned me in Philadelphia, where I was appearing in a play and headed for a New York opening. A new seven-year Sherlock Holmes radio contract had been negotiated by MCA—was I about ready to return to the Coast? It was then that the seriousness of my "condition" became evident. The climax was reached in a long-distance telephone call from Jules in Los Angeles—*No!* I was not coming back—I had sold my house in Bel Air and was heading for the Plymouth Theatre in New York. Supremely confident and relaxed, sipping a gin and tonic, I lounged in a comfortable chair in my room at the Ritz Hotel, Philadelphia. Eventually, I seemed to break through the clouds of dismay and bewilderment occasioned by my ingratitude, and I shall forever be grateful to Jules Stein for his acceptance of my decision—and his most generous attentions to my well-being on my return to New York, which eventualized in a contract that he made for me in 1947 to appear as Dr. Sloper in Jed Harris's memorable production of Henry James' classic *The Heiress*.

Ever since I said good-by to Mr. Sherlock Holmes there has lingered somewhere inside of me a sentimental attachment for this memorable character. I am not gifted enough to pay him the tribute I would—but a few years ago I made an attempt. And so by kind permission of Esquire Magazine, I give you

DAYDREAM

I had always loved the county of Sussex. It held for me some of the happiest memories of my life—my early childhood. Early in June I had slipped down, for a few days' much-needed rest, to the little village of Heathfield, to dream again of the past and to try to shut out, for a brief period at least, both the present and the future.

The last afternoon of my holiday I was walking across the gentle countryside when I was rudely stung by a bee. Startled, I grabbed a handful of soft earth and applied it to the sting; it's an old-fashioned remedy I had learned as a child. Suddenly I became aware that the air about me was swarming with bees. It was then I noticed the small house with a thatched roof and a well-kept garden, with beehives at one end, that Mrs. Messenger, my landlady, had so often mentioned. She had told me that "he" had come to live in the thatched cottage many years ago. As he bothered no one, no one bothered him, which is an old English custom. Now, in 1946, he had become almost a legend.

I saw him now, on this late summer afternoon, seated in his garden, a rug over his knees, reading a book. In spite of his great age he wore no reading glasses; and though he made no movement there was a curious sense of animation in his apparently inanimate body. He had the majestic beauty of a very old tree: his features were sharp, emphasizing a particularly prominent nose. He was smoking a meerschaum pipe with obvious relish. Suddenly he looked up and our eyes met.

"Won't you come in?" he called in a surprisingly firm voice.

"Thank you, sir," I replied, "but I have no right to impose on your privacy."

"If it were an imposition I should not have invited you," he replied. "Pull up a chair and sit down."

He gave me a quick glance of penetrating comprehension. As I sat down I had an odd feeling that I was dreaming.

"I'm sorry to see that you have been stung by one of my bees."

I smiled; the smile was intended to say that it didn't matter.

"You must forgive the little fellow," he continued. "He's paid for it with his life."

"It seems unfair that he should have had to," I said.

"No," mused the old man, "it's a law of nature. 'God moves in a mysterious way His wonders to perform.' May I order you some tea?"

"Thank you, no," I said.

"I used to be a prolific coffee drinker myself. I have always found tea an insipid substitute by comparison." He smiled. "Do you live here?"

"No, sir, I'm on a short holiday. But I was born near here."

"Really!" The smile touched his eyes. "It's a comforting little corner of the earth, isn't it, especially in times like these?"

"Have you lived here all through the war, sir?" I asked.

"Yes." The smile disappeared. Slowly he pulled an old Webley revolver from under the rug which covered his knees. "If they had come, six of them would not have lived to tell the story. . . . I learned to use this thing many years ago. I have never missed my man."

He cradled the gun in his hand and left me momentarily for that world which to each of us is his own.

There was quite a pause before I had the courage to ask, "Were you in the First World War, sir?"

"Indirectly—and you?" He replaced the gun on his knees.

"I'm an Inspector at Scotland Yard."

"I thought so!" As he spoke the book in his lap fell to the ground. I reached down, picked it up, and handed it back to him.

"Thank you. And how are things at the Yard these days?"

"Modern science and equipment have done much to help us," I said.

"Yesss." His hand went to a pocket and brought forth an old magnifying glass. "When I was a young man they used things like this. Modern inventions have proved to be great timesavers, but they have dulled our natural instincts and made us lazy—most of us at least."

"You may be right, sir. But we either go forward or back."

He put the magnifying glass and revolver back into two voluminous pockets of an old sports jacket which had leather patches at the elbows. Then he took a deep breath and released it in a long-drawn-out sigh.

"I've followed your career very closely, Inspector. The Yard is fortunate in your services."

"That's kind of you, sir."

"Not at all. I knew your father quite well at one time."

"You knew my father!" The words stumbled out.

"Yesss. He was a brilliant man, your father. He interested me deeply. His mind was balanced precariously on that thin line between sanity and insanity. Is he still living?"

"No, sir; he died in 1936."

The old man nodded his head reflectively. "These fellows with their newfangled ideas would have found him intensely interesting subject matter. What do you call them? Psycho-psychoanalysts!"

"Psychoanalysis can be very helpful, don't you think, sir?"

"No, I don't. I't's a lot of rubbish—*psychoanalysis!* It's nothing more than a simple process of deduction by elimination."

We talked of crime and its different ways of detection, until a cool breeze crossed the garden with its warning of the day's departure.

He rose slowly to a full six feet and held out his hand. "I must go in now. It's been pleasant talking with you."

"I am deeply indebted to you, sir." I wanted to say so much more, but felt oddly constrained.

He held out the book in his hand, *The Adventures of Sherlock Holmes.* "Do you know these stories? They are often overdramatized; but they make good reading." Once again the smile danced in his eyes.

I acknowledged an intimate acquaintance with all the works to which he referred and he seemed greatly pleased by my references to "The Master." He accompanied me slowly to the road and we spoke briefly of S. C. Roberts, and Christopher Morley and Vincent Starrett.

"The adventures as written by our dear friend Doctor Watson mean a great deal to me at my time of life," he reflected. "As someone once said, 'Remembrance is the only sure immortality we can know.'"

On my return, Mrs. Messenger gave me an urgent telegram from Scotland Yard, requesting my immediate return. I didn't speak to her of my visit to "him." I was afraid she might consider me as childish as the youngsters in Heathfield who still believe "he" was the great Sherlock Holmes.

Which they did, until they reached an age when he was dismissed, together with Santa Claus and those other worthwhile people who, for a brief, beautiful period, are more real than reality itself.

14

The Heiress

It wasn't instinct, (or was it perhaps?) but just luck that we decided to return to New York in June of 1946. Most of our friends considered us mad and pleaded with us not to throw away my career and our home. However, there were many contributing factors that influenced this move at this time. Los Angeles had become a very cosmopolitan city during the war, and our war work had been most stimulating to us both. Without it, and no longer meeting continuously with interesting people from all over the world, we felt the community would slip back into a conventional pattern that might prove to be a tremendous letdown. Also we felt I had accomplished as much as was coming to me in motion pictures at this time, and that I needed another springboard in order to return successfully. I had had seven years of Sherlock Holmes and was not only tired and bored with the series, but felt myself losing ground in other fields of endeavor. And last but not least I was literally aching to get back to my first love, the theater.

We certainly had no idea how lucky we were to be getting out at this time, for in the next two years motion pictures were to take one of the biggest nose dives in their history.

Ouida had rewritten and modernized an old play called *Jealousy*, and retitled it *Obsession*. There are only two characters in the play. It was a melodrama that required sustaining by every means at the theater's disposal. Stewart Chaney designed a lovely set. Reginald Denham did a most expert job of directing. But the major burden fell on Miss Eugenie Leontovitch and myself as a newly married couple very much in love, but with "a skeleton in the closet." It was her skeleton. I had married her not knowing she had had an elderly lover who refused to leave her alone in her new-found happiness. This third character never appeared except on the telephone. In her efforts to shake him off I became suspicious of her. When I found out who he was and suspecting her of still carrying on an affair with him I murdered him. The murder was to be the perfect crime and she was never to know I had killed him. The final scene was a complete breakdown on my part and a lengthy confession to her of my crime and the suggestion that it was only a matter of time before the police would arrest me and charge me with murder. It was a wonderful postgraduate course for us both and we met with considerable success to begin with. But as a very hot summer developed we were less successful as we toured the Middle West. Coming to the Plymouth Theatre in New York in September of 1946 we received mixed reviews and managed to run only three weeks. In spite of Ouida's work on the play and all our efforts it was generally considered old-fashioned and audiences were not particularly interested in watching Miss Leontovitch and myself walking a tightrope for over two hours! Had we brought the play into New York at the end of a season for a limited run we might have got away with it.

A Mr. Reeves, who had a lovely apartment at 10 Gracie Square in New York, overlooking the East River, wanted our house in Bel Air. So we arranged to swap places, each living rent-free, as it were, with an option to buy at the end of a year.

Of the dogs only three remained to us. Cullum and Judy and Happy were all buried in our garden. We boarded Leo and Moritza until we were settled and could fly them East. Bunty was to travel with us. Cynthia, now seven years old, was deeply upset at leaving her home.

Our year's tenure at 10 Gracie Square was a very happy

experience. The ships of all nations were continuously passing up and down the East River day and night. The apartment was comfortable, even if the furnishings and decoration were not our taste. Snow came early and we had a
white Christmas. Cynthia, and the dogs who had been flown
out from California, had never seen snow before and went
wild with excitement. Moritza (the black German shepherd)
would charge madly at a snow drift and then roll over and
over in it trying to eat it away! We had some nice parties
with many old friends. Richard Tauber and his Diana were
in town and one night Richard went to say good night to
Cynthia in her room. It was a memorable occasion. Richard
cradled the little child in his arms and sang her to sleep . . .
sang to her in a most exquisite, controlled pianissimo. I have
known of no lyric tenor like him, save John McCormack.

Only one thing troubled me. I could not find a play or
anyone willing to consider me for one. One well-known
author came to see me. I wanted to do his play about King
David, and there was no question that *he* wanted *me*. But
both he and the producer decided against me because of my
seven years' identification with Sherlock Holmes. They felt
this identification would be a hazard to them. So during the
season of 1946–47 I did nothing but guest spots on radio,
not one of them worth mentioning except an appearance
with Fred Allen and a couple with The Theatre Guild of the
Air. Fred Allen was one of the most generous stars I have
ever worked with in any medium. Added to this he had a
brilliant mind and a caustic humor. Most of his programs
were contemporary satires. He had contempt for radio as a
medium and his loathing of television was unsparingly expressed in a piece he wrote, I think it was for *Life* magazine.
I think he enjoyed having me on his program as a guest star
because he always wrote for me most amusing and intelligent
"spots." I say "wrote" because, although he had writers, he
was the originator of a great deal of his material, and most of
the best ideas in his scripts emanated from him. He was a devout Catholic and never missed Mass on a Sunday if he could

possibly help it. He was also extremely charitable. There were old friends of his that he literally "kept," and if he left town for any time his secretary was instructed that remittances were to be sent out regularly every week.

One of his writers told me a delightful story about Fred Allen, a story that exemplifies his kindly if caustic humor and his indomitable hold on realities. There was a Major Bowes connected with this story. Major Bowes had a very successful radio program at this time and was also a devout Catholic and extremely wealthy. He had just died.

It was Christmastime and Fred and his writer were wandering up Fifth Avenue. As they passed St. Patrick's Cathedral Fred indicated to his friend that he would like to go in for a few minutes. His friend, who was Jewish, decided to wait outside. As he waited, Fred's friend became aware of the big "face lifting" job that was being done externally on the Cathedral at that time. It must have cost a pretty penny and he said so to Fred as they walked home.

"Granted the Catholic Church is a wealthy organization, but that's a lot of money to spend on a church," said his writer-friend.

"Sure—sure," replied Fred.

"How much do you suppose it cost?"

"Oh, about three million dollars."

"Wheeeww!" gasped the writer. "In return for a weekly Mass to be said for him for eternity after his death, do you suppose some rich guy made an outright gift?"

"Sure—sure," answered Fred dryly. "Major Bowes— He died with Cardinal Spellman's hand in his pocket."

I had always heard that Cardinal Spellman was a magician at raising funds, and that equally he was a most dedicated priest of the Church—witness his visits overseas every Christmas to spend this Holy Day with the armed forces of the United States.

One day in the spring of 1947 Jed Harris sent me a play, *The Heiress*, by Mr. and Mrs. Augustus Goetz, from the novel of Henry James entitled *Washington Square*.

As *Washington Square* it had failed miserably on a tryout in Boston earlier in the year. Jed had seen it in Boston and his keen, perceptive, professional eye had spotted a quality in it that excited him. So he bought the play. In the two leading roles he saw but two people, Wendy Hiller and myself. If he could get both of us he would do the play in the fall. Failing to get either one of us, he would not. But as with all real creative inspirations Jed had not asked himself "How?" He was flat broke at the time, but the entire production was complete in his mind and he was avidly changing and rewriting the play to meet his requirements.

I read the play and loved it. Then I gave it to Ouida, and for one of the few times in our lives we did not agree. She was not anxious for me to do it, and not happy about my playing Dr. Sloper. I have never been able to pin-point her reasons, but I believe her reaction was based on the major change that had to take place in me as an actor if I were to play this role, and I believe her reaction to have been a very simple one. Leading man or villain, my roles previously, in all mediums, had had a texture of glamor. Dr. Sloper was in his late fifties, a difficult complex man, *and!* as with all doctors of his time he wore a beard! (For more information on this you must inquire of my wife.)

A few nights later (we were going for the summer to Sharon, Connecticut) Jed insisted on seeing us both. He brought with him Ruth and Augustus Goetz. After a brief introduction Jed went after Ouida with that enormous charm he has when he needs it. I was left with Ruth and Augustus Goetz. But Ouida had known Jed previously and was immune to his magic. I heard her telling Jed she would like nothing better than to have him direct me. Then, as most writers will, particularly Ouida, who had been renowned for her sound construction in pictures, she proceeded to reconstruct the play along lines as she saw it. I indicated to Ruth and Gus to let Jed and Ouida go to it—good creative minds like theirs might come up with something of value. But, whatever happened, I told them, I intended to do the play and that I was fascinated by Dr. Sloper, who I believed would open up a whole new professional life for me.

There were drinks and sandwiches and the battle between Ouida and Jed raged on.

"Oh, come on, Jed," I heard Ouida say, "I have known you too long so I'm immune to your charms—just listen to me." And they went to it again.

I liked Gus at once, very much. With Ruth I felt less secure. I can't remember if she told me, or Gus or Jed, but I remember someone telling me that Ruth's personal life had been influenced by something in the nature of the tragedy of Washington Square.

The meeting ended somewhere around 2 A.M., and as was to be expected with two such dynamic personalities, Jed and Ouida had agreed about nothing! I took the play up to Sharon, Connecticut, with me and gave it much thought. Ouida was too bright to be ignored, but her version of the play would require major revisions, and I knew Jed was not sympathetic to them. So I made my decision and told Ouida, who wished me luck. "At least you will be working with a great director," she said.

Then one night Jed turned up in the country without any warning and told us he could get Wendy Hiller, and he must know my decision at once before signing her. Of course my answer was, "Yes—I'm yours, body and soul." I heard Ouida mumble, "You better be careful because it may *be* body and soul. Jed has the charm of the devil, and I mean the *devil!*"

From that moment on, throughout the rest of the summer, Jed phoned me frequently. "Got your script handy?" he would ask. "Well write down this line. It's for you at the end of the first scene—got it?—how's that for a line?"

"You are a genius, Jed," and I almost believed it. Our "honeymoon" was starting off most delightfully!

The house we had in Sharon, Connecticut, was a charming one. It stood on a high hill in considerable grounds of its own overlooking the Berkshire Hills. We were very happy there, except for domestic problems in regard to our help. A Mexican cook and an English maid who had both been with us for over ten years quit at the end of the first month. Both had learned, from some "political" influence, to think and refer to us as "capitalists!" From then on to this day we were often to meet with this "accusation" by employees! Wages doubled and tripled, and in most cases their end of the bargain became more and more unsatisfactorily fulfilled. The house in Sharon was completely dependent for water on a primitive pump, which was continually breaking down, and there was a plague of some kind of beetle that ate up all the lawn and destroyed the trees. However, we enjoyed good weather, and with the help of a wonderful local Lithuanian woman we managed to keep the house clean and produce three meals a day, on time! When she feels like it, Ouida is a very fine chef. But her dishes are all somewhat complicated, highly seasoned, and take hours and hours and hours to produce. Her salmon mousse and her duck are *pièces de résistance*. Cynthia also contributed with chocolate fudge and angel cake. You can't buy a better angel cake anywhere. When we had week-end guests they were warned of conditions and expected to help, which they did with varying stages of incompetence.

Mr. Reeves had bought our home in California and we had bought a house at 9 East Ninety-second Street. The buying price on our apartment at 10 Gracie Square was prohibitive and the maintenance exorbitant, and I refused to buy so many square feet of just air! Once again Ouida organized our move into the new house completely alone. I was rehearsing *The Heiress*. Our furniture and effects were transported from California across the country by road. One day two colossal vans arrived at our door and the bill was backbreaking! What with alterations to the house, painting, and a new Esso oil heater in place of the old inadequate coal one, it was essential that *The Heiress* be a success. Early in August, with both Wendy's and my contracts signed, Jed had not only been stony broke but could not find a co-producer, with money, to finance his venture. The failure of *Washington Square* in Boston in January was a hopeless handicap. The story is told that one very hot Sunday early in August Jed took Freddie Finklehoff for a walk in Central Park and so brilliantly did he dramatize his play that Freddie was completely enthralled. It is said that whenever Jed saw the slightest sign of weakening in Freddie he would walk him on to another location in the Park. At last, in self-defense, sweating like a pig and completely exhausted, Freddie capitulated and gave Jed a check for some $50,000 dollars!

Rehearsals for *The Heiress* were unique. I have never experienced anything quite like them. There was to be no try-out period out of town. We were to open "cold" at the Biltmore Theatre on September 30. Four weeks to the day we started rehearsals. We arrived at the theater and were allocated our dressing rooms. Jed insisted that from the very beginning I wear my beard in order that I might become so used to it that I would eventually be completely unconscious of it. I looked about my bare dressing room as I put on my beard, and my imagination ran riot. There were glorious dreams of tremendous success and equally vivid pictures of a hopeless failure! Then down to the stage, where a long table had been set up with chairs for the cast, Mr. Harris, and our stage manager, Mr. Shapiro. Punctually at 11 A.M. we were all in place. Wendy Hiller, myself, Patricia Collinge, Kate Raht, Peter Cookson, and the other four small roles, a cast of nine. In the theater about row ten on the aisle sat Mr. and Mrs. Augustus Goetz, the authors. A moment later Jed entered with Freddie Finklehoff, now co-producer. Jed strode past Mr. and Mrs. Goetz without so much as acknowledging them. Freddie stopped for a moment to greet them. Jed came up onto the stage and welcomed us all in a most friendly manner. He then introduced the cast to one another, announcing the roles that each of us would play. Then he turned and, looking out into the theater, he said, "Those two people sitting out there are the authors." Then turning back to us with an impudent smile, he continued, "If I catch any of you talking to those people out there you will be sacked immediately. Mr. and Mrs. Goetz know nothing about this play. I have completely rewritten it. Now let's get to work!"

For ten days from 11 A.M. to 5 P.M. we sat around that table and read and reread that play. Jed had done a wonderful job on his homework. There was no facet of any situation or character that he had not delved into deeply, and what is more he was always right in his analysis. He had our complete confidence and respect in a matter of hours. By the end of the first day (I do not exaggerate) we were completely inspired, and so remained until our opening. We asked questions, and in sheer self-defense strove to find something he had not thought of, but all to no avail. From about the fifth or sixth day we became restless and edgy, just as Jed had wanted us to. If any of us got up and started to walk around as we spoke our lines we were ordered to sit down again. Every day at 3:30 P.M. we had tea, provided by the management in Wendy's dressing room. Mrs. Finklehoff, Miss Ella Logan, would bring in homemade cookies and Scottish scones. She was working at the Palace Theatre in vaudeville, at the time, to provide the last $5000 necessary for our production costs. She just turned over her net salary to her husband, who turned it over to production.

At the end of the tenth day of rehearsal, Jed said to us, "All right, tomorrow at 11 A.M. we get on our feet." And in the remaining two days of that week Jed put the complete play on its feet, as if he had done it all a hundred times before. The movements and business he gave us during those two days, with minor exceptions, were those we followed on the opening night. On the Monday of the third week the set and furnishings were brought in and we worked in them daily. We had been excused rehearsals from time to time for costume fittings, and on the Monday of the fourth week they were all delivered to our dressing rooms. Both the period set and costumes were in exquisite taste and beautifully made. During this fourth week we dress-rehearsed on alternate nights with an invited audience. Monday, Wednesday, and Friday we worked alone with Jed. Tuesday, Thursday, and Saturday we performed to an audience, and on the following Monday we opened. I don't think there was one of us that came down to the theater for that opening that had the slightest doubt we would be a success. We received a tremendous ovation. But that was no indication as to what the critics might say. On Tuesday the *Times* and the *Tribune* were lukewarm, and I said to Ouida, "Well, darling, I guess you were right, we didn't make it." I had a radio rehearsal for the Theatre Guild at 2 P.M. that Tuesday, and it was there that I learned that all the afternoon papers were for us. Then Jed and Freddie made a brilliant publicity move. They paid for a full page on Wednesday morning in the *Times* and the *Tribune* and printed in full the reviews of Mr. Morehouse and Mr. Garland from competitive newspapers! Also, these two reviews and excerpts from others including the *Times* and the *Tribune*, carefully chosen, were blown up and exhibited outside the theater, and except for the first few performances we were virtually sold out all season. What an experience it was. And what was all this nonsense Ouida and others had talked about Jed being difficult. How could they be so unfair! He was certainly no saint (but then who wants to be a saint. What a dreary existence, forever holding on to one's dubious halo) but he was certainly no devil. Throughout the entire run of the play he was out front at least twice a month. We never knew when. Before the last scene the stage manager would send word to each of us, "Everyone on stage at the end of the play, please," and we knew it was Jed to see and talk with us, to make some minor alteration or adjustments or to get us back on the line where we might unintentionally have slipped off a little.

Re: Jed's and my "honeymoon!" For months in New York I would go to the theater and there on my dressing-room make-up table would be a piece of torn paper on which was written, "Love you—love you—love you—" signed Jed, or "What a joy to work with you," signed, "Ever yours,"

Jed, or "You are not only a wonderful actor, you are a wonderful man," signed Jed. I learned later that he had heard of my exploits in World War I for which I had received the Military Cross. His admiration and affection for me at this time were completely sincere and I shall always be most deeply appreciative of his warm friendship.

A year or so later when we went out on tour Jed came to Philadelphia to re-rehearse us, and then again when we opened in Chicago and in Los Angeles. His dedication to this play was unquestionably reflected in our performances. I remember Pat Collinge saying to me as the curtain was about to go up on the last performance in Boston, "Good luck, dear Basil. Let's make this one as good as our opening night in New York nearly two years ago." And we did. It was during these last weeks that Jed asked me to do another play with him. I read the play and didn't like it, and I told him so. He called me one night in Cincinnati and blew my head off. Then he called Ouida, who hadn't even read the play (I knew she wouldn't like it), and tore her to pieces! I talked to Pat Collinge about it. All she said was, "Looks like your 'honeymoon' with Jed is about over!" And it was. I have only met him once since then, on a train. He tried to avoid meeting me, but I forced myself on him and was nearly frozen to death for my trouble. Dear Jed, it was wonderful while it lasted, and I thank you from the bottom of my heart. Maybe it was wise for us both to have ended our "honeymoon" as we did. Who knows? There are worse endings.

Shortly after we opened *The Heiress* in New York I was the cause of very nearly closing the play. It was my habit each morning to walk the dogs. At Ninety-sixth Street and Fifth Avenue the park is some eight feet above the sidewalk. It was a nice secluded spot with trees and brambles and grass, where I could let the dogs off the lead, and they loved it. The perfumes of Canine No. 1 and No. 2 were most pungent there and seemed to be most conducive to the purposes of our morning visits. On this morning of November 13 I was aware of some broken glass. I picked it up and dropped it onto the sidewalk of Fifth Avenue below, where I figured it would be more visible and do less harm. In a split second I was conscious of falling. Then there followed a complete blackout. When I came to I found myself cradled in the arms of an elderly woman on the sidewalk on Fifth Avenue. Then I looked at my right hand and passed out again. Except for the skin it was completely separated at the wrist from my arm by about half an inch. When I came to again there were several people standing idly and inquisitively by. The dogs had somehow found their way to me and stood waiting, curiously. A policeman came up and said a New York Yankee bonesetter had his offices across the street. So the policeman and the dear lady and I and the dogs called on him. The doctor gave me a sedative and put my arm in a temporary sling. Then the ambulance arrived, called by the policeman. Two very efficient looking men walked into the doctor's office and one of them said, "Sign here."

I looked at my arm and replied, "With what?"

Anyway I told them I didn't need them as I lived only a few blocks away and was going home. And home I went with the policeman and the dear lady leading the dogs.

Ouida took one look at me and nearly fainted herself. Then I went off to my own doctor who gave me another sedative and took me in a taxi to Doctors Hospital. There I was X-rayed, and Ouida joined me. This was about 11 A.M. I lay on a cot in a small room downstairs for hours. Doctors came and went and examined my X rays outside. An anesthetist visited me periodically, but seeing there was nothing doing left me to administer sleep to some other patient. I could hear Ouida talking incessantly, the question being apparently whether to use the knife or manipulate. The consensus seemed to be to use the knife. In the meanwhile Ouida had phoned Jed, who had phoned *his* doctor, who had phoned a Dr. Balensweig. About 5 P.M. a short, rather fierce red-haired man walked into my room.

"Is this the patient?" he said. (He had seen the X rays.)

"Well, put him to sleep and let's get on with it." It was Dr. Balensweig, of course. I knew by this time that it would be impossible for me to play that night, but I said, "Look, Doctor, I've got to 'go on' tomorrow, come what may."

"You will," he replied and they put me to sleep.

It appears that Dr. Balensweig's coming had created a furore in Doctors Hospital. This was not his hospital, and to add insult to injury I am told he ordered the other doctors around, using them as his assistants! The fracas meant nothing to me—all I know is Dr. Balensweig set my broken bones in a most miraculous manner. (The other doctors all having said it was impossible.) I awakened an hour or so later in a private room with my arm in a cast, resting on a pillow, and through that first haze I saw Ouida and Jed and "Gussy" Goetz standing around my bed. Gus was crying. "I'll be on tomorrow night, Jed," I said. I was as high as a kite.

"You were on tonight," Jed replied. "The whole time they had you 'out' you were going through the play, speaking everyone's part—you bloody old ham!" and Gus cried some more. Then I slowly and peacefully went out again and slept till morning. I was up early and according to Dr. Balensweig's instructions I was in his office on Madison Avenue by 10 A.M.

"I *can* 'go on' tonight, can't I, Doctor?" I said.

"But of course. Why not? You're O.K.," he replied, and my heart took a triple beat. He later told me that going back to work immediately probably negated any possible shock effects.

Jed called me at home and said there would be a make-up man at the theater every performance to make me up.

"Get rid of him," I said. "I can do it myself. I would rather."

Jed continued, "I'll come up to the house. I've worked out all your business for you so you can do everything you have always done with your left hand only."

"Don't worry," said. "I have been through it all myself —it's quite easy."

Pure bravura, but it was all a very exciting experience.

My dear old colored dresser, John Hart, called for me that night in a taxi and we arrived at the theater about an hour earlier than usual. I went slowly but surely to work, with my left hand only of course, even to the putting on of my beard. At "the quarter" I was ready, made-up, and dressed.

Since Dr. Sloper opens the play, entering into his living room after having delivered a neighbor's baby, Jed was afraid that the broken arm in a sling might cause a laugh. It never occurred to me, I was much too "high." After my first scene Jed came backstage.

"You're doing fine," he said. "But bring it down a little— you're overexcited. But you're great, just great. We all love you."

At the conclusion of the play, when the curtain rose for the calls, the entire company stepped downstage, and facing me with the audience gave me a tremendous ovation. It was then that my pent-up emotions rose up like a flood. It was over. I had done it, and would do it again and again and again; which I did for eight weeks. There were actually those who came back and thought Dr. Sloper was supposed to have his right arm in a cast and a sling! Why, I shall never know. It was nowhere so indicated in the play. Perhaps it was that I was so deeply convinced in all I was saying and doing, and Dr. Sloper was such a challenging role. And so before leaving him I would like, very briefly, to state his case. There were those who came backstage with understanding and those who had none. These latter would say, "Oh you wicked man. Up to your evil tricks again," or something equally puerile and silly.

Dr. Sloper was a gentleman and a dedicated children's doctor. He had married young, a very beautiful woman with whom he was deeply in love. They had gone to Paris for their honeymoon and when they returned she was pregnant. She died in childbirth leaving him with a daughter, Catherine. He worshiped this child as a baby, but not so much for herself, as in the image of her mother. Then later when she

grew up it was obvious to all that she had none of her
mother's attributes and nothing of her beauty. Catherine became self-conscious, and Dr. Sloper grew intolerant. I make
no excuses for his intolerance, but I understand it. Both he
and Catherine were deeply to be pitied. Then turning thirty,
the heiress to a considerable fortune, Catherine is introduced
to a Morris Townsend at a party at the end of Act I. Dr.
Sloper realizes from Morris's rather superficial manner and
conversation that this is someone to take note of and beware
of. Morris Townsend makes love to Catherine and proposed
to her. He is curtly turned down by Dr. Sloper as a fortune
hunter. Dr. Sloper then takes Catherine to Paris with him—
a bitter experience, during which he lives in the past with
his dead wife while Catherine waits daily for letters from
Morris. On their return Dr. Sloper realizes that the trip to
Paris has done nothing for Catherine except increase her love
for Morris Townsend, and in a cruel, bitter scene he cuts
Catherine out of his will. Now Catherine and Morris have
planned to run away together this very night. But when Morris hears what the doctor has done and that Catherine will
only inherit her mother's money, he deserts her as Dr.
Sloper had most surely known that he would. The play ends
tragically with Dr. Sloper's death as his daughter denounces
him. Then Morris returns and finds in Catherine a granite
replica of her father. She plays with him mercilessly like a
cat with a mouse, and eventually orders him out of the house
as the curtain falls on the virtual assurance that Catherine
will one day die an old spinster, a living reminder to all of her
father's image.

There is no villain here, unless it be Morris Townsend. It
is rather the tragic story of intolerance, lack of understanding, ineptitude on Catherine's part, and a great love that eventually bordered on, if it did not actually reach at times,
hatred. A powerful play, most sensitively written and directed, and one of the most challenging parts I have ever
been called upon to play.

It was Easter of 1949 that I became involved in the most appalling *faux pas* of my life, one that, to this day, brings me out in a mucksweat every time I think of it. It was Good Friday morning and I had returned home a few days before from the tour of *The Heiress* and I was still very full of our success. Ouida and I had just enjoyed a leisurely breakfast in bed together and I had retired to shave. I had soap all over my face when the telephone rang. Ouida answered it, calling to me. "It's for you, darling. Bishop Sheen."

What on earth was she talking about?

"Darling, please," she continued, "do get on, its for you. Bishop Sheen."

Now what ass did I know who wanted to talk to me this morning and would think to dream up this ridiculous means of getting me to the phone. Anyway, whoever it was, I was in a good mood and would play along with his crummy joke. So I picked up the phone in my room.

"Hello, Bish, you old poop, why aren't you in church this morning?"

"May I speak to Basil Rathbone please," a voice with a slight Irish inflection replied.

"No, I'm afraid you can't. He's out in the Park flying his kite!"

"When do you expect him back?" the voice on the phone continued.

"Well, his mummy likes him home before dark of course. But he's such a willful little boy—I say, cut it out, who is it?"

"Bishop Sheen," the voice insisted.

"Don't tell me!" I sank deeper in! "Now don't tell me it's that dear little cock robin of Horn and Hardart fame!"

Silence reigned at the other end of the phone.

"All right, Jed [Jed Harris], Freddie [Freddie Finklehoff], Peter [Peter Cookson], who the hell is it?"

"Bishop Sheen," the voice steadily persisted. "I have two seats for Mr. Rathbone in St. Patrick's Cathedral for the three-hour service today over which I shall preside. He can pick them up at the Roosevelt Hotel desk at his convenience.

Thank you." And the phone at the other end went dead, and I began to wish *I* were. I called the Roosevelt Hotel. It was true the seats were there! Ye gods, what could I do? Nothing, just drown the whole incident and refuse to admit it was me on the phone. Ignore it, write a gracious formal thank-you letter in due course and let the Bishop think what he would. Some time later I met with him at his domicile on Park Avenue and Thirty-fourth Street. I had forty minutes alone with him: forty memorable minutes during which my flagrant indiscretion was never so much as mentioned. How had all this come about? My dear friend Sister Mary Marguerite at Mercy College, Detroit, had arranged the whole thing. She knew how much I admired Bishop Sheen, particularly via his outstanding and brilliant half-hour T.V. series, and she had put the wheels in motion through a certain monsignor who was very close to the Bishop.

My "crack" on the phone with the Bishop about "cock robin" was based on a story I am reliably informed is true. During rehearsals of one of his T.V. shows the Bishop had gone across the road to a Horn & Hardart for a cup of coffee. He had done so in full regalia. Completely engrossed in his forthcoming program the Bishop was aware of no one and nothing, including the fact that he was resplendently dressed and wore on his head his little red beanie. An attendant at Horn & Hardart's, clearing up the tables, looked at the Bishop quizzically, probably thinking he was a guest star on Milton Berle's program, which was rehearsing and later performing nearby! Passing the Bishop's table, he quipped, "Hello there cock robin and what can we do for you?" Bishop Sheen must treasure the incident; he has a wonderful sense of humor. He usually started his T.V. programs with a joke. There was one I particularly liked. His entrance was always magnificent. He strode onto the stage, using to full effect his colorful "costume." During the tremendous applause in the theater that inevitably greeted him, those deep-set Savonorola eyes virtually demolished the camera lenses, but there was a hint of a smile in the mouth. "Tonight," he said on this particular occasion, "I want to read you a letter I have received. This letter makes me very happy for it would seem to indicate that my little talks with you each week reach out and encompass many people of varying faiths." The letter he read went approximately as follows. "Dear Bishop. We listen to you every week and enjoy you so much. If by any chance some household chore should be engaging my attention at the time of your program my little boy always calls out to me, 'Hey, Mom, quick, Rabbi Sheen on the air.'" The letter was signed by a Mrs. Shapiro. In an earlier chapter I have referred to Bishop Sheen as an entertainer rather than an actor. This somewhat arbitrary classification I believe to be justified, but it cannot do justice to a personality and dedication that defies pigeonholing. In conclusion, the Good Friday service at St. Patrick's Cathedral was one of the most inspiring and dramatic experiences I have ever been exposed to. The understanding and appreciation of "good theater" was deeply impressive and Bishop Sheen, who spoke periodically during the three hours on the last words from the Cross, was spiritually and intellectually most moving. His command of our language and his simplicity in the use of it were a lesson to all of us.

15

Good-by, My Friend

In the fall of 1950 I sold the house on 9 East Ninety-second regretfully. Ouida had done a superb job of its decoration, but the burden was too much for me to carry, and the problem of "help" was growing steadily worse. We moved into an apartment in a new modern building, just around the corner from where we had lived, and in this apartment we were to stay for the next three and a half years.

Sometime late in 1951 I suggested to Ouida that she write a Sherlock Holmes play for me. I had been away from Mr. Holmes for approximately five years and felt I might risk a renewal of my acquaintance with him. Ouida read all *The Adventures* very carefully, making copious notes. After some months she came up with what seemed a masterly construction, using material from five of the Conan Doyle stories. I was immensely intrigued. We did a lot of thinking and talking and discussing. It looked like a "sure fire" success, especially since I was still closely identified with the character of Sherlock Holmes, by which name I was still more often than not greeted by strangers almost everywhere I went. I was trying out my *Evening with Basil Rathbone* around the country and each time that I returned home for a rest period I was delighted by Ouida's significant progress. Bearing in mind that the play would have to be O.K.'d by the Conan Doyle estate, Ouida had stayed closely to legitimate Sherlockiana. Wherever she could she used the original dialogue, borrowed from any and all of "the adventures," and where this was not possible had written a most excellent facsimile thereof. It was a workmanlike job, and most faithful to the traditions that made these stories classics. Mr. Adrian Conan Doyle came to New York (the executor of his father's estate) on private business. We met with him and his charming Dutch wife and found them both most enthusiastic about the play. Adrian told us he was sure it would have his father's blessing. Adrian Conan Doyle is a devout member of the British Psychical Research Society. It pleased him that his father and mine had known each other in South Africa in years gone-by. He offered to prepare me for a future meeting with his father's spirit, which he estimated might take as long as six months, and invited both Ouida and myself to visit him in Algiers, where he was living at that time. Adrian indicated he spoke with his father frequently. These matters have always intrigued me deeply and I would be the last to doubt their reality, any more than I doubt the appearance of the spirit of Hamlet's father to his son before three witnesses, Horatio, Marcellus, and Bernado. I am under oath to Adrian not to repeat much of what he told me at this time in regard to his own and other reliable persons' experiences in this field of psychical research. I can only assure you, my dear reader, that this is no matter for hasty conclusions, pro or con. There are perhaps extra-extrasensory perceptions that you and I do not have. Outright denial is impossible, however difficult acceptance may be.

With Adrian's complete acceptance of the play we sent it to several New York theater managers, and it was read by several friends whose opinions we valued. From no one did we receive an affirmative response. This is a particularly difficult and dangerous period in the life of a play. One must keep an open mind and try to be completely objective toward suggestions made. There were many suggestions. Ouida and I weighed them carefully. Some seemed to have value and Ouida took advantage of them, doing a considerable amount of rewriting. At last, early in 1953, Bill Doll, a very well-known and respected press agent, going into manage-

ment, read the play and fell for it "hook, line, and sinker."
We agreed to share the burden of raising the necessary production money. My share was to be $25,000, which I had
little difficulty in raising from generous friends who were
convinced of our unquestioned success. But Bill Doll was
not so lucky in the professional field. When Bill's close
friend Mike Todd would not give him a penny I was disturbed. The Theatre Guild gave it a paid professional reading and turned it down. But all in all we were not too much
worried. This had been the story of so many phenomenal
successes in the past. Stewart Chaney was engaged to design
the sets and costumes, Reginald Denham to direct. Our cast
included Thomas Gomez as Moriarty, Madame Novotna as
Irene Adler and Jack Rains as Watson (my good friend
Nigel Bruce had suffered a serious heart attack and was
unable to join us). We rehearsed for three weeks in New
York and then went to Boston for a three-week tryout before coming into New York.

Cynthia, Ouida's niece Ouida Wagner, and all our friends
were greatly excited for us. There would also be some un-
knowing beneficiaries to our success, needy friends who had
problems, problems we had promised ourselves they should
have no more.

The first warning that all was not well came when I
went down to the Shubert Theatre in Boston on the Monday
morning to unpack. I had walked Ginger across Boston's
Common. (Ouida and Ginger and I were staying at the Ritz,
one of the most charming and civilized hotels in America.)
There was no line-up at the box office, only desultory buying. We would open slowly, it seemed. Everyone in the front
of the house wore masks and spoke hesitantly as to our prospects! Of course the reviews would help a great deal, and the
local chapter of "The Baker Street Irregulars" were with us
to a man.

The Boston membership of "The Baker Street Irregulars," if I remember correctly, numbered about fifty. This
organization has chapters all over the world. Its members

meet periodically to discuss *The Adventures*, and they have a magazine to which members contribute. Theories are advanced and propounded, dismissed or tentatively accepted. Some of the most eminent men in all professional fields are devoted members, including famous lawyers and doctors and scientists. There used to be an annual dinner at the old Murray Hill Hotel in New York, a momentous occasion. The story is told that one year, with Christopher Morley in "the chair," with Edgar Smith, Vincent Starrett, and other dignitaries surrounding him, a very young and new member asked if he might read a telegram he had just received. I have never attended one of these dinners but I understand they are very much protocol and everyone very dignified and on their best behavior. It was unusual that so young and new a member should so naïvely push himself forward on such an auspicious occasion. However, Mr. Morley gave permission for the telegram to be read. The young man thanked "the chair" for this privilege and proceeded to read the telegram, which went as follows:

"To the Members of the Baker Street Irregulars Murray Hill Hotel New York City, N.Y.
"NUTS TO YOU!"
signed EDGAR ALLAN POE."

The membership froze with horror. What happened to the young man I never heard. There were no doubt hopes that he would speedily be condemned to suffer the agonies of *The Pit and the Pendulum*.

The first dress rehearsal at the Shubert Theatre on the Monday night was catastrophic. Everything went wrong, including the stage manager, who fainted at his desk from a mild heart attack. Even the prospects of sabotage occurred to us. But by whom? Edgar Allan Poe's ghost? We returned to our hotel at 4 A.M. in the morning, worn-out and deeply concerned and depressed. At the next night's dress rehearsal things went a little better after a hard day's work on technical problems. But tempers were frayed and everyone was "passing the buck." It was the most incompetent stage crew I have ever worked with. The fact that the sets, beautifully designed, proved to be impractical did not help, and tired actors, including myself, started to muff their lines. So many high hopes were bending perilously before the blast, while the ugly spectre of failure lurked in dark corners. Only dear little Ginger seemed unaware of it all as he slept peacefully on the floor of my dressing room. Ouida, as ever, was her courageous self, facing facts but refusing to allow them to undermine her morale and unconquerable optimism. She was a tower of strength to this tottering edifice.

The opening on Wednesday was a nightmare. Shattered with tiredness and nerves I blew up badly in the very first scene! I never quite recovered and gave a hesitant, mechanical performance.

The reviews, however, were more than kind, they were encouraging. They said we needed work, but that our prospects seemed bright. As the star of the play, in a character with which I was so indelibly associated, I was aware of an added burden of responsibility; the responsibility of "laugh clown laugh." It was up to me to put on an "antic disposition" and to play-act the optimist until the curtain dropped with a sickening thud on the opening night in New York. A considerable crowd came backstage. There was laughter and the "yackety yack" of those curious intruders, and we—"how oft when men are at the point of death have they been merry"—We laughed with them and chattered inconsequentially.

"Coming over to Sardi's for supper and wait up for the reviews?" It was Bill Doll speaking to me.

"No thanks, Bill," I said. "With two shows tomorrow I think I'll be wise and get some rest."

It was a Tuesday night and Wednesday was a matinee. As Ouida and I went home we avoided the obvious. But I imagine we were both prepared for the worst. Business in Boston had been bad—very bad. Even the reviews had not helped us much. The opening night audience in New York had seemed listless and only modest applause had greeted our efforts.

The Wednesday morning reviews dug a deep grave for us. The afternoon papers shoveled us in, and in due course the magazines covered us up.

The notice was up on the board as I went to my dressing room for the matinee. We were closing that night after three performances. Ouida joined me for dinner. We walked to the Plaza Hotel holding tightly to one another.

"Don't worry, darling," she said. "Everything's going to be all right, you'll see. Anyway let's forget all about it and have a wonderful dinner together, shall we?" How much she was hurt I shall never know, because her only concern was for me and that half-empty, papered house I was to give my last performance to. We played that last show all out, for all we were worth, as "my people" will do on such occasions. And when I made a little speech at the end and said we were closing that night there were cries of, "Oh—no—no—no." A trickle of compensation, like a sip of cool water to a dying man. But Edgar Allan Poe's ghost had followed us to New York, and during that last performance we played one very dramatic scene in complete darkness. A main switch had burned out!

We called Cynthia at her convent school. She was deeply upset and cried bitterly. The next day I received from her a little piece of paper on which she had written: "Despair is dangerous for men. Despair means that a man has given up hope. A man without hope has nothing to live for, nothing to seek, nothing to gain. He can neither respect himself, nor others, nor love God. Since he no longer trusts the divine power, he has no means by which to advance to God, and the mercy God will give him to draw him from despair." I have carried this little piece of paper with me everywhere, all over the world. I am never without it.

AN AUTOPSY

How could so many intelligent professional people have
been so hopelessly mistaken?

For myself be it said that, like Conan Doyle at the end of
the first *Adventures*, try as I would my heart was not really
in it. I hoped to be carried by the volume of public opinion
that had supported me so enthusiastically from 1939 to 1946.
But this was 1953. Seven years had passed—yes, we were at
least seven years too late! I believe it possible that had I returned to New York from the West Coast in this play in
1947 the results might have been very different. Then there
was this new gadget television that was sweeping the country
with one-hour and half-hour plays. With our Sherlock
Holmes play we were leisurely, thoughtful, and purposefully
analytical, in the mood of the period. With television it happened fast, and was most times all over in about twenty-four
minutes, allowing six minutes for introduction and closing
and commercials. We were outdated, hopelessly outdated.

In Boston I had noticed there were rarely ever any *young*
people in our audiences. I should estimate the average age at
well over thirty. That meant that nearly fifty per cent of our
potential audience were not interested. No doubt due to some
extent to the fact that I could be seen in these stories on
television, to which my motion pictures had been sold.

The sets and the direction and even a "slow moving story"
came in for some criticism. And one famous New York
critic said that only Tommy Gomez as Moriarty lived up to
expectations! But such criticism would have played little
part had the flood waters still been flowing. But they had
receded too far, and my ship was stuck on a sand bar. Only
the remembrance of her many memorable cruises and exploits remained; but as time goes, not for long. One day her
hulk would break up and she would be lost forever, and even
her name would be committed to the limbo of eternity.

GOOD-BY, MY FRIEND

It is my custom to take long walks in Central Park whenever the weather permits. The autumn of 1953 had been
more beautiful than any I can remember for many years.
Day after day and week after week a soft sunlight had
bathed the city in many and varying colors. The air was
crisp and invigorating. The trees shed their leaves with a
calm and patient resignation, then stood naked and strong to
sleep peacefully in the promise of spring. It was indeed difficult to associate the perils of our times with one's instinct
to accept, without reservation, Robert Browning's unique
expression of faith, "God's in His Heaven, all's right with
the world."

One afternoon in mid-November I paused in my walk to
sit down on a park bench and empty my mind of everything
but the pervading beauty about me.

The distant sound of children playing mingled inexplicably
with excerpts from Schubert's Ninth Symphony. Or not so
inexplicably, perhaps, since a recording of this great work
had so often relieved my studies in preparation for the play
that had just closed after three performances. It may be that
I dozed off. Of this I cannot be certain. There was still the
sound of children playing, of this I am sure; and together
with the Schubert Ninth there was woven a delicious pattern of half-forgotten memories through my reveries. Suddenly I had the feeling that someone was looking at me. I
opened my eyes slowly, cautiously, to become aware of a
man seated on the bench beside me. He was not looking
directly at me, but with a sort of sidelong glance that could
have been disregarded had I so wished. It was a quizzical
look from a face I seemed to remember. Since my instinct is
always to enter into conversation with anyone who indicates
the slightest interest in me (a normal curiosity and an expression of one's ego prevailing on such occasions) I turned

toward him. "What a day!" I said. To which he replied with a long-drawn-out, "Ye-e-s-s!"

He not only intrigued my curiosity and my ego, but he also startled in me a vague sense of remembrance. Where have I seen that face before, I thought to myself. He was a large man, at least six feet tall, immaculately dressed in clothes that had obviously been well cared for; and their style indicated that they had been tailored in the early part of the century! He wore a bowler hat of a kind I had not seen since I was a very little boy, and wore soft-topped button boots. From a round, well-tanned face there twinkled two pale blue eyes that seemed to belie his age, for there was no question in my mind that he was very old.

Without looking my way he said suddenly, "Is your name Rathbone?"

"Yes," I replied.

He paused for a moment; then he turned to me and held out his hand.

"How do you do? My name is Watson. *John* Watson."

Taking his hand, I ventured, "What a curious coincidence!"

"Coincidence?"

"Yes."

"Why?" And his whole face took part in a most provocative smile.

"Well, it's an unusual name . . . and . . ."

"Not at all," he interrupted. "There are fifteen John Watsons in the New York telephone book."

". . . and associated for me," I continued, "and many others, I imagine, with the famous Dr. John Watson, who chronicled the adventures of Sherlock Holmes."

"I knew him well," my companion said softly.

"Who? . . . Sherlock Holmes?"

He nodded his head in assent.

During the pause that followed, I found myself wondering just how far the game would go before one of us became bored and decided to go home.

"Of course I knew Dr. Watson even better," he continued eventually, and at this he laughed heartily. Then he suddenly turned, and quite seriously added, "I don't expect you to believe me. Why should you?"

To which I replied instinctively and with equal sincerity, "One is more inclined to believe than to disbelieve the unusual."

Again the voices of children playing, to the accompaniment of the Schubert's Ninth . . . the rustle of leaves as a soft breath of wind brushed gently across my face . . . I heard his voice again.

"I saw your play a few nights ago. I'm sorry it had to come off."

"Did you like it?" I turned to him.

In the pause that followed, I noticed that the laughter had left his eyes, and his mouth had assumed a petulance that surprised me.

"You shouldn't ask questions like that," he said at last.

"Why not? It seems natural enough to me."

"It wasn't what you said. It was the way you said it."

"I'm sorry, sir, but I don't understand."

Without looking at me he continued. "Forgive me. I'm a very old man. Even as a young man I was a slow thinker. In my old age I am virtually at a standstill."

The smile crept slowly back into his eyes. "I hope you will forgive me if I don't answer your question, for two reasons. We could *both* be hurt, under the circumstances, by almost anything I might say." He paused again for a moment. When he continued it seemed to me he did so with some difficulty.

"The tone in your voice suggested your need for consolation. But I am afraid I would find it difficult to talk to you about anything so extremely personal to us both. . . . I was educated in a school and at a time that gave early priority to self-discipline. One sought for consolation within one's self rather than from others. To be truthful with one's self was one's only criterion of success. If you have been truthful with yourself in this play, you have been successful with it."

I felt no desire to interrupt him. For the first time since the play had closed, I felt relaxed and at peace with myself again; and I was very grateful to this man who sat on the park bench beside me.

"For my part," he continued, "I find your theater of to-day too much concerned with the problems that emanate from a major world revolution that first showed its purpose and direction in 1914, and will probably continue for another fifty years. Of course, at my age, it is impossible to adjust myself to an era of atomic energy and purely material progress . . . and which has so little time for autumn leaves, the scent of a rose, and the eternal promise of spring. Your theater is earth-bound my friend. It lacks reverence for the unknown, and the simplest and most beautiful of all human relationships—love."

I could resist it no longer; I had to look at him. I was much disturbed to see the petulance creep back into his mouth, and to hear an odd harshness in his voice. "In my young days I wanted to be a writer, a great writer, but I had to compromise with myself because I needed money." As he continued his mouth lost its petulance and his voice grew soft again. "I was associated for many years with a man of incredible talents. I was devoted to him, but he absorbed me completely. I don't think I ever quite found myself . . . never compromise, if it's humanly possible. Good-by my friend, I am glad to have had this opportunity to talk with you. You must not regret anything you have attempted with a sincere affection. Nothing is lost that is born of the heart."

He rose slowly to his feet. His back was turned to me. A huge back, with slightly stooping shoulders. He lit a cigarette. I closed my eyes. I didn't want to look at him again for fear it might not be true. I sat very still for quite some time. . . .

Yes, there it was again—the laughter of children, the soft wind on my face, the rustle of leaves, and that ever-recurring

theme from the Schubert Ninth. When I opened my eyes—
only minutes had passed, surely!—the sky to the west was
multicolored from the setting sun, and one little cloud hung
"like a pink feather from some gigantic flamingo."

Yes, Vincent Starrett was right—painfully, beautifully
right—"Only those things the heart believes are true!"

16

J.B.

From *Judas* in January of 1929 to my association with Archibald MacLeish's *J.B.* in May of 1959 is a leap of thirty years. But I became involved in *J.B.* for somewhat the same reasons that had impelled me toward my collaboration in the writing of *Judas*, and my playing of the name part. Both *J.B.* and *Judas* come under a heading we might call "restless plays." Both are based on Biblical stories that have always, I should imagine, intrigued the inquiring mind. They are anti-fundamentalist, but most certainly not anti-Christian. In fact, in both plays I found that audiences were stimulated by the sincerity of the provocative questions posed.

Mr. Alfred de Liagre, Jr., the producer of *J.B.*, assures me that I was his first choice for the part of Nickles, and I quote from Mr. MacLeish's Prologue. "Mr. Zuss, followed by Nickles, enters . . . *Both are old* . . . Mr. Zuss . . . is large, florid, deep-voiced, dignified, imposing. Nickles is gaunt and sardonic." I did not play Nickles until late September of 1959, and only then after considerable resistance had been overcome.

The original production, which opened in New York in December of 1958, was an immediate and tremendous success. It had been brilliantly directed by Mr. Elia Kazan. When Messrs. de Liagre, MacLeish, and Kazan first met to discuss the play and its production, Mr. Kazan asked for a major change in one of the leading roles. He contended (so I am substantially informed) that the part of Nickles should be played by a *young* man who should be something of a "beatnik." Mr. Kazan's arguments were so persuasive that before long he had Mr. MacLeish in the palm of his hand and they were soon in complete agreement. An exchange of letters and/or communications between Kazan and Mac-Leish relating to this "argument" were published later by *Esquire Magazine* and make stimulating reading.

The part of Nickles was created by Christopher Plummer, who gave a very exciting and completely convincing performance.

In May of 1959 I was rather despondent. A particularly hot summer had come upon us very early that year and I was dreading the prospect of those long, hot, empty months in New York with nothing to do. "Summer stock" was of course a possibility and Ouida and I had involved ourselves to a considerable extent in a tryout of a new play of hers, *Dark Angel,* which she had "tailored" for me. But the heat was terrific, and summer stock is an arduous existence under the most favorable conditions. You play eight performances a week, and then every Sunday you travel most of the day to your next "date." You arrive hot and tired, and that night you do a "technical dress" of the play in a theater in no way resembling the one you have left and just become accustomed to. Often on Monday afternoon there is another technical dress and Monday night you open again. To live through this kind of summer one must have considerable endurance and a stimulating objective—such as some play you saw on Broadway and always hoped one day to play somewhere, somehow! Plays such as *The Winslow Boy* and *Separate Tables,* both of which I enjoyed playing in tremendously in summer stock. But a new play like *Dark Angel* presented added problems. Summer audiences are hesitant to support an unknown property—the assembly of an adequate cast within a modest budget—new sets to be designed every week by a new scenic artist, and each week the inevitability of rewrites and consequent re-rehearsing for the greater part of the tour.

Then one day early in May 1959 I received a telephone call from my agent, Mr. Milton Goldman, indicating I was wanted by Mr. de Liagre to play the part of Mr. Zuss in *J.B.*, owing to Mr. Raymond Massey's leaving the cast in June. I did not want Mr. Zuss, but almost anything seemed preferable to a long, tiring tryout in summer stock. So I determined to gamble, since I knew the play was scheduled to tour in the fall and Mr. Plummer was not going with it, owing to other commitments. I made no mention of my gamble to anyone except Ouida, who was very distressed by my contract, which called for me to play Mr. Zuss for the balance of the New York season and the tour, which was to follow. I felt that the signing of the contract was an unpropitious time to indicate an important and ulterior objective in so doing. For when an actor is as good as Mr. Plummer was as Nickles, a management is reluctant to even consider his eventual replacement, and when they do so it is only in terms of someone as near to the original conception as possible. I also knew that Mr. Kazan's vote must inevitably be cast against me, and quite possibly Mr. MacLeish's also, since he had "bought" Mr. Kazan's conception of Nickles "lock, stock, and barrel," and it was Mr. Nickles that I was after by however devious a route, or obstacles to be overcome.

I was rather dreading meeting with Mr. Kazan. Being much younger than myself, and with a theater background I felt might be unsympathetic to my own classic apprenticeship and development as an actor, I anticipated an incompatability that could be somewhat frustrating to us both. I could not have been more mistaken. He greeted me warmly at my first rehearsal, and at the end of an hour or so I felt I had known him for a long time. He proceeded at once to define his ideas of Mr. Zuss as related to me, and he was attentive and interested in the picture I had drawn in my mind's eye of Mr. Zuss for myself. It was a stimulating discussion that quickly and concisely adjusted the character to what I might bring to it. Mr. Massey and Mr. Kazan had pictured him as a rather seedy old actor with delusions of grandeur. Mr. Kazan and I agreed to retain the old actor with delusions of grandeur, but we changed my outward appearance. "Gadge" (Mr. Kazan's nickname) soon built up a most intriguing background for me. My bed-sitting-room-kitchenette he was sure I kept spotless. I did my own laundry. I had only two suits of clothes to my name, but these were cleaned and pressed by me every day until they shone with antiquity! Zuss for me was to be a precise, disciplined fundamentalist. Alternately, Gadge would be walking around, or very close to me, looking curiously at me, or lying stretched out full-length on the stage, but always talking, talking, talking. I asked him how I could appear to tolerate this bumptious young man Nickles as a companion? We decided I had once had a very unhappy love affair, which had produced a son who had died very young, and that in spite of my fundamentalist ultraconservatism there was a paternal complex here that enabled me to put up with Nickles' provocative modernism, and retain the picture I had created for myself of the boy I had lost. I was completely fascinated by Gadge, who almost succeeded in making Zuss an interesting part to play! I rehearsed for nearly three weeks under the direction of Mr. Bob Downing, Mr. Kazan's stage manager, who most helpfully and intelligently prepared me for my opening night.

I played Mr. Zuss for some ten weeks, and during this period Chris Plummer would sit with me in my dressing room during intermission and tactfully and most stimulatingly endeavor to help me in the development of my performance. It was very hard work for us both because Mr. Zuss and I had virtually nothing in common! I even came to dislike him! For me, he was a doctrinaire-puritan-Calvinist. He had made up his mind long ago not only about himself but about other people. Where there was disagreement as to his principles *he* was always right and the *opposition* was always wrong! Frankly, his self-satisfaction irritated me and it was always a fight to perform him convincingly.

Somewhere in August, I think it was, rumors reached me

that Chris Plummer's replacement was under consideration. As I had suspected, the management were thinking in terms of someone as near as possible to the original conception. I spoke to Mr. de Liagre, who tentatively accepted the idea of my playing Nickles, but pointed out that he would have to consult with Mr. Kazan and Mr. MacLeish. Both these gentlemen were at first opposed to the idea. It was a case of do or die and so I offered to read the part for them one night after the play. I had watched Chris closely for weeks and had studied the part carefully at home. The reading was a success and I got the part, Mr. MacLeish falling back to his original conception of the role and Mr. Kazan saying he would not stand in my way, but that he could not see Nickles as an older man. Since Mr. Kazan was not to direct the touring company, but his direction was to be followed, this decision by Mr. Kazan on my behalf I feel was a generous one. To me, an older man seemed entirely acceptable since I had always seen Nickles as a sort of devil's advocate, his maturity giving a weightier and more dangerous quality to his questionings and arguments. And in spite of Chris Plummer's youth there was in him a maturity far beyond his years that made him an extremely dangerous opponent. My performance and his, from which I borrowed freely and much to my advantage, were not really so far apart in their presentations except in the matter of our ages.

Nickles I found tremendously stimulating. There could be no pallid acceptance of anything for him. He questioned profoundly when he was not satisfied, and he was rarely satisfied. If he appeared to be a little vicious at times it was perhaps that he despised the obvious and resented conformity for conformity's sake. He was not evil, though evil might have resulted from his violent refusal to accept platitudes in place of answers. He was strangely attached to Mr. Zuss, perhaps recognizing in him a way of life that gave Zuss a peace of mind that Nickles was jealous of but was unwilling to compromise with. Like the Judas of my play he was a zealot, but a zealot without a cause. But had destiny marked him for Judas' role in history there is no question in my mind that he would have accepted this opportunity to prove himself. At the conclusion of Mr. MacLeish's play I feel it is not unreasonable to consider the possibility of Nickles' suicide.

The tour of *J.B.* was a tremendous success. In Boston at the Colonial Theatre we broke the house record. In Rochester, New York, I was invited to stay on over the Sunday and "they" would fly me up to Toronto on the Monday. "They" were a church that invited me to preach a Sunday morning sermon on *J.B.* I replied to the rector of the church that I was willing to do so provided he played Nickles on the Saturday night! And that was the end of that. It would have been more than inadvisable for me to sermonize on *J.B.*, particularly since I was a devout supporter of Mr. Nickles and had a strong distaste for Mr. Zuss' conventionalities, and also not much sympathy with Mr. and Mrs. J.B. and their family's problems and afflictions.

In January of 1960 in Columbus, Ohio, I awakened one Saturday morning feeling dizzy, and upon rising found I was insecure on my feet. I had retired at a normal hour on the Friday night and had slept well. My condition bothered me, particularly since we had a matinee and evening show at the Hartman Theatre, both of which were sold out with standing room only. I ate a light breakfast and struggled to pull myself together. Later I walked quietly to the theater, passing an Episcopal Church where I had decided to take Communion the following morning. The church was closed. I tried several doors, but all had been locked. I had wanted to go in and sit there awhile, to give thanks and to ask for help through the coming day.

It has always seemed to me a pity that churches should not remain open for twenty-four hours every day throughout the year. There is no time at which someone in need of help, comfort, or consolation should find the door closed, particularly the lonely and often troubled traveler who is passing by.

And so I proceeded on to the Hartman Theatre feeling despondent and ill. As I made-up and put on my costume in my dressing room the dizziness recurred at intervals, and I did something I had never done before. I asked for and drank a triple Scotch whisky, straight! It had absolutely no effect. At the intermission I sent word to our company manager that I would like to see a doctor between shows and get something to help me through the evening performance. As the second act progressed I became more and more unsteady on my legs and found difficulty in articulating. During the last few minutes of the play I was holding on desperately, my knees were giving way and I was afraid of falling. After the final curtain call I walked unsteadily off the stage to be met by two stage hands and our company manager, George Osherin, who literally picked me up and carried me to a waiting ambulance. I protested without effect. All I needed was a doctor and an injection. But my condition had been so apparent out front that Mr. Osherin was taking no chances and had asked the fire department for immediate assistance. One aspect of this precipitous but entirely justified action was that the press and the radio got wind of it and fired their reports across the country in such headlines as BASIL RATHBONE COLLAPSES ON STAGE FROM HEART ATTACK—BASIL RATHBONE HAS STROKE DURING PERFORMANCE OF *J.B.* And this is how my wife and daughter were first informed of my condition!

In make-up and costume (somewhat resembling the devil —a black knitted jersey with tight black trousers and a red sash) I was raced to Mount Carmel Catholic Hospital. There, in the emergency room, I was met by Dr. Bowers, who examined me thoroughly. I told him I must leave the following night for Milwaukee, where I was due to open on the Monday. Dr. Bowers replied there would be no Milwaukee for me, or anywhere else, for perhaps many weeks. I absorbed the shock and then a few moments later determined to prove him wrong, come what may. I was allowed to phone home to New York and assure Ouida and Cynthia that reports were much exaggerated and that all I needed was a few days rest. Ouida joined me the following morning after I had had a wonderful night's rest and was feeling fine. It was poor Ouida who looked like the sick one I was supposed to be.

I had a private room and on the door there was a notice, NO VISITORS—QUIET PLEASE. Dr. Bowers' instructions were that I was to rest and sleep as much as possible until the results of his examination could be determined. But the notice on the door and Dr. Bowers' instructions proved to be entirely ineffective. Nuns and nurses, doctors and priests visited with me in ever-increasing numbers. The parade was a delight and I thoroughly enjoyed myself! The telephone in my room rang frequently and many dear friends called to ask after me—Mr. and Mrs. Brian Aherne from California; Katharine Cornell from New York; and Mr. and Mrs. Alfred Lunt, inviting me to recuperate on their farm nearby in Wisconsin—such expressions of concern and sympathy were deeply heart warming and I am sure contributed much to my rapid recovery.

My stay at Mount Carmel Hospital was a beautiful experience. There was a gentle, ever-present aura of both physical and spiritual assurance in the days to come, whatever they might hold for me.

At morning the whole hospital was gently awakened by celestial music that floated down the corridors and drifted into each ward and room. This recorded music had a therapeutic influence unlike anything else I had ever known. It happened again in the evening as the hospital bade its patients "good night." One was given to remember one's childhood —prayers by the bedside in the nursery with Mother and Daddy and Beatrice and John. And one prayed again as then, so many years ago; and those who had gone before came back for a fleeting moment and a reunion in blessed memory was consummated.

The rector of the church of the closed doors phoned and asked if he might bring the Sacrament to my hospital room.

This he did, and Ouida and I were communicants together. There was no question in this Catholic hospital of an Episcopal priest officiating. He was welcome.

There was the little nun who had been on duty in the emergency room when I had arrived. She was delighted in telling me of a companion sister who had asked her what I looked like as I lay there in costume and make-up. "Like the devil," she had answered with appreciative humor.

Monsignor Applegate was a frequent visitor and one evening we had debated *J.B.* until well after midnight when the night nurse came in and threw him out almost physically —and she was such a little woman and he was such a very big man!

After a week the time had come to say good-by to these dear people and return to my job as the devil's advocate in St. Paul, Minnesota. And now I would have to find him again—Mr. Nickles, that troubled, hurt man who would no doubt question me much about all I had experienced since seeing him last in Columbus, Ohio. Perhaps my short visit to Mount Carmel would help me to play Nickles with a greater understanding and not to be so intolerant of Mr. Zuss. I like to think that I did.

17

Last Act, Please. Curtain Going Up.

Emerson has said of friendship that "a friend is a person with whom I may be sincere. Before him I may think aloud." It has also been said that you are lucky if you can count your true friends on the fingers of one hand. Ouida of course is the greatest friend I have in the world. There is nothing she would not do for me, including giving her life if that were necessary. She has loved me as few men have been privileged to be loved. Then of course there were my mother and father and my brother John and Jack Miltern and Cynthia—Well that exactly makes up the five fingers of one of my hands and one finger on the other—nice going! But what of those I have not had the opportunity to share life with so intimately? I believe that Ouida and I are blessed in the knowledge that we have many true friends. "Treat your friends for what you know them to be. Regard no surfaces. Consider not what they did, but what they intended," Thoreau says. Give this consideration to many an acquaintance and you may find that you have a friend. We have tried to I think—I hope—There are Betty and "Augie" and Dorothy and Alex and Hershal that spring to mind immediately and oh so many others who have brought laughter and warmth into our lives. Then there are those who have influenced our lives by their example, men like Bishop Sheen, Stokowski and Rubinstein, Bruno Walter and Richard

Tauber, and women like Diana Tauber, Lilly McCormack, and Irene Ravensdale.

The one single and greatest abstract influence in our lives I believe to have been music. As some will seek out and "worship" men of letters, others painters and sculptors, and some even actors! Ouida's and my "gods" have been worshiped in a world that was and is and remains a world of music. And not alone as musicians but as fellow human beings have we loved them and been loved by them.

Fritz Kreisler was one of the gentlest men I have ever met, besides most certainly being *the* greatest violinist I have ever heard. There are a couple of little personal incidents about him that I think deserve recording.

After one of his concerts we were invited to supper at his hotel. Arriving early, before the other guests, we were waiting in the living room. The door to the Kreislers' bedroom was open and one could not but hear their conversation. Harriet, his wife, was helping Fritz remove his wet, evening dress shirt, while Fritz was making the most tender but ardent love to her. He swore by all that was holy there was no woman like her in all the world, that without her he would never have amounted to anything and that but for her his life would not have been worth living! And there was much truth to all that he said, for before he met Harriet many of Fritz's friends were much worried about his future.

On another occasion, after lunch at some mutual friends', a fellow musician wanted Kreisler to listen to a new record made by the London String Quartet. Fritz sank back into an easy chair and closed his eyes. After the record had been playing a few seconds one of the little children present climbed up onto "Uncle Fritz'" lap and started to talk to him. Fritz brushed the child roughly aside and she tumbled onto the floor and started to cry. It was as if Fritz were in a coma, his concentration and appreciation of the recording were so great. Eventually the child's crying brought him slowly out of it. I am sure he had no idea of what he had done. But when it was explained to him, he picked up the child with infinite tenderness and cradling her in his arms beseeched her forgiveness.

It was during *The Swan* that Lilly McCormack invited Ouida and me to drop in after the play. The only other guest was our mutual good friend Philip Merivale. There were also present Fritz Kreisler, Rachmaninoff, and of course John McCormack! The occasion was a rehearsal, which continued far into the early hours of the next morning, for recordings of some of Rachmaninoff's songs (with himself at the piano) sung by John McCormack, with violin obligato by Fritz Kreisler. The very thought of it now staggers the imagination—that such an experience could have happened to us seems almost unbelievable. And yet it happened, as on another occasion in 1941 in Los Angeles.

It was just after lunch on a Sunday that the telephone rang. It was Jascha Heifitz. Would we care to motor down to his place at Newport and go for a sail on his yacht. We gladly accepted and were soon on our way. As we approached the Heifitz home we noted his yacht was still anchored in the harbor with sails furled. When we drove off the highway and into the driveway to the house, familiar sounds reached our ears—violin—piano—viola and cello—Schubert . . . was it Schubert—yes, it was Schubert. But who besides Heifitz was playing? We tiptoed into the living room, overlooking the harbor. Mrs. Heifitz greeted us silently and we seated ourselves unobtrusively. It was now about 3 P.M. They had decided not to go sailing but to rehearse some recordings that were shortly to be made . . . Jascha Heifitz, Artur Rubinstein, Emanuel Feuermann, William Primrose, and Kauffman —trios, quartets and quintets—Beethoven, Brahms, Schubert, Schumann, and the Lord knows what else. All the artists were in shirt sleeves, completely oblivious of us (Mrs. Heifitz, Mrs. Feuermann, Ouida, and myself) or any previous invitation to go sailing! We were immediately aware of being in for a unique experience. Rubinstein and Heifitz need no introduction, but Emanuel Feuermann died in his early thirties after giving promise of being one of the greatest cellists of our time. William Primrose is recognized as a great viola player and Kauffman a violinist of outstanding ability.

After about an hour there was "a break" when we were introduced to the Feuermanns and Kauffman, whom we did not know. I had known William Primrose for many years, and intimately when he was a member of the famous London String Quartet.

When these gods from Olympus returned to work a few minutes later I was struck not only by their comaraderie but by the precise and disciplined attention they paid to their leader, Jascha Heifitz, as first violinist. Where an instrument predominated in the score that instrument was given its proper balanced value. There were no stars except the composer and every player was the composer's dedicated and humble servant, irrespective of their world-renowned reputations as soloists.

At 10 P.M. Mrs. Heifitz served a buffet supper, after which Ouida and I wandered down to the water's edge bewitched by the music we had heard. A full moon reflected her image in the sea, the stars shone like Christmas candles in the sky, and the night-blooming jasmine wafted her amorous perfume about us.

We were suddenly awakened from our romantic mood by the sounds of music again. The Olympians were at it once more!

A rose pink sky was heralding the dawn as they put down their instruments for the last time and we bade each other good night. This occasion still remains the most fabulous experience in music of my whole life. There was another which came very close to it.

Ouida had arranged a small dinner party for our very dear friends, Mr. and Mrs. Richard Tauber, a day or so after his concert in the Philharmonic Auditorium in Los Angeles, which we had been unable to attend owing to a family bout with a flu epidemic. Richard and Diana arrived with a large suitcase and Richard's accompanist! The extra man threw Ouida's table out completely, and even more distressing to

her was the fact that Richard would not eat or drink anything of the very special menu Ouida had arranged for him.
When coffee was served Richard rose and announced that
since the Rathbones had been unable to attend his concert
he was bringing his concert to us! So we all took our places
in the living room and for the next two hours Richard sang
his entire concert for us and our guests.

When Richard Tauber died of cancer of the lungs some
years later we lost a great friend and the world a great voice
and a great musician. Of Richard and Diana so much more
remains to be said, but I am leaving this for Ouida to record in her book.

One day about this same time Vladimir Horowitz phoned
Ouida to ask if our house in Bel Air was for rent. Ouida
told him most definitely, "No." But he insisted on coming
over. We had known Horowitz for many years, first meeting him at John McCormack's home in London shortly after
our marriage. He approached the question of renting our
house somewhat tentatively, but it was not long before he
strolled casually over to our Steinway grand piano and sat
down to it. No one looks quite like Horowitz at the piano,
though many of his pupils have tried to. The body crouches
as if ready to spring forward. His contact with the piano
makes them as one being (as when a lamp connection is fitted
into an electric socket in the wall).

Those beautiful hands rippled up and down the keyboard
a few times and he struck a few resounding chords. Then
for the next hour he played a concert for himself. I am
reasonably sure he had completely forgotten we were there.
He had fallen in love with that piano as passionately as if it
had been a woman; as had his great rival at that time—
Artur Rubinstein.

Of Artur and Nella Rubinstein a whole chapter in this
book would be entirely inadequate. They deserve a whole
book to themselves and, no doubt, some day such a book will
be written. Artur is for us *the* greatest pianist we have ever

heard or ever expect to hear, besides having been a warm and generous friend for more than thirty years. I am sure that some part of his greatness comes from the fact of his being such a well-rounded human being. He is extremely well informed, a brilliant raconteur, and his energy in his seventies is still limitless. I asked him quite recently who would take his place when he had gone and he replied, "My dear Basil, there are at least half a dozen young men who play much more expertly than I do; they never play a wrong note—*but they don't make music like I do*." He also told me he had never been bored in his life but once. This occasion was when Nella, for Artur's sake and her own and the children's, took a chalet for a couple of weeks in Switzerland for a much-needed rest and vacation. Artur plays about seventy concerts each winter season in America, and his summers are crowded with European engagements. The morning after they arrived in Switzerland Nella took Artur out onto the terrace to enjoy the wonderful view. "Isn't it beautiful, Artur . . . what a rest we can have here." "Yes," replied Artur somewhat dubiously, "but what do we do?"

After a couple of days Artur became so restless that he took off for Monte Carlo, where he spent his days and nights at the gambling tables! Some of us need rest, Artur needs continuous stimulation. His exceptionally active mind and tremendous energy are like an electric battery. It charges itself with usage; unused it will die. And Nella keeps up with him. God alone knows how! Theirs is a tremendously successful marriage and they have four beautiful children. We shall never forget when Nella (with her delicious Polish accent) called up one morning to announce her eldest daughter's engagement. The approach suggested unutterable tragedy! The conversation went something like this:

NELLA: "Ouida, oh, my darling Ouida, it's too awful . . .
OUIDA: "What is it Nella dear!"
NELLA: "Artur and I are just frantic—but what can we do?"

OUIDA: "Nella dear, tell me—is there anything *we* can do to help you?"

NELLA: "No, my darling, no—it's too ridiculous, too absurd . . . you know Artur is Jewish and I am a Catholic . . . well darling, believe it or not, Eva is engaged to marry a Presbyterian minister!"

The marriage has proved to be a great success and Eva has presented Artur and Nella with two lovely grandchildren and Presbyterian is no longer a second-class word in Nella's and Artur's vocabularies.

I met with Leopold Stokowski in 1941. I was engaged by him to be narrator in his recording of Prokofiev's *Peter and the Wolf*. It was a most successful venture. I am still receiving royalties on this record twenty years later. Before the recording session, for two or three evenings, I rehearsed with Mr. Stokowski at his home in the Hollywood hills. *Peter and the Wolf* is approximately an eighteen-minute piece, but many hours were spent on my contribution as narrator, with piano accompaniment, Mr. Stokowski following me carefully and critically from the full orchestral score. Several word changes were made in the narration at Mr. Stokowski's suggestion; to these changes I readily and happily agreed since they were all so instinctively and unquestionably right. The experience will always remain for me as stimulating and inspiring as any I have ever had in any field of endeavor. Since that memorable occasion Mr. Stokowski and Ouida and I have become good friends. There were evenings with him when he would dine with us alone in California, and afterward we would sit out in the garden and listen to him talk. These evenings are rich in remembrance. I think he appreciated our love of music and our yearning for a better understanding of its mysteries, its magic and its mechanics. "Stoky" is a dedicated man and would sooner say nothing rather than say something merely for the purpose of making conversation. He talked much to us during those nights after dinner in the garden and I think we proved apt pupils of this master in music. He was particularly interested in a play of Ouida's that she was working on at the time about Franz Liszt—in my opinion and in his a very beautiful play that, alas, was completed at a time when the theater costs were rising rapidly and there was no practical solution to its production cost. These costs have doubled and tripled since then (the mid-40s) and this tender romantic work I fear will never be seen. Mr. Stokowski was interested in being the play's musical adviser and director. Our admiration, respect, and affection for Mr. Stokowski is not alone based on his meticulous attention to every detail of any work he is engaged in, his profound knowledge of music, his creativity as a conductor, but upon that youthfulness in him which makes him one of the great crusaders for contemporary composers. He was asked to participate in The Empire State Festival at Ellenville, New York, a few years ago and agreed to do so if he could perform some new work. And so it was that he gave us Carl Orff's *A Midsummer Night's Dream* in which I played Oberon. It is a score of unusual inventiveness and imagination and I would not care to play in *The Dream* again without it, or without Mr. Stokowski on the podium. It was as if Shakespeare and Carl Orff were wedded, with Mr. Stokowski the officiating priest! These three are sublimely satisfying when heard together.

To these friends of whom I have spoken and many others, I owe a tremendous debt of gratitude. They have not only been an inspiration, but examples of constancy in affection and true friendship. If I have advanced in my own work I owe a great deal of any success I have had to them. We all need our "heroes" to whom we may hitch our wagon. And we who are less gifted can never repay our debt of gratitude to those who have so greatly inspired our lives and, unconsciously perhaps, imposed their standards on us.

But what of the thousands of gifted musicians who by their sensitive and masterly playing of the great composers, in orchestras all over the world, have given us such infinite pleasure, solace, and inspiration? To them, too, Ouida and I owe a deep debt of gratitude.

There is a story about a musician that I have long wanted to write, and now I shall write it. The musician's name for my purposes here is Herbert Greenfield. It was Herbert who said to me once in a moment of desperation, "So much to do, so little done." And, "So much to do, so little done" is I am sure so often the cry from an artist's aching heart, when at last he realizes that his vision has proven to be greater than his talent and opportunities. And what creative artist (for all artists have a degree of creativity) can ever escape that cry of the lonely heart, "So much to do, so little done."

Very often an author will write a preface to the effect that all the characters in his story are purely fictional, and in no way related to any living person known to him. And yet, quite frankly, upon inquiry, one finds that such an author, if not consciously, then subconsciously, has been influenced by persons and events that have unquestionably motivated his story.

A series of circumstances concerning many different people I have known over a considerable period of my life motivate this story. Each character is a composite, so that no one character may be said to be a true portrait of real life. Living or dead, not even Mr. Sherlock Holmes, himself, would be able to identify them!

I knew Cheedie very well indeed in my early days in the theater. She came of a family of fine artists in the musical world in London, and she and her brother had received considerable professional acclaim. Returning with her from an opera—or a ballet or a concert—in 1912–13, Cheedie would sit down at her piano and, by ear, play almost anything from that evening's program. She had married "above her station," a man who cared nothing for the arts and was a devotee of all sporting events.

Seated one evening at a performance of *Romeo and Juliet* in London, played by a great star as Juliet, who was a friend of Cheedie's, Robert, her husband, read his newspaper, checking the cricket scores and the form of the horses entered on the following day for the races at Ascot. Then he fell into a deep sleep from which he had to be awakened at the conclusion of the play. It was a strangely happy marriage, under the circumstances.

Gloria I have known in fragments. Her real life story belongs to a friend of mine, and to a particular item I read in a newspaper one morning.

Herbert is a composite character of many of the young artists who hung around Cheedie's salon, young artists of that day, including myself, who owed much to Cheedie's motherly encouragement in the development of our careers. She would have "evenings" in which we all performed, and then would sit around for hours commenting upon each other's contributions. I would recite Shakespeare—Eric, with his beautiful tenor voice, would sing—Jack would brilliantly mingle Chopin with jazz, by ear, he couldn't read a note—and so on—and so on—and so on.

Herbert came to life for me, as it were, one evening on Pacific Palisades, in Los Angeles—early in the 1950s. I was taking an after-dinner stroll. Nearby the house in which I was staying was a vacant lot. From this lot there was a sheer drop of two to three hundred feet to the main coast highway below. It was a clear moonlight night.

At the very edge of the lot I saw a rather small man teetering, as if about to throw himself over. I called to him, a dangerous thing to have done under the circumstances, but he turned sharply in my direction. Then, in dressing gown and pyjamas, he ran hastily away from me across the lot and up the road and into the night.

CHEEDIE

Boredom is a very dangerous state of mind. It is a form of self-indulgence that is often both unreasonable and unreasoning. By this state of mind I found myself seriously

affected early in the year of 1952. In my own defense I must
tell you that I write for television, which I found a mitigat-
ing circumstance to my condition, even if the reader should
not! I am one of many thousands, no doubt, who have been
intrigued by the "art of letters." I have read considerably,
and I am observant and imaginative.

I started my career with reasonable success in the short-
story field; turned out a couple of novels of modest dimensions, both in size and theme, which barely met their cost of
publishing; suffered through the writing of a play, which
appeared briefly on Broadway and was sold to pictures, but
never found its way onto the screen! So that the advent of
television was little short of a life saver to me. I could at
last, and did, indulge in a spree of prolific mediocrity for
which I was extremely well-paid. For some considerable
time I was delighted by my increased standards of living. I
also enjoyed the added respect with which my friends apparently viewed me. For years my telephone has stood beside me reproachfully and, believe me, there is nothing more
reproachful than a silent telephone. Now it rings, I may
even say sings, incessantly!

But these illusions of well-being were in due course dis-
pelled by a formidable realization that "mediocrity knows
nothing higher than itself," as the great detective Sherlock
Holmes once said, and a sense of deep dissatisfaction with
myself gave birth to a state of boredom in which I indulged
with increasing degrees of intensity. Surely the dreams of
my youth deserved something more than the hack pedes-
trianism to which I had accustomed myself in writing for
television. It was nonsense to delude myself with the hope
that public demand would one day produce "clients" and
advertising agents with standards of artistic integrity and
appreciation that would be an inspiration to the whole entertainment world! Besides, I was being unfair to myself and
my employers in accepting their money with this sense of
superiority and self-importance that I found, in my saner
moments, hard to justify.

So it was that in May of 1952, with the summer hiatus in T.V. approaching, I accepted the invitation of a friend in Santa Monica, California, to "spend a few days at the beach." I had not recovered sufficiently from my doldrums to have the courage to do otherwise, for I had never enjoyed my previous visits to Southern California. But anything was preferable to New York in the summer, and my present state of indecision became the decisive factor!

My friend in Santa Monica was a Mrs. Edith Greenfield, known to her more intimate friends as Cheedie. The origin and definition of this diminutive, as far as I have been able to discover, is unknown. Phonetically it had always suggested to me one of Edith's outstanding qualities, a talented child with a tireless ability to absorb admiration. She loved to be listened to and held herself an authority on everything. Discussion was impossible, agreement was essential. But since she was extremely well-informed and enormously talented it was not difficult to relax and let her have the stage, particularly when she went to the piano, an instrument she played with much feeling, understanding, and technical ability. She played entirely by ear, being much too lazy to sight-read. I shall never forget hearing *Boris Godunov* for the first time with her, many years ago in London. After the performance we returned to her house for some supper, and later, to my amazement, she sat down at the piano and played large portions of the score from memory, with masterful execution and feeling.

Cheedie resembled, only somewhat of course, a cross between the late Queen Victoria and Madame George Sand! Short and stout, with a slightly petulant baby face, she dressed extravagantly and in very bad taste. She always appeared to be in some sort of costume, and when she came into a room it was definitely an "entrance." She talked incessantly in a pleasingly low and modulated voice and never remained seated in one place very long. She had a passion for moving furniture from one place in a room to another. "Help me move this sofa, dear, will you?" she would say.

"There now, it looks much better under the window. I've always wanted it there and I knew I was right." A day or so later we would move it back again, to the accompaniment of the same dialogue, completely oblivious of its contradiction in fact! And I would look at those fat little shapeless hands and wonder where their strength came from.

Herbert had looked at them too, without much concern, I should imagine. Herbert was Cheedie's second husband and seemed interested in little but his advertising business, so it appeared to me. But superficial impressions can be very misleading, as was later to prove to be the case with Herbert Greenfield.

Cheedie had married her first husband when she was barely eighteen. A man of independent means, Sir Robert Hoarthwaite had idolized his young wife, and in spite of his advanced years—he was in his fifties when they married—they had appeared to be extremely happy together.

He was Cheedie's escort at all times and on all occasions, even to her *couturier's*, where he would sit patiently reading the newspaper or listening to the radio. In his younger days he had been passionately fond of sports, playing an excellent game of polo, tennis, and golf. After his marriage he had become an avid baseball fan. His knowledge of the game was second to none, which was considered by his friends to be "quite extraordinary" since he rarely went to a ball park, and the very mention of the game was forbidden in the presence of his wife, who "just adored" bullfights. Frequent visits to Spain and Mexico were made for this express purpose, a great strain on Sir Robert, who abhorred "the bloody business," which he would only admit to, somewhat apologetically, to a very intimate friend. His general complaisance was partly constitutional (he had put on considerable weight) and partly a very genuine pleasure in everything that his Cheedie said or did, at whatever cost to himself. He had died in his sleep while listening, on the radio in the butler's room, to a world series baseball game. And in so doing he had left Cheedie a very considerable fortune.

For many years her widowhood and her fortune were the object of much obvious attention. But Cheedie had managed to weather the storm, and had settled down to a sort of "grand salon" existence, which amused both her and her guests, mainly composed of artists, visiting celebrities, Washington diplomats—in fact anyone with a name or some fame. Yes, there was no question about it, Cheedie the hostess had definitely arrived! She became a patron of the arts, made liberal contributions to charity, and gave "the best parties ever, my dear."

It was generally conceded that unless she should meet another Sir Robert she was unlikely to marry again. She had been virtually independent during her marriage and was now completely so, and she let it be understood that she had no intention of sharing her good fortune with anyone who might make the least demand upon her time and inclinations.

But, as time passed, the years were not too kind to Cheedie. Her physical indolence, her spasmodic exercises in mental gymnastics, during pseudo-intellectual conversations with some famous guest, her increasing boredom and the ever-increasing attempts to alleviate it had made her older than she was before her time, and periodically she looked positively unattractive. And, as will happen in such circumstances, all this became an insidious topic of conversation and Cheedie lost quite a number of those old "friends," whose sincerity had always been conspicuous by its absence.

It was about this time that she had met Herbert Greenfield. He was many times her junior, fair-haired, with pale blue eyes, short, small, and trim he was, however, much older than he looked. He rarely smiled, spoke hesitantly, for the simple reason he had very little to say, but he played boogie-woogie superbly. "A friend" had brought him to a party and Cheedie had been enchanted by his playing. After cocktails he had stayed for supper. Three months later, they were married.

That was in April of 1953, and I had seen them both and met Herbert on their way through New York for a honeymoon in Europe. Cheedie, for a woman of her age, was embarrassingly "in love." Her protestations and demonstrations of affection, especially in public, made me uncomfortable and self-conscious, particularly since Herbert seemed to be detached and entirely unresponsive. He neither drank nor smoked, only speaking when he was spoken to. We dined together, went to the theater, and had supper in their suite at the Plaza. It was after supper that I first heard him play his boogie-woogie, a form of music I have never appreciated or enjoyed but, on this occasion, had to admit required some considerable skill, if not definite talent. Cheedie listened to him as if he were playing Chopin or Beethoven, but her effusive demonstrations of approval seemed to be those of a mother for her child. I was also disturbed by the way she was dressed. Perhaps it was a *studied* carelessness. Or was it merely the acceptance of a situation she refused to admit she couldn't cope with by the normal application of her undeniable charm and her ruthless individualism? What on earth was it that she saw in Herbert that had made her wish to share her life so intimately with him? Oh well, I thought, it's the same old story. She was lonely and old age was just around the corner. And even if in due course he left her, a few years of borrowed happiness would help to delay the inevitable last few chapters of her life.

But Herbert . . . what of Herbert? There was no stardust in his eyes! And it would appear that he had little, if any, appreciation of Cheedie's exceptional qualities and the milieu in which she was accustomed to live. If he were honest with himself, and her, his acceptance of Cheedie's fortune was perfectly understandable, particularly since he had insisted on continuing in his advertising business. Cheedie had wanted him to give it all up and live like "a gentleman." To Cheedie a gentleman was a man who did not work, or only occasionally; and definitely never when it might interfere with anything *she* had planned to do. *Robert* had never worked and they had been divinely happy.

"When we come back," she had said after Herbert had

retired to bed and we were alone together the night before they sailed, "when we come back I'll make him give it all up and I'll buy him a seat on the stock exchange or something." As if she were buying a toy for a child. "Dear boy," and she smiled with a deep inner satisfaction, "he's so maddeningly conscientious."

I finished my drink and prepared to leave. I wanted to be tactful, but I also wanted to register quite definitely what was on my mind.

"Don't rush him, darling," I said. "He has a considerable adjustment to make. I like him for wanting to retain his independence, and he's obviously a little sensitive about it. Watch out he doesn't develop an inferiority complex. He's obviously not had the same opportunities that you and I have had."

"Oh *you!*" and she laughed her pretty little tinkling laugh. "Always looking for material for a new story. Go home, you bore me," and she kissed me affectionately.

I saw them again when they returned from Europe. Cheedie looked tired, which she attributed to a heart condition that a London specialist had diagnosed as needing treatment, chiefly rest. She had had a couple of rather painful and unpleasant attacks in Paris and in Rome, and on her return to London her doctor had prescribed a small nitroglycerin pill to be taken whenever an indication of these attacks occurred in the future. She was instructed to carry them with her at all times. But Cheedie, who had never known a day's illness in her life, consistently neglected these instructions and on the boat coming home she had had another attack and the pills were nowhere to be found. They were later discovered in an evening bag that she rarely used. She had no recollection of putting them there. But this was not unlike Cheedie, who rarly knew where anything was, and always relied on someone else to find whatever had been lost.

Herbert had collected a nice tan on their trip and a lot of new clothes. He was also more loquacious. Like many

others who have never traveled abroad, he was opinionated
on matters of which he could only have acquired a superficial knowledge. I found him a little tiresome in this respect.
But Cheedie puffed like a pigeon whenever he talked and
encouraged him to express his thoughts and impressions.
Knowing my ebullient Cheedie of years past I could not help
wondering how long this would last!

A few months later Herbert was in New York alone,
"on business." He phoned me and we dined together. We
spent an uneventful evening except that I was distressed to
hear that Cheedie had not been at all well. She had been, as
a consequence, unable to do much entertaining and at
times, quite naturally, became restless and a little irritable.
A couple of months later he was back in New York again
and we went to a theater and had supper at "21." It was on
this occasion that I ventured to ask him exactly what his
business was.

"Oh, nothing that would interest a writer fellow like
you," he had replied. "Cheedie wants me to give the whole
thing up you know. But I can't do that . . . what would
people say . . . I mean, I don't think it would be fair to
either of us, do you?"

"Well you are a bit young to retire, I suppose."

He gave me a quick look, and the suggestion of a smile
that lingered hardly long enough for me to even guess at its
intent or meaning.

"I adore Cheedie of course," he continued.

And before he could finish I heard myself say, "But of
course," and a moment later I was wishing I hadn't. He
finished his drink and paused to a light a cigarette. He was
no longer a teetotaler and a nonsmoker. Since his marriage
he both drank and smoked, in moderation, and seemed to
enjoy his release from these self-imposed abstinences.

Then quite suddenly he said, "You've never liked me very
much, have you?"

He took me completely by surprise and I was considerably
embarrassed by his directness and the fact that I had so

obviously been unable to disguise my feelings about him. It was true that I had never really liked him very much. But I had never actually *disliked* him. My feelings toward him were not that positive. In his own humdrum way he was not a bad chap, but as Cheedie's husband he was a ridiculous anachronism. I was very fond of Cheedie, I had never been in love with her, and Herbert had come with his nasty little pencil and scribbled all over the picture I had cherished of her for years! But to be fair I had to admit that if it was anyone's fault it was not his, but Cheedie's.

"If I have ever caused you to think I didn't like you, Herbert, I am extremely sorry. At my age I don't make new friends too readily. And I suppose my English background is something of an obstruction to any change—I have never been able to adjust myself to the warm, willing acceptance, so charmingly expressed in this country, between men who hardly know each other. There are risks involved in both approaches of course. The American way is most generous, but the English way is less of a gamble I think, don't you?"

I was conscious of having been rather verbose in my explanation to him. But how else was I to cover my embarrassment, and my evasion of the whole truth.

He quietly continued smoking his cigarette. Then, without looking at me he said, "That's a lot of baloney and you know it. You just don't like me and that's all there is to it. I don't blame you, being what you are . . . an intellectual snob . . . and like most intellectual snobs you're unsure of yourself. You pretend to be watching the world go by . . . you think you're objective . . . you're really completely subjective . . . your major interest in life is yourself."

He flipped his cigarette across the room, firing it with amazing accuracy into a finger bowl on an empty table opposite. The whole thing was so completely spontaneous, and I laughed without restraint. But my laughter seemed to aggravate his mood.

"You think I'm a nonentity," he continued. "You think

I'm second class . . . you can't understand why Cheedie married me, and a lot of other things . . . here, give me that bill and let's get to hell out of here!"

He paid the bill and we left. Outside he got into a waiting taxi, and without so much as "good night" he slammed the door and drove off.

From the doorman I heard, "Can I get you a cab, sir?"

"No, thanks. It's rather a nice night. I think I'll walk a few blocks."

I was very much disturbed by what had happened, and when I arrived home I phoned Herbert, but could get no reply. The next morning I phoned him again without success. So I wrote him. But I never received any answer to my letter. This was in April of 1954. In June he wired me that Cheedie was dead.

I flew out for the funeral, staying at the Miramar Hotel in Santa Monica. Cheedie was buried at Forest Lawn Cemetery. The occasion turned out to be as bizarre as any that has ever taken place at these celebrated burial grounds. Herbert was costumed completely in black. I use the word "costumed" advisedly, for it was not only his suit that was black but he wore a black silk hat, a long black cape, and black gloves. Upon his arrival at the chapel he spoke to no one and went straight to the organ loft, where he improvised lightly as we all took our places "in church." The service was taken by an Episcopal minister and at its conclusion that barbarous custom of viewing the dead was in process when, suddenly, the organ broke forth into the wildest boogie-woogie. The shock to everyone present was so great that for a moment we stood as if paralyzed, looking accusingly at one another. Then, without a word being spoken, we drifted slowly away as if each were personally guilty of some secret and horrible crime. As I left the chapel I started to run, but the dreadful profanity continued to ring in my ears and, believe me, I think I shall hear its hideous mockery as long as I live.

When I returned to my hotel I endeavored to adjust my

thinking to the shocking events that had occurred. I could only conclude that Herbert was completely unbalanced by Cheedie's death, and I determined to see him that very evening, come what may.

I had my dinner sent up to my room and watched a matchless sunset kaleidoscope the western sky with magic colors that found a brooding reflection in the Pacific Ocean. The tall top-knotted palm trees that lined the Palisades stood like black sentinels against an opaque sky, motionless in their salute to the dying day. I sipped my coffee and a deep sense of uneasiness filled every part of my being. The sky and the sea and the trees, Herbert and Cheedie, and what I felt I must do filled me with an ominous premonition of evil.

I decided to walk to his house on Huntington Palisades. It was not very far. As I approached Corona del Mar the moon came up, a full moon, that gave to everything a sense of ethereal unreality. I walked as in a dream that had its origin and being, but as yet no indication of a conclusion.

The home was dark and the iron gates to the driveway were closed. The stillness was oppressive. The bark of a dog nearby jolted me back to reality again as I moved out onto an empty lot next door that overlooked the coast route several hundred feet below, and a phosphorescent sea that faded at the horizon into a brilliant starlit sky. I wanted to see if there were any lights in the rear of Herbert's house, so I walked slowly to the edge of the cliff and looked back. The whole place was in darkness. I decided to return and ring the front-door bell and see what would happen. As I turned, my attention was arrested by a figure at the other end of the lot, standing motionless at the cliff's edge. It was obvious that he was not conscious of my presence and I would have left him standing there had I not become aware that he was whimpering softly to himself like an injured animal. I paused momentarily in subconscious recognition. Suddenly he threw his hands over his head and all but lost his balance. Instinctively I called out and ran toward him. Startled by my cry he turned and I saw that it was Herbert.

He was in pyjamas and dressing gown. When he saw me coming he hesitated a moment, then ran from me as fast as he could back to the street and on into his house.

I was fully aware of my participation in what had appeared to be a near-tragedy, and the realization of what might have occurred before my very eyes stunned me into frustrated immobility. I stood in the empty lot and looked at the dark house. And its darkness seemed to envelop me, hiding the moon and the stars and driving my imagination into a whirlpool of violent conjecture. Should I call on Herbert and insist upon seeing him? Should I call the police and warn them of my fears for this man? But, in so doing, might I not help to precipitate the very thing I sought to prevent? My decision was finally influenced more by pure selfishness than anything else. I decided not to become any further involved in a situation that was no business of mine and could only implicate me in considerable unpleasantness the more I pursued it. So I persuaded myself to walk home and do nothing about it.

At the hotel I was told that New York had been calling me. I answered the call and was delighted to accept the request of some friends that I occupy their beach house for a couple of weeks. Their tenants had vacated and, not wishing to leave the house empty, would I act as caretaker pending their delayed return to the Coast? I accepted. But within myself I had peculiar reservations. I had planned to fly back to New York the next day, thus putting 3000 miles between me and the events of the day as soon as possible. But like a criminal, I was, as it were, magnetized to the scene of the crime. My friend's place was a charming house, comfortable and well appointed. It was situated on the coast route below, and not very far from Herbert's residence, so that one could look up into his rear windows.

I moved the following morning and decided to stay there alone. I am a reasonably good cook and the place was spotlessly clean. All that was necessary was to keep it so by occupying as little of it as possible and closing up the rest of the house.

The weather had turned very warm and for a couple of days I enjoyed the sea bathing and the privilege of complete solitude. On the third day a heavy fog rolled in and I awakened with a deep sense of melancholy. It was the first day upon which I had been unable to keep watch on Herbert's house, where the blinds in the rear had remained drawn and there had been no signs of life in the small garden that edged onto the cliff. I had been tempted to visit the Palisades again and view the front of the house, but had not done so for fear of running into any further complications. After providing myself with a modest breakfast I decided to do some writing. I went back to my bedroom, sat down at my desk, and looked out of my window—the fog rolled in with monotonous persistency and my room felt damp and cold and unfriendly. For over an hour I sat, pencil in hand and paper before me. It was nearly lunchtime, and nothing accomplished, before I decided to take a quick dip to shock myself out of this lethargy. The tide was high and it was not long before I was diving through the first wave. The water was much warmer than the air and most invigorating. I swam some distance out to sea, then turned on my back and floated. A slight swell rocked me pleasantly for a few minutes. Then I rolled over and swam back to shore. I would have Boston baked beans and some hot tea for lunch. I picked up my towel and ran up the beach, almost falling over someone seated on a newspaper and smoking a cigarette.

It was Herbert! He was still wearing pyjamas and dressing gown. He did not look up and could not possibly have known who I was. Lunch was now out of the question. I dressed quickly and warmly and took myself a liberal Scotch and water. This done, I walked quietly out onto the beach again.

Herbert was still seated where I had left him. He stubbed the cigarette he was smoking into the sand and lit another. The fog formed a thin screen between us as I stood there watching him. Once again the compulsion to speak to him and that answering voice of caution not to involve myself in his affairs.

I returned to my room, turned on the radio, and opened my window so that the sound of the music might reach him and perhaps disturb his brooding contemplations. All afternoon I watched his dimly outlined figure through the fog, motionless except for the continuous lighting of endless cigarettes. About seven o'clock a faint perception of the oncoming night joined with the fog to almost obliterate his image. A moment later he rose and moved toward the ocean and I lost sight of him.

I was instinctively aware of impending disaster. I rushed from the house and out onto the beach. I found the newspaper he had been sitting on and rapidly followed his footsteps to the water's edge. A wave broke across me knee-high and I saw him floating some fifty yards out, his dressing gown spread out over the water like a colored petal from some gigantic flower.

When I reached him he struggled frantically, and for a time the combined weight of our wet clothing made our return to shore problematical. At last I dragged him up onto the sand. He was completely exhausted and near choking to death with the quantity of sea water he had swallowed. I myself had very little strength left also, so I sat quietly beside him, watching him retching and vomiting. Suddenly I felt very cold and my sense of self-protection impelled me to immediate action.

"Let's go up to the house—it's just over there—we both need a good stiff drink," I said.

He turned over, burying his face in the sand, and made no reply. This time I was determined in what I must do. I looked at the outline of his slight figure, every limb closely defined by his wet dressing gown and pyjamas.

"I'll knock you cold if you don't do as I say, Herbert, and I'll keep you that way until somebody comes to help me."

He remained motionless.

"Come on, old man," I continued, "I know you don't think of me as a friend. But, if you'll let me I will be. And then, later, when we've talked we can decide what's the best thing to do . . . please."

There was a moment's pause. Then, slowly he sat up and looked at me. His eyes were bloodshot and tired beyond knowledge or feeling. His face was a mask of the man I had known. His body was rigid and desperately cold. For a time he just stared at me meaninglessly until his breathing became more regular, and a faint color began to tinge his ashen cheeks. At last he rose painfully to his feet and I took his arm and led him firmly back to the house.

I took him to my room and rubbed his aching body with alcohol. Then I gave him some of my clothes to wear. They were ill-fitting—I was a much larger man than he—and he looked like a scarecrow in a wheat field, quite ridiculous and utterly helpless. But I wouldn't leave him; I never even took my eyes off him for fear of what he might do. After I had myself changed we went downstairs and I cooked the baked beans and made some hot tea. This finished we went into the living room and sat silently smoking a cigarette. Neither of us had spoken a word since I had led him up from the beach. It was I who eventually broke the enveloping silence.

"Feeling better?" I asked.

He got up and walked over to the window and looked out. I followed him closely. A slight breeze had come up and the fog had lifted. A few stars were plainly visible. It would probably be a fine day on the morrow. Suddenly, without turning to me, he said, "Don't worry. I promise not to do anything. I want to talk to you and then, as you said, maybe I can decide what to do."

I lit the fire and we sat on either side of it as he started to unburden his soul. He spoke in an impersonal monotone, as I imagine some confessions are made by those who feel they *must* purge themselves, even though there be no hope of redemption. Here is what he told me as faithfully as I can remember it.

"I loathed my father and I cannot believe that he could have ever loved me. My mother was a woman of infinite patience but she hadn't the courage to defend me, and her love for me was silent and sorrowful so that I developed a loneliness it would be hard to describe. The old man considered himself a solid Christian, but his so-called religion was empty and meaningless. He was a regular churchgoer—every Sunday, fifty-two weeks in the year, and he professed certain precepts and preached certain dogma of which his whole life was the complete antithesis. . . . For as long as I can remember I've been passionately fond of music. He hated it. I think he was afraid of it emotionally. Certain emotions went very deep with him—fear of hell-fire—a terrible temper and a sadistic cruelty. . . . I don't want to talk of my mother . . . I loved her too much, but there was nothing either of us could do for the other in a home like that. . . . She died when I was sixteen. . . . The day after her funeral I packed a bag and walked out on the old bastard and left him cold. I've never seen him again."

"Is your father still living?" I ventured.

"I've no idea and I couldn't care less."

He paused for a moment to add another cigarette to the endless chain he'd been smoking. Then he continued.

"I got a job in a store and lived in the proverbial garret. I saved enough money to rent an upright piano and taught myself to play. I learned very fast and practiced religiously every night, often into the early hours of the morning, until my neighbors complained and I had to move. As luck would have it I managed to get another job in a men's shirts concern and was soon traveling for them. This changed my circumstances considerably and, with further advancement in the business, I could afford to live quite nicely. I bought a baby grand piano, on time of course, and continued to work at my music in every spare moment I had. Then I bought a record player and started collecting records. I developed a small group of friends, musicians and music lovers, and continued to dream of the day when music would be my life. Quite frankly I never doubted that the day would come, and I worked as hard as I could at my job to expedite the materialization of my dream. Sounds silly to you I suppose."

"Certainly not," I replied. "After all I'm a writer and I too have had my dreams."

"Ever realize any of them?"

"No, I can't say I have."

"I have. There have been moments when I knew I was among the greatest. Would you like to hear me play?"

Before I could answer he had gone to the piano. He opened it and sat down before it silently. For some little time he remained there motionless with his eyes closed. When he opened them again he did not look at me. His hands went to the keyboard and rested there momentarily. Then after a deep sigh he played me Chopin's "Revolutionary Etude" with magnificent technique and feeling. I found myself strangely moved as he came back to his chair and renewed his endless cigarette smoking. When he spoke again he seemed to be coming from a great distance.

"I never had anything to do with women until Gloria came into my life. Believe it or not, I was past thirty when I met her. Until that time my music had satisfied me completely. It seemed to absorb and exhaust every emotion I had and leave me strangely indifferent to the opposite sex. I knew that people said unpleasant things about me but I didn't give a damn. It was something I just couldn't explain to anyone, perhaps not even to myself. . . . But Gloria changed all that . . . she had soft brown hair, huge blue eyes, and the most beautiful little body you can imagine—she was Irish and Polish and twenty-three years old when I met her. For nearly a year I abandoned myself completely to her delicious resourcefulness so that no day was complete without the contentment of her body. My music suffered considerably but I rarely gave it a thought. Then one day she taught me to play boogie-woogie and I practiced incessantly to please her. But at the same time, there was born in me an underlying resentment that anyone should so possess me to the exclusion of all my earlier dreams of accomplishment. So I tried to see less of her and returned to my music. But soon the lure of her body had me back with her and, like an animated puppet, there I was playing boogie-woogie again." He laughed audibly, something I could not remember his ever having done before. The release of confession was working miraculously.

I sat very still and watched him intently. I cannot truthfully say what I felt. This atom of human frailty, so grotesquely dressed in my clothes, *frightened* me more than anything else, I think. I was not afraid of him physically; there was no need for that. But I felt as if someone else was in the room with us, some evil spirit that lived with him and would not let him go; his father perhaps or the girl . . . perhaps even Cheedie. But whoever it was I wanted him to be rid of it . . . yes . . . I felt *that* was how I could help him, if help him I could . . . but why Cheedie? What on earth had Cheedie to do with all this? And this laughter that had come to him in the midst of his anguish recalled to me the question asked by Rama of Valmiki at their parting in *The Ramayana* by Aubrey Menen. "You have shown me how many things are illusion. But in your way of looking at the world, is there anything you believe is real?"

Valmiki said, "Certainly, Rama. There are three things which are real: God, human folly, and laughter. Since the first two pass our comprehension, we must do what we can to live with the third."

Could it be that this faint echo of life that lived in his laughter might prove to be the beginning of his ultimate salvation?

When he continued he seemed more at his ease. And though what he had to say was both poignant and terrible he remained strangely impersonal, as if talking of someone else.

"Then once again, after a while, those brief moments in bed with her lost their purpose of complete satisfaction. After a time, I realize now of course, that my subconscious intent was an all-consuming assertion of my ego. Earlier in my life, I suppose I would have found Gloria a normal outlet for my excess of emotion, pent-up since my childhood and inflamed by my imagination that I might be something very near to real greatness . . . even genius. . . . But the Spartan discipline I had imposed on myself in search of my quest, well . . . once the floodgates were let down I was as powerless as a man in the path of an avalanche."

If he were not so deadly serious I would have been tempted to consider what he had just said as being as corny as anything I had ever listened to. But there was absolutely no justification for such an assumption under the circumstances.

"Of course, I had to take her out to dinner and the theater and things like that," he continued. "Then there were times when she just wanted to be with me and talk. At first I found in this no unsurmountable difficulty, for one took pleasure in teasing her and insinuating into everything one's ultimate desire to possess her. . . . She was anxious to "better" herself and developed periodically a slight veneer of pseudo-sophistication. . . . She "adored" Aldous Huxley, she said and was "just fascinated" by modern art and sculpture. . . . She went to dramatic class with some group that studied contemporaneous self-expression, some cult derived from the teachings of Stanislavsky, I suppose. The whole thing could be quite nauseating at times, with its monotonous mediocrity. . . . She had a small income from a deceased uncle on which she managed to live simply if somewhat severely. Of course this kind of thing had its inevitable limitations. All we really had in common was a chemical affinity to one another which, with a man like myself, found a natural saturation point where it eventually became almost repulsive to me. I tried . . . half-heartedly I know, but at least I tried . . . to integrate what she had to give me with my dreams and ambitions, but I only succeeded in nearly destroying them both. . . . She became possessive and made little scenes. . . . Why was I late? . . . Why had I not phoned her the previous day? Why had I become so distant and funny? . . . Of course her woman's intuition knew the true reason. I was through with her but I hadn't the courage to tell her.

"At last I returned to my music with an even deeper dedication, for I had planned to create a new and most fascinating world for myself."

He closed his eyes and his mouth relaxed in a gentle smile. He spoke as someone who had been put into a trance.

"Something told me I would never realize my ambitions . . . but I made up my mind that no one and nothing should stop the fulfillment of my dreams. . . . I would *be* Chopin and Schumann and Brahms and Debussy . . . I would *be* Toscanini and Ormandy and Walter . . . I would compose and conduct with the greatest of them. You have no idea how easy it was to be anyone I wanted once I had learned to create the complete illusion . . . one could never do it in the presence of other people . . . only in the secret places of one's heart and mind. . . . It requires enormous concentration, but the thrill of the accomplishment is simply beyond description. . . . You sit very still and just wait . . . and then it comes to you . . . Brahms, Beethoven, anything you love very much. Then you go to the piano and you *are* Brahms or Beethoven. And what you play is your own and has never been heard before. It's the most beautiful experience imaginable . . . and completely exhausting. . . . Another night you will sit there and it will be a symphony that comes to you. Then you open your heart and your mind and a great conductor walks in, and completely possesses you. You and he are as one in shadow and substance, and slowly but surely you absorb and assume all his greatness. . . . You raise your baton . . . those first few bars are the nearest approach to heaven I shall ever know."

He opened his eyes and looked at me. But for a moment I am sure that he did not see me. He had to retreat from his self-hypnosis and find me again. When he did he spoke quite naturally. He was completely relaxed.

I have an enormous collection of recordings, you know . . . almost any symphony that 'comes' to me, I have it and can conduct it from start to finish."

"Where did you learn to conduct?" I asked.

"By watching and working whenever I could."

I had been waiting patiently for the climax of his story and now he was looking at me intently as if he were reading my thoughts.

"You want to know about Cheedie . . . of course . . . of course . . . you were her friend."

He spoke with an abruptness that startled me, so much so that I felt the need of a drink to help me accept what was coming—something I had subconsciously anticipated for a long time but had been fatefully unwilling to attempt to define for myself. I rose from my chair.

"Can I get you a drink?"

"No, thanks. But get one for yourself. You may need it."

It was the old Herbert I had known in New York, the Herbert who had seemed to dislike me so much. Again he seemed to be reading my thoughts.

"I know just what you are thinking," he said. "But you're wrong . . . I never really disliked you . . . I was jealous of you . . . but let's not go into that now, I haven't much time."

I tried not to understand what he meant by not having much time, but it was a foolish pretense on my part especially in view of the circumstances in which I had found him. But why? . . . *Why* his determination to end his life? And why of all people was he talking it out with me?

As I sat down again the hands of the small clock on the table beside me stood at just after midnight.

"I'm going to tell you everything and I want you to pray for me because, if there's an eternity, I'm damned beyond hope. . . . You *will* pray for me, won't you?"

"I'll try to," I said.

"But you *must!* You're the only one. That's why I let you take me out of the water . . . and a million years from now perhaps your prayers will release me from hell . . . if there's nothing, just an eternity of nothing . . . not even darkness but completely nothing, your prayers may help *you* to forgive me." He covered his face with his hands. There was a moment's pause, and then without looking up he said, "Is that a record player over there?"

"Yes. Why?" I replied, somewhat taken aback by his abrupt change of thought, as it appeared to me.

He got up and went over to the Victrola. Looking into it he said, "You play this thing?"

"Sometimes."

"There's a record on there now. What is it?"

"I think it might be the Overture to Wagner's *Flying Dutchman*."

Looking closer into the Victrola he said, "Yes, it is." Then he went over to the window and stood there silently looking out into the darkness and the fog. Suddenly he turned and spoke to me as if he had made an irrevocable decision—a decision that was, however, posed in the form of a question, but which nevertheless had a finality to it that was unmistakable.

"Will you promise me something?"

"Under the circumstances . . . until I know what it is how can I?"

He turned away from me and sat down again, slowly and calmly. Then he lit a cigarette and continued.

"If you don't promise I shall not tell you anything more . . . and not knowing the end of my story would haunt you for the rest of your life. . . . You see, whether I tell you or not it's the end of me, one way or another . . . there's nothing you can do about that I assure you."

Yes, the decision he had come to was irrevocable now, that was obvious, whatever had been the slight hope he had clung to when I had dragged him out of the water. The trace of a smile crept into his eyes as he looked straight into mine.

"If I tell you you'll be the only one to know . . ."

Then slowly the smile faded and was replaced by a deep and desperate tiredness.

"And if I don't no one will ever know . . . take your choice."

I was myself a little tired. Too tired to resist a terrible sense of pity for this fellow traveler so near the end of his journey. A sense of pity that whispered in my heart . . . "There, but for the grace of God." So I said, "I promise."

He rose and threw his cigarette into the fireplace. For his sake and my own I was glad that I could not see his face.

"Perhaps you will never fully understand what you are doing for me. But it isn't really necessary for you to understand . . . only to accept . . . and perhaps one day even to forgive. . . . When I finish talking please don't say anything . . . I shall go to that Victrola and I shall conduct for you the Overture to *The Flying Dutchman*. I have never done this for anyone before . . . I shall do it for you because it's the only way I have of thanking you, and because—when I have finished conducting I shall not be quite myself, and what I have to do afterward will come easier . . . and you will just sit here—and that will be the end." He paused and I repeated again, "I promise."

Placing his hands on the mantelshelf he told the rest of his story without once turning to address a single word to me. His body remained absolutely motionless. But for the sound of his voice he could have been a piece of the stone fireplace to which he had attached himself.

"As you know I met Cheedie at one of her parties to which someone had taken me . . . no one you know, and someone she hardly knew herself. It was a big party and we crashed it, as you might say. She was in wonderful form that night, playing and singing to a small group of us who had stayed on after the crowd had gone. During a snack, about 3 A.M. she asked me about myself in a casual sort of way, and as we were talking I remember looking at those funny fat little hands that seemed so incongruous a part of her . . . what a strange contradiction they were to the keen brown eyes and the enormous vitality that was the very essence of her whole being in those days. . . . As I was leaving, she said, 'I'm going to hear the Philadelphia Symphony on Tuesday, would you care to go with me?' I told her I would love it. She asked for my address and telephone number so that she could call me about where we should meet.

"This was the first of a number of concerts and shows she invited me to. We always dressed and dined first at her apart-

ment. Then one night she invited me back for a bite of supper.
I can't explain it, but I would have given anything not to have
gone. I had a sort of presentiment or something. During supper she put one of those horrible fat little hands on mine and
just left it there. Without looking I just raised her hand to my
lips perfunctorily. Then our eyes met . . . she had beautiful
eyes, dark brown and deep-set in that baby face, which looked
extraordinarily young at the moment. . . . She said she was
desperately lonely for some real friendship based on mutual
interests, a companionship she had never known in her life
even with her husband Robert. 'Robert was a dear of course,'
she said. 'He never denied me anything. He loved me, but
with a sort of patient forbearance for what he called my
charming "eccentricities" . . .'"

He paused briefly to continue a moment later in the same
calm, toneless voice.

"She asked me to marry her . . . and I accepted. I was so
very tired of being so much alone myself . . . alone within
myself that is . . . of course I know now that's something we
can none of us ever escape from completely—and I thought
she might understand about my music . . . and Gloria was ill
and I wanted to help her . . . that's why I made it a condition
of our marriage that I could continue in my business . . . so
that I could help Gloria. . . . "No," he said as if once more
reading my thoughts, "Cheedie never knew about Gloria . . .
every month I sent Gloria most of my salary, keeping just
enough for my personal needs so as not to be completely
dependent on Cheedie.

"The trip to Europe was not what I had hoped it might be.
I was out of my depth all the way, if you know what I mean,
and Cheedie never wanted me out of her sight. We saw nothing of Paris but the Ritz and other Americans traveling
abroad. It was the same everywhere we went, London, Rome,
Madrid . . . oh, those sickening bullfights she made me take
her to . . . she would cling to me desperately or cover her
face or gesticulate grotesquely when the poor beast was
killed. . . . I looked everywhere, anywhere, at the crowd all

about me, even into the arena itself to escape those wild masochistic little hands, soft and pudgy and red with the abuse she had given them. . . .

"When we arrived back in New York I phoned Gloria from a pay booth in a drugstore. Whoever it was that answered the phone said Gloria had been taken to the hospital. It was TB, they said, and was there any message. I said no, but would like to know the name of the hospital. I couldn't see her because the next day we went on to the Coast. But I couldn't wait to return . . . on the pretense of my business requiring my immediate attention after so long a visit away I returned East about a week later. . . . Gloria was pathetically pleased to see me . . . she didn't know I was married and I didn't tell her . . . I never told her . . . she found out somehow, and the next thing I knew she was dead. . . . She wrote me a letter . . ."

He paused for a moment and I could sense the effort he was making to continue. But he never moved a muscle.

"She told me to be happy and to have no regrets about her, and that she was glad she was going now that she couldn't see me any more. . . . You see, I came East as often as I could and would sit with her for hours . . . that's when I would see you and we dined together. . . . By some intuitive sense, or perhaps it was my own sense of guilt, Cheedie suspected something—of course I'd been away more than usual, and she began to nag and complain . . . and her heart attacks became more frequent . . . so I gave up my job . . . I had to . . . it didn't mean anything any more anyway . . . I couldn't work . . . I couldn't even think clearly.

"Very soon I became obsessed with the idea of getting away from Cheedie. But I didn't know how to do it . . . it would probably have killed her . . . so I decided to kill her myself."

At last it was out. All that I had seemed to have known from the very beginning was now a horrible reality. In a sense I was relieved for, though I had never spoken of it to anyone, I had been under a great tension for a long time, a tension I found quite inexplicable under the circumstances, for I was in the best of health and had become quite prosperous.

"She had those pills, you know, that she was supposed to take whenever she had an attack . . . and she was always misplacing them . . . and whenever I could I helped her misplace them . . . once I even threw them away. . . . Don't ask me why one does these things because I couldn't tell you. It was almost as if someone else were doing it for me. . . . I just knew I had to be rid of her and this was the only way. . . . I knew she was dying that day and the pills were in my pocket. . . . I couldn't stand there and watch her die, so I rushed downstairs and called her maid hoping that by the time I got back it would all be over . . . and that's how it happened."

I waited and waited and waited, but no more words came from him. I was sick to my stomach and wanted to vomit. I tried to think, but the thoughts would not arrange themselves into any continuity. It seemed like all eternity before I saw him move over to the Victrola like a man walking in his sleep. I heard him breathe deeply several times, and then at last he turned on the player. I watched him askance, half in horror, half in pity. But I knew one thing, that I must keep the promise I had made him. Then I heard and saw something that will live with me to the day of my death. I am not a musician, but all my life I have known and loved the best in music and admired its great soloists, orchestras, and conductors. And now here was Herbert with my ill-fitting clothes hanging grotesquely on his frail body, a changed man, a complete metamorphosis, tall, slender, and infinitely magnetic, conducting the Overture from *The Flying Dutchman* with a deep sense of musical appreciation.

When he had finished he seemed to shrink back visibly into the dreadful reality of his miserable destiny. Slowly he removed the clothes I had loaned him until he stood before me naked. He did this quite deliberately I am sure, so that when his body was found I should in no way be implicated. His was a frail little body, with sloping shoulders; he was sway-backed and the veins in his legs showed a deep blue and were swollen. But God had made him as he had made all the rest of us, and now he was to return to his Creator all that was left of his earthly being.

There was absolute silence in the room, not even the sound of his breathing, as he moved slowly through the French windows and out into the night. For a long time I sat motionless, listening to the rhythmic beat of the sea on the soft sand.

At last the sun rose with imperious calm and chased the shadows of the night into some dark corner of my mind, there to remain until the night released them once more and for many, too many, nights to come for the rest of my life.

18

And So Good Night

In 1954 we had moved again, to Central Park West. This apartment house was built in 1902, and is one of the last to be built with spacious rooms and high ceilings. Our view from the eleventh floor looks north, east, and south. The whole of Central Park is spread out beneath us. The city's sky line is sheer magic. Every day and night, particularly at the turn of the seasons, there are kaleidoscopic changes in lighting and effects. Storm clouds brood like huge monsters over the city, swallowing up the Empire State Building, or are chased murderously across the skies by tempestuous winds that shriek and howl like tormented lost souls. There are burning hot days in summer when a myriad different colored little row boats laze on the tepid waters of the lake, while at night the strains of the band drift up from the Park, and thousands of people lie on the burning grass half listening, half dreaming—some sleeping, exhausted by the day's simmering heat. And in winter the lake looks like a Currier & Ives, with the skaters speeding over its surface, and the bandstand is empty and deserted. There are evenings like paintings by Turner—clear days in spring or fall when the reality of this fabulous city, climbing up and ever up into the skies, staggers the imagination.

Ouida, as usual, had moved into our apartment alone. Cynthia and I had gone to the Coast, where I was to make the picture *My Three Angels*. It was during this month that Cynthia asked me if we might go out to 10728 Bellagio Road. The indulgence of sentimentality has always seemed to me a great risk, but I decided to take it. So I rang the front-door bell, and a butler answered. Mr. and Mrs. Reeves were out, but he was willing to let us go over the house when he knew who we were. Everything had been so completely changed both inside the house and in the gardens that I felt the risk I had taken would pay off. Cynthia and I said hardly a word to one another during our visit over the house, and not a word was said on the way home, or ever again. Her childhood home could now become a dream that she could remember without pain or regret. I was happy for her—happier than I have ever been in my own memories of Greenbank Cottage—and I am glad that it turned out as it did. During this period, Cynthia wrote several poems. They were imaginative, well-formed, and had meaning and feeling beyond anything that might be expected of a girl of fifteen. It was her mood of the moment.

It had been a very hot summer in the East, and when Cynthia and I returned from the Coast, we found Ouida in bed, completely exhausted. She just cried like a child as we came into her bedroom. She was so upset that the apartment was not ready for us! She had packed and unpacked all our books herself. Several hundred of them. The furniture was in place. There were even a few flowers in some vases! Ouida cannot live without living things about her, flowers and birds and dogs. "Ginger" too was glad to see us back and "kissed" us both profusely!

But Ouida's resilience is amazing and with her family reunited about her again she was soon on top of the world and we were planning a few parties for the following season. During our four years at 15 East Ninety-first we had been unable to do much entertaining, as in these new apartment houses the rooms are very small and unsuited to much more than a half-dozen friends in to dinner. Ouida and I like to give (and enjoy) about three parties a year. We have friends we love, acquaintances we enjoy, and even some people we don't particularly like or dislike but who are both amusing and intelligent, and are often good for my business! Our rooms in our present apartment are enormous, and with Ouida's genius for decoration, her good taste, and that sense of "home" she has always given to any place we have ever lived in, she has managed to give some very glamorous evenings in our ivory tower overlooking Central Park. These events are "catered," but in every detail Ouida's magic touch is discernible. Ouida, as Lady Mendl was the first to admit, is a truly great hostess, *and* a very economical one. She has a list of the strangest people from all over New York, the Bronx, and Long Island who seem to become involuntarily involved and infected by Ouida's enthusiasm for what she is doing, and who will do just about anything for her at a price far beneath that charged by less personal and more obvious contacts. The buffet supper menu is of her most careful choosing, the added staff for the occasion are hand-picked, the floral designs are like paintings, and there is genius in the way that she mixes and handles her guests. Eric Remarque and Paulette Goddard, Dick Watts of the New York *Post*, Mr. and Mrs. Artur Rubinstein, Laurence Olivier, my daughter's boss Miss Hockaday of Hockaday Associates, Mr. and Mrs. Goddard Lieberson of Columbia Recordings, Sol Hurok, Bruno Walter, Stokowski, Marlene Dietrich, the Baroness Ravensdale, to name but a few, all mixed up with close and near-close friends and acquaintances and a village idiot or two for laughs!

My professional and artistic life in recent years has had its ups and downs, but this is normal for an actor, or anyone who pursues the arts for his livelihood, or anyone who devotes a good proportion of his time to the life of the imagination. And I should like to recall, in this connection, Edgar Allan Poe's famous sonnet *To Science*. It seems terrifyingly apropos.

SONNET—TO SCIENCE

by Edgar Allan Poe

Science! true daughter of Old Time thou art!
    Who alterest all things with thy peering eyes.
Why preyest thou thus upon the poet's heart,

Vulture, whose wings are dull realities?
How should he love thee? or how deem thee wise?
Who wouldst not leave him in his wandering
To Seek for treasure in the jewelled skies,
Albeit he soared with an undaunted wing?
Hast thou not dragged Diana from her car?
And driven the Hamadryad from the wood
To seek a shelter in some happier star?
Hast thou not torn the Naiad from her flood,
The Elfin from the green grass, and from me
The summer dream beneath the tamarind tree?

What is this dream which the heart pursues so relentlessly?
All my life, I have had one dream or another constantly before me. If one has withered another has sprung up in its
place. . . . If for me the Naiad has not been torn "from her
flood," or the Elfin "from the green grass," or "the summer
dream beneath the tamarind tree," for this I must to a large
extent thank Ouida who shares with me this dream world
within and beyond a world of reality; a dream world that
can be at times more real than reality itself for all those who
with their hearts and from childhood have believed that one
can "dream true."

In the last years of his life, when we had come to know him
well, Max Reinhardt, that great man of the German theater
of his time, pleaded desperately during his visit to the United
States in the thirties for our help in sustaining the "illusion" of
the theater and to keep theater-going a "festive event." But
science and the increasing problems of the economics of our
day left him "to seek a shelter in some happier star." Since
his death the pattern of our days has followed a relentless pro-
gression. This I think has been largely due to the sudden
and unexpected explosion of television. The theater unquestionably suffered a further relapse. The motion picture
experienced some very lean years, and there was a general
shuffling and reassortment of talent that gave the whole entertainment world a sense of insecurity that had not been experienced since the talking picture revolutionized the future

prospects of all those to whom the theater had been a major source of employment. Some of us, including myself, have been able to take it in our stride. To those with considerable theater and motion picture experience, television did not seem to present any insuperable problems. We were to find later that this early optimism had its foundations in sand.

Never has so much been said by so many about so few! (with apologies to Mr. Churchill). In the past few years television in particular, and the entertainment world in general, has taken a terrific beating from the F.C.C., the press, and the public, much of it thoroughly deserved. But please, dear reader, bear with me briefly if I touch on some personal expressions of opinion in relation to this subject matter. I shall not stay with it long for the time approaches when, shortly now, I must say "and so good night" to you.

In the early fifties it was considered a "must" to get one's foot into television. It was mostly "live" in those days, the majority of shows emanating from New York, and there were indications that the medium, as it developed, might contribute much good, adult entertainment. Robert Montgomery, among others, produced a most promising program, and the comedians had a ball for themselves. I personally did everything and anything, irrespective of quality or my suitability! I was "a guest star" on Milton Berle's or Sid Caesar's programs, or played for "Chevy" automobiles in Pushkin's *The Ace of Spades*, or on The Theatre Guild U. S. Steel program as the Duke in Mark Twain's *Huckleberry Finn*. The atmosphere, from the first rehearsal to the final "signing off," was frantic with the pressure of competition and the inadequacies of time for preparation and rehearsal. Like a monster New York garbage truck the industry was devouring material each day of every week. An original script was rare; adaptations of plays, books, stories, just anything was the order of the day, and like yesterday's newspapers, millions of pages of typewritten paper were consigned to thousands of greedy wastebaskets. Never had the wastebasket lived so well, gorged day and night with desperate, discarded thoughts, and dreams that had died on the sponsor's desk, like flowers wilting in a factory.

Big names soon started dropping out from sheer exhaustion and "overexposure," from which some never recovered. There was little pleasure or pride in one's work. Television soon became a means of employment and a source of income. The pace was terrific and one was haunted by fears of inadequacy owing to time limitations for preparation and proper rehearsals, and the knowledge that no one could help you if anything went wrong once you were "on the air." You were like an astronaut with all ground contacts cut off. One would come home after a show the family had watched and they would be "kind" about it and eventually someone would ask, "How much did they pay you for doing that?"

It was a miserably frustrating existence. Now we have tape, which helps to some extent. But the major frustration is a complete lack of illusion. Surrounded by cameras and sound equipment snaking their way in and around and about you, sometimes looking right into your face like huge prehistoric monsters, you mechanically move through the hour with a wing and a prayer that you won't forget your lines or fall over a camera cable. From time to time you glance at the floor manager, who holds a stop watch in his hand, and he signals to you to pick up the pace or "spread" or that "we are right on the nose." I do as little television as possible now. Just enough to meet exposure requirements (Jack Parr's program is invaluable for this), and to qualify annually for the benefits of the A. F. T. R. A. Welfare and Pension Fund (American Federation of Television and Radio Artists). Fortunately for me I have had considerable exposure of late years. All my Sherlock Holmes pictures have been run again and again all over the country and many of my best pictures have been sold to television. Here, surely, is a frank, personal admission that, as with many others, the monster Mediocrity had won his first round with me. Half consciously as yet, I was hiding miserably behind the obvious excuse that science and technology were masters of the future and that their "peering eyes" were

searing "the poet's heart . . . with dull realities," and there
was nothing I could do about it.

Another source of income during this time was paid advertising. I have advertised cigarettes, liquor, a new accident
policy for a well-known insurance company, a diet food, etc.,
etc., etc.

The number of persons employed to produce this form of
radio or T.V. advertising is incredible. For one product I was
contracted to do six one-minute radio "spots." It took a whole
afternoon. There were present at the session: someone representing the product; two or three men representing the
agency; a couple of copy writers, besides the usual team of
studio technicians.

First we sat around and read the spots, everyone tense and
apprehensive lest one little word might detract from the sala-
bility of the product. Then a "spot" would be rehearsed, after
which they would all go into a huddle and in due course they
would come up either with the deletion of one line somewhere (we were three seconds over!) or a word change.

"Try 'delectable' instead of 'delicious' will you please, Mr.
Rathbone? All right, let's have another try. Keep it bright and
interesting!"

Then we would do it again—and again—and again. This
procedure was followed the whole afternoon until the six
one-minute spots were finished and "in the can." I sat numb,
with the endless repetitions and the atmosphere of increasing
sterility occasioned by the frantic efforts to assure an omniv-
orous public that "X" tablets were better than "Y." One
learns to be very patient under such conditions. But the
knowledge that I was allowing the monster Mediocrity to still
further encroach upon "my summer dream beneath the tamarind tree" disturbed me considerably.

There was, however, a breath of hope and encouragement
in brief but very pleasant interludes of recording for Caedmon
Records, Inc. This firm was organized and functions solidly
under the personal management of two most charming and
intelligent young ladies, Miss Marianne Rooney and Miss

Barbara Cohen. They are concerned first, last, and always with quality in every department of their product. Recordings are carefully rehearsed for days by Mr. Howard Sackler, a young man of considerable talent and knowledge of all that is best in the field of letters. Mr. Sackler also directs the recordings sessions and assembles and edits the tapes. The sound engineer is Mr. Bartok, son of the eminent composer, a most sensitive artist. Mr. Sackler and I worked many hours on Poe's *Raven* alone, and my recordings of Poe works, Oscar Wilde's fairy tales, and two of Nathaniel Hawthorne's New England tales have had considerable success not only in the United States but abroad.

Plays I have enjoyed performing in during this period (1950–61) have been A) *The Winslow Boy* in summer stock, Sir Robert Morton, the brilliant attorney in this play, will always remain one of my favorite roles; B) *Julius Caesar*, in the round, at the Edison Hotel, in which I played Cassius; C) a version of Somerset Maugham's short story *Jane* dramatized by S. N. Behrman and produced by The Theatre Guild, in which I played Mr. Tower. Mr. Tower is supposed to represent Mr. Maugham himself. And, of course, there was *J.B.* Pictures included *My Three Angels* with Humphrey Bogart, and the *Court Jester* with Danny Kaye. In television one likes to remember *The Lark* with Julie Harris for Hallmark, in which I played the chief inquisitor; and but recently again with Julie Harris and for Hallmark, *Victoria Regina* in which I played Mr. Disraeli (Lord Beaconsfield). These two television shows stand out for me so far beyond anything else I have done in this medium that there is little point in mentioning other and more fragmentary contributions. The Hallmark Hall of Fame television presentations always maintain a very high standard, and much of this is due to George Schaeffer's sensitive direction and dedication to quality. There are others in the industry, but they don't come any better than George. In all of this there were signs at least that one could and would adjust to conditions and that "the poet's heart" once more could and would be one's guide and inspiration in

the future, a different future no doubt, but a definite challenge
to character and integrity of purpose. To live with oneself
(and one's dear ones) in the present, and in approaching the
future, one cannot be continually looking backward over
one's shoulder and sighing for the past. I speak particularly of
those of us who are connected with the arts.

Science and technology have advanced our way of life to
an almost unimaginable degree of physical comfort and well-
being, irrespective of one's income bracket. I well remember
when there was no air conditioning; when carpets were
strewn with wet tea leaves and swept by hand with a long-
handled broom; when every pot and pan and dish and plate
and glass and cup and saucer was washed by hand; when the
running of a home was a full-time job, as it was with my
mother, and the organization of a home life was as much a
profession as any other profession followed by women today.
Days when to have been a good wife to her man and a good
mother to her children was not a daily chore but an inspiring
and rewarding experience. But science and technology have
changed all that. To have the many added comforts, conveni-
ences, and luxuries that are available (mostly on the credit
system) to almost all of us, most families find it impossible to
meet expenses on father's pay check alone. And so it is that
mother too has had to go to work, and more often than not
at a considerable cost to family life that no added pay check
can compensate for. Children have been thrown more and
more together and upon their own resources, in a life of their
own that has set them apart from their elders. I hear "youth"
continuously spoken of as if it were a tribal organization precariously attached to some outworn and outmoded "traditions" that have become no more than antiquated slogans of a
dead past. The pace of our lives has so increased that youth
is unavoidably caught up in its vortex. The young dreamer
soon becomes a neurotic for want of mature companionship
and understanding. The young "artist" seeks out his own people and often finds himself hiding with them behind false
values he is not ready to evaluate. Modern art and modern

music revolt against a past they feel they cannot compete with and so ineffectually compete with each other in sheer desperation and with often distorted and hideous results. Much of our modern literature protests with an angry and frequently ignorant tongue against a life it fails to understand, and consequently falls into an abusive pattern of crude violence and sheer lewdness that it miserably mistakes for reality. Unguided and unguarded, young people, quite early in life, become involved in the "realities" of sex, and "love" becomes a discarded word in their vocabulary because it suggests to them an unacceptable frustration to the immediacy of their emotions. And to a considerable extent much of all this is inevitable when companionship and mutual confidence within the family has been lost and many are strangers to one another in a house that has never been a home.

The theater has unhappily allowed itself to be slanted too much toward these conditions and, with obvious exceptions, it has never in my lifetime been more unlovely and unloving. Within the motion picture industry there is an organization know as The Academy of Motion Picture Arts and Sciences. I would suggest that the science of making motion pictures far exceeds an appreciation of the arts. The whole procedure of making a moving picture from its inception to its final screening before the public is a series of purely technological and mechanical devices. There is little if any direct audience participation since there is nothing "live" up there on the screen to participate with. The same applies to television, but to an even greater extent. What then can be done to resuscitate for us and our children and our children's children that quality of respect, admiration, and inspiration that must exist between the art of entertainment and its audiences if entertainment is to play a serious part in our cultural development now and in the years to come. Surely Shakespeare, Molière, and Shaw, Eugene O'Neill, Bob Sherwood, and others are as worthy of perpetuation as are Michelangelo, Raphael, Rubens, Rodin, and Mario Korbel; as Beethoven, Bach, Brahms, Prokofiev, Britten, and Gershwin. Music and art have permanent homes all over the world, supported by private or government subsidy. The theater here in the United States has none, or so little as to be virtually unrecognizable. Motion pictures and television being purely commercial enterprises must be left to their own devices. But with a thriving and inspired theater they will automatically follow an upward trend. The theater cannot remain (as it is today) a purely commercial enterprise and survive. *It must be subsidized in one form or another.* And here I would offer a practical, plausible blueprint as a solution to this problem, leaving all details of its consummation to those fully qualified (of which there are an abundance) in our business, both producers, directors and actors, stage hands and musicians. *We have the talent. There is the money to promote such an addition to American culture.* There is also the ever-present challenge from the national theaters of France, Germany, Russia, and Britain that remains unanswered; and I am unable to accept any excuse for some such idea not being put into effect, unless we are shamelessly to admit that we are fettered and festered with mediocrity, apathy, and self-indulgence.

I would like to see consideration given to a national theater represented in six, seven, or even eight districts or areas of this great country; a northwest national theater in Seattle, a southwest in Los Angeles, two Middle West theaters in Denver and Chicago, a Northeast theater in Boston and a southeast theater in Atlanta, leaving New York to continue its precarious commercial career, and to those speculators who cannot resist the temptation of making a fast buck or losing a fortune overnight! These national theaters would exchange productions in some form of rotation. Each national theater producing three plays per season would mean that each of our six national theaters would have the opportunity of presenting eighteen plays a season—Each national theater agreeing not to duplicate productions of the same play in any one season. There should be seasonal membership tickets and special accommodation for student groups. This is asking no more for the theater than the great orchestras of this great country receive annually; and it is not improbable that such a national institution might create a better international understanding of American culture throughout the world as has already been done with music and ballet. With a national theater of this stature a repertoire of great plays past, present, and *future* would be presented before thousands upon thousands of young people (besides a considerable number of older ones!) many of whom have never seen live professional theater. Such a venture might also induce young playwrights to consider the theater again where they may be heard, and with the possibility of adding some jam to their bread and butter. The economics and inflationary costs on Broadway make present-day playwriting a bigger risk than horse racing or roulette. The motion picture industry and television hold promise of adequate and immediate financial rewards which no bad press can unduly influence. But alas, these media remain a vast playground for the monster Mediocrity, and many a potential playwright has, I feel sure, been swallowed up in this jungle of frivolity and pseudoviolence.

If this is dreaming, so be it. But dreams have come true as in the case of the new theater at Utah State University at Salt Lake City, where the dream of Dr. Lowell Lees is now a *fait accompli* after many years of dreaming (which I have been privileged to share with him) and tireless work in this one-man adventure. The new theater at the University of Utah is the most beautifully constructed and practical theater I have ever seen anywhere in the world and is to be made available, from time to time, to anyone seeking to produce a play worthy of the high standards that Dr. Lees has always insisted upon in his own work.

Universities and colleges all over the country spend considerable time and money in theater activities and there is great enthusiasm within student bodies to understand and appreciate good theater. They feel it to be a part of their heritage; they want it, they demand it, and more often than not they experience it. I know this from close personal contacts through my "show" *An Evening with Basil Rathbone*, which

I present primarily at universities and colleges throughout the country. This show is my answer to my own personal theater problem. I cannot wait ten years between worthwhile plays, which has been the case since I returned from the Coast in 1946. *The Heiress* was produced in September of 1947. In the years that followed its closing in Boston in April of 1949 I made two or three abortive appearances in plays on Broadway—plays I had no right to accept because I did not believe in them. It was not until June of 1958 that my enthusiasm and faith in a play were renewed by my participation in Archibald MacLeish's *J.B.*

It was Charles Laughton who pioneered the "one-man show" and proved without question of doubt how hungry huge ready-made audiences were for "live" entertainment all over the country. Taking a leaf out of Laughton's book I began to study my own prospects in this field. By trial and error, through spasmodic bookings over a period of about three years I arrived at a format. From this format I developed a program that has been booked solidly from early October to late April for the past two seasons; a program from which I derive much pleasure and great stimulation and which has completely erased the ugly specter of that monster Mediocrity that had haunted me.

The first half of my program is devoted to those I call "the neglected men of letters," the poets. In presenting them and their work I have found that personal identification with one's audience is extremely important. For example, I was much disturbed at first to find that Shelley's *Ode to the West Wind* received only modest acceptance. Discussing this great work with members of my audience who visited me backstage after the show, I realized it lacked personal identification for them, whereas Shakespeare's eighteenth and one hundred sixteenth sonnets, Browning's *Evelyn Hope*, Elizabeth Barrett's "How do I love thee?" were greeted warmly. With each of these latter there proved to be considerable personal audience identification, and they remain permanent selections in my program. The second half of my program is devoted to Mr. Shakespeare and in it I endeavor to break down certain barriers that seem to exist for both young and old in their approach to this most commercial box-office-minded playwright of all time. The fault would seem to be largely in the introduction of Shakespeare's plays in the classroom. It is not generally appreciated that there can be no satisfactory contact between Mr. Shakespeare and his players except upon a stage, with all that a stage has to offer in familiarizing and *releasing* oneself to the magic of these masterpieces of "theater." It has been deeply gratifying to experience how easily one can break down these barriers with short introductions and performed selections from *Hamlet, Macbeth, Romeo and Juliet,* and *The Tempest.* The enthusiastic reception of the second half of my program far exceeds that of the first. My program adequately meets my financial responsibilities and enables me to pick and choose from what else may come my way in the theater, motion pictures, or television. For instance, at this moment I have a play that has tremendous potential. It needs work, and with work may eventualize into one of the truly great plays of our time. My program enables me to wait patiently for this play, which alas we feel we cannot risk launching on the rocks of Broadway. All being well we hope to produce it in London in about a year's time, at a reasonable cost both in production and maintenance and with a consequent more hopeful chance of success. In London I can buy the best seat in any theater for about three dollars, while in New York I must pay anywhere from seven to ten dollars for the same location. Consequently London audiences are not so dependent on newspaper reviews, whereas New York audiences rely upon their reviewers to guide them in the considered outlay of a considerable sum of money!

"An evening in the theater with Basil Rathbone" takes me away from home a good deal, but I try to arrange my bookings so that I have periods of time at home in between groups of four or five consecutive dates (as much as ten days to two weeks at a time). Both Ouida and Cynthia have "reviewed" my show and I have their approval of it, I may even say their enthusiastic approval. Cynthia is happy and extremely successful in her work for Hockaday Associates, where she is their art buyer and consultant. Ouida is back at her writing again, a book she has entitled *They Gave Me Red Roses.* Soon we shall celebrate having known each other for thirty-nine years, and on April 18 of 1963 we shall celebrate our thirty-seventh wedding anniversary. Our next milestone will be April 18, 1976, our golden wedding anniversary! So come on, Ouida darling, let's go—there is still so much to do, and so much of life for us to enjoy together.

Let me not to the marriage of true minds
Admit impediments. Love is not love
Which alters when it alteration finds,
Or bends with the remover to remove:
O, no! it is an ever-fixed mark,
That looks on tempests and is never shaken;
It is the star to every wandering bark,
Whose worth's unknown, although his height be taken.
Love's not Time's Fool, though rosy lips and cheeks
Within his bending sickle's compass come;
Love alters not with his brief hours and weeks.
But bears it out even to the edge of doom.
If this be error, and upon me proved,
I never writ, nor no man ever lov'd.
(CXVI Sonnet—*William Shakespeare*)